THE DEPUTIES

TO THE ESTATES GENERAL

IN RENAISSANCE FRANCE

Studies Presented
to the International Commission for the History of
Representative and Parliamentary Institutions

XXI

The Deputies to the Estates General in Renaissance France

J. RUSSELL MAJOR

Madison

The University of Wisconsin Press

1960

Published by the University of Wisconsin Press,
430 Sterling Court, Madison 6, Wisconsin

c

LITHOPRINTED IN THE UNITED STATES OF AMERICA BY
CUSHING - MALLOY, INC., ANN ARBOR, MICHIGAN, 1960

TO BLAIR

PREFACE

This book is one of several I plan to write analyzing the French Estates General and related institutions during the Renaissance. Later studies will deal with the procedures used in the Estates General and the cahiers prepared by the local, provincial, and national assemblies. At the same time I am preparing a narrative history of French representative institutions during this period. One volume, Representative Institutions in Renaissance France, 1421-1559, is being published at this time. A bibliography is also planned.

This study has been made possible by the generous assistance of many foundations and individuals. Fulbright and John Simon Guggenheim Memorial fellowships enabled me to spend two years in the French archives and libraries, a three-year Faculty Research Fellowship of the Social Science Research Council provided the free time to write this volume, and Emory University granted my many requests for leaves of absence. Numerous French archivists and librarians have assisted me in locating and microfilming manuscripts. Without their efforts there would be many more omissions and errors in this volume. Professors Helmut Koenigsberger of the University of Manchester, Walter Love of Emory University, and Gaines Post of the University of Wisconsin have read and criticized this manuscript. My wife has contributed generously with her time in many ways. To each and all these foundations and individuals I wish to express my appreciation.

TABLE OF CONTENTS

TABLES

MAP

THE DEPUTIES

TO THE ESTATES GENERAL

IN RENAISSANCE FRANCE

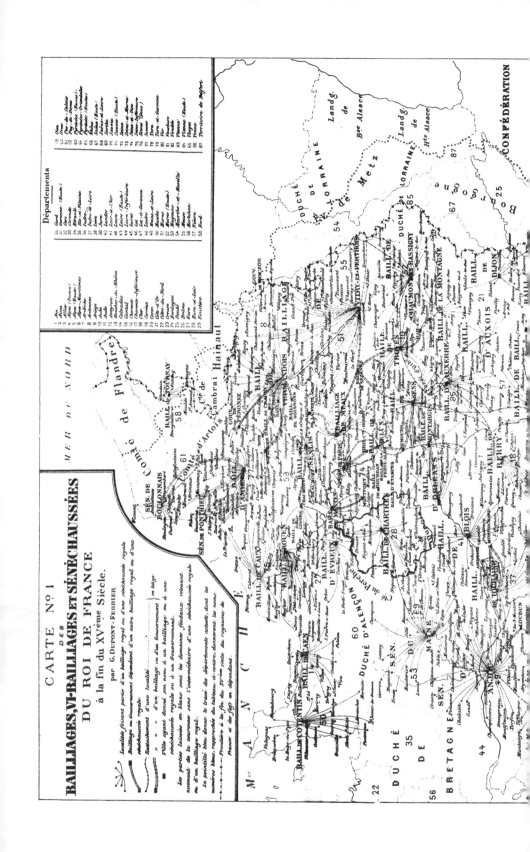

CARTE N°. 1
DES
BAILLIAGES, VI-BAILLIAGES ET SÉNÉCHAUSSÉES
DU ROI DE FRANCE
à la fin du XVème Siècle.
par G. DUPONT-FERRIER.

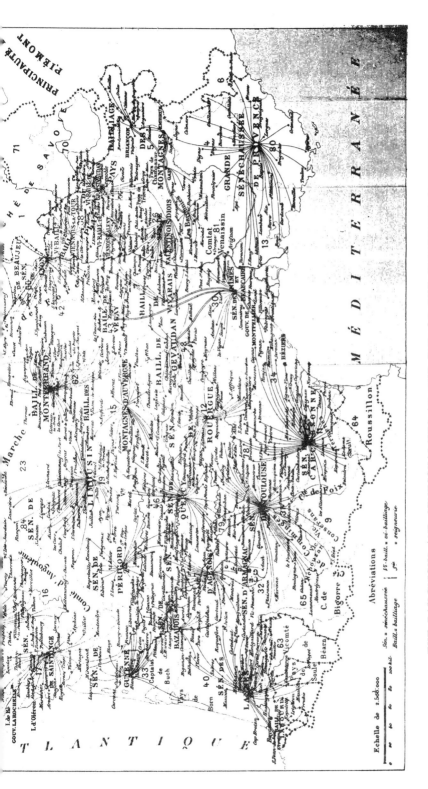

THE BAILIWICKS AND SENESCHALSIES AT THE END OF THE FIFTEENTH CENTURY

From Gustave Dupont-Ferrier, Les Officiers royaux des bailliages et sénéchaussées
et les institutions monarchiques locales en France à la fin du moyen âge
(Paris, 1902), Bibliothèque de l'Ecole des Hautes Études, vol. 145.

1

THE ELECTIONS IN PROSPECT

Introduction

The Renaissance was not a disciplined age. Everyone except the Latinist still enjoyed the happy freedom to write and spell as he pleased. Neither the meanings of words nor the composition and functions of institutions were carefully defined. System and uniformity were seldom desired. Instead, the love of detail and the acceptance of infinite variations that Huizinga has so brilliantly shown to be at the heart of late medieval aesthetic concepts still prevailed in the ceremonies and governmental practices of the sixteenth century.[1] Nowhere do these facts appear more clearly than in regard to representative institutions in France.

The French kings had at their disposal a wide variety of assemblies. At the local level there were assemblies of the three estates of viscounties, provostships, and the still larger bailiwicks and seneschalsies; at the provincial level there were assemblies of duchies, provinces, and governments; and at the regional level there were assemblies of two or more provinces such as the estates of Languedoïl. In addition, the clergy, the nobility, or the third estate of this or that locality was sometimes told to meet alone. An equally bewildering array of assemblies could be found at the national level. Before 1483 the king sometimes summoned individually important ecclesiastics and nobles and directed monasteries, chapters, and towns to name deputies; after 1483 he sharply reduced the number who were individually convoked and directed the assemblies of the bailiwicks and seneschalsies to elect deputies representing the three estates. In both periods he sometimes summoned only one estate, usually the clergy or the deputies of the towns; at other times he held meetings composed of only judicial, military, economic, or fiscal specialists, and there the elective elements, if present at all, were reduced to a handful of deputies from the sovereign courts or the towns.

Except for the assemblies of the clergy or of the towns, no definite name was assigned to each of the various types of national assemblies. The difference between a large and restricted meeting was recognized, but the Renaissance man did not distinguish between them in his terminology. All of them were referred to as being "assemblies of notable persons," "assemblies of the three estates," and, from the late fifteenth century, "Estates Generals." The term, "assembly of notables," did not come to mean a particular type of meeting until the dawn of the seventeenth century. Thus the assembly of 1468 which was composed of individually summoned ecclesiastics and nobles and the deputies of the towns, the assembly of 1484 which was made up primarily of the deputies of the three estates of the bailiwicks and seneschalsies, and the restricted assembly of 1558 with its handful of magnates, judges, and deputies of the towns were indiscriminately referred to as being "assemblies of notable persons," "assemblies of the three (of four) estates," and "Estates Generals."[2]

It would be virtually impossible to discuss the deputies to all the meetings

3

that were called Estates Generals. The smaller less important assemblies will therefore be relegated to a secondary position in this book. The same fate will be meted out to the large assemblies prior to the inauguration of bailiwick elections in 1483 because there is not enough evidence to make possible a detailed study. What remains are those meetings of the Estates General in which most of the deputies were chosen in bailiwick and other local assemblies. It is the purpose of this book to show who these deputies were, how they were elected, how they lived during the meetings, and how they were paid.

This information is important because the events that took place during the meetings of the Estates General and the tragic fate of national represent-ative institutions in France depended in part on the deputies who participated. Furthermore, it reveals much concerning the nature of the Renaissance Mon-archy. It shows the local government in action; the activities of the bailiwick officials in relation to the royal directives for holding the elections, the tra-ditions of a particular bialiwick, and the desires of the local inhabitants. The structure of society, the relations between the social orders, and the policies of the crown are also illuminated.

The bailiwick and other local estates, then, must be given considerable attention. There are ample documents to show the structure and procedures that were followed in the electoral assemblies of many places, but where the sources are inadequate, it is necessary to study the local estates when they met for other purposes such as to codify customs and ratify treaties. Care must be taken in using this material, however, for the composition of the local estates varied somewhat with the purposes they were designed to serve. Thus the assemblies to codify the customs during the late fifteenth and early sixteenth centuries favored the lawyer class at the expense of other members of the third estate. On the other hand, the same trend towards increased suf-frage may be found here as in the electoral assemblies to the Estates Gen-eral. The curés were added to the first estate, seigneurs with middle and low justice to the second, and the deputies of the bourgs, villages, and parishes to the third as the sixteenth century progressed. The composition of these meetings, and of course, of those regularly organized provincial estates that sometimes elected deputies, may therefore be considered with the electoral assemblies.

One is tempted to make sweeping generalizations concerning the proce-dure followed in the bailiwick electoral assemblies, but to do so is dangerous for it varied from place to place and from year to year. Only after the re-markable diversity of electoral practices has been stressed can satisfactory conclusions be reached. Too often historians feel obligated to bring order out of chaos by ignoring exceptions and slighting details; but when exceptions become the rule and confusion the most significant characteristic, a brief and general account distorts history. To understand the evolution of electoral practices in Renaissance France, it is necessary to study the electoral pro-cedure bailiwick by bailiwick. But first we must consider the instructions contained in the royal letters of convocation and the mandate system.

The Letters of Convocation and the Mandate System

The letters convoking an assembly, whatever the size and composition, were similar in certain respects.[3] They were issued in the king's name un-less he was a minor. In this case the regent and often the princes of the blood and the council were mentioned as advocating the step. These letters were sent either directly to the individuals who were summoned or else to them through the hands of local officials. When corporate groups were involved, the letters were sent to the officials whose duty it was to order the elections whether in the town, bailiwick, or province. In the towns the convoking authority was usually the mayor and échevins, in the bailiwicks it was the bailiff or his lieutenant general, and in the provinces it was the governor or special royal commissioners.

The letters of convocation told why the national assembly was convoked, when and where it was to meet, how the deputies were to be elected, and in what number. The kings determined the size and composition of an assembly by the purpose it was to serve. Generally during the Hundred Years War and the Wars of Religion they preferred large assemblies, because they desired to use them to influence public opinion. The more people who heard explanations of the royal policy, the more there were to spread the desired information when they returned to their homes. There is little precise evidence of the numbers who attended prior to 1484, but the presence of twenty-seven deputies from the towns of Languedoc at Bourges in 1440 indicates that attendance was large. What is known of the earlier assemblies bears out this conclusion. The estates of 1356 drew 800 persons, and the late Capetians were in the habit of summoning about 300 nobles to stand for the second estate. About 400 deputies usually attended when bailiwick elections were held.[4]

Louis XI and his immediate successors generally preferred smaller assemblies. They sought advice, and for this a few experts were of far greater use than the large confused mass that kings like Charles VII had convoked to publicize the crown's financial difficulties. When Louis XI wanted to deal with economic problems, he thought that asking from twenty to twenty-five towns to send a couple of deputies each was sufficient, and his successors kept to the same number when they desired to consult the municipalities.[5] Only in 1468 when Louis wanted to rally popular support against the rebellious feudal magnates did he indulge in a larger meeting. Then, in addition to the royal officials, about fifty prelates and nobles were listed as attending and other members of the second estate were said to be present in great numbers. Sixty-four towns sent about 200 deputies from the lesser clergy and the third estate, bringing the minimum possible attendance to 250 and the maximum probable figure to 350, which was still only half the size of the great medieval assemblies. The meeting of the three estates held in 1596 by Henry IV was even more restricted. Only 150 individuals were convoked and out of these, only 80 attended. The nonrepresentative consultative assemblies were smaller still; the 54 who took part in the meeting in 1617 and the 55 in 1626 were probably typical of those of an earlier period.[6]

When the king decided to have bailiwick elections, he instructed the bailiff to have the members of the three estates meet in the accustomed manner in the principal town of his jurisdiction to prepare the remonstrances they wished to propose in the Estates General and to elect the deputies to attend. The use of the phrase "in the accustomed manner" was of significance because it gave royal permission for innumerable local variations. These variations make it necessary to study each jurisdiction to see how the elections were actually held and the remonstrances prepared. In 1560 the king asked that the bailiwicks elect one or more deputies from each estate, but in 1484, 1576, 1588, and 1614 the crown was more specific and ordered that one deputy be chosen from each order. In spite of these directives, the local estates chose as many or as few deputies as they wished, and in 1614 only twenty-six of the ninety-nine bailiwicks that named delegations to the Estates General complied with the royal order to send one and only one deputy from each estate. When the towns were convoked, the king usually asked that a specific number of deputies be elected. However, different towns might be told to elect different numbers to the same meeting. Thus in 1468 Lyon and Poitiers were told to name three laymen and one clergyman, Blois and several other municipalities were told to send two laymen only, but the majority of the towns were asked for two laymen and one clergyman.[7] Probably the relative size and importance of each town were the determining factors.

When the purpose of an assembly was purely advisory, the king usually requested that the deputies selected be notable persons, well informed on the matters to be discussed. When he wished to win consent for taxation or to bind the electorate to support his policies, he usually stipulated in the letters of convocation that the deputies be given the necessary powers to act in the name of their constituents. The powers to be given the deputies and the remonstrances or cahiers they were to carry to the assemblies lead to the question of the origin and nature of the idea of representation. The earliest national assemblies had been composed of ecclesiastical and noble magnates, but with the advent of towns, the custom developed of having several of their leading citizens attend as well. These assemblies were satisfactory as means of giving advice and information to the government, but the decisions reached therein were neither legally nor morally binding on the other inhabitants of the kingdom.

In the twelfth century, renewed interest in Roman law brought the use of proctors with powers of attorney to represent individuals and communities in court in private matters. It was but a small step to employ similarly empowered persons in the assemblies of the kings, and at the dawn of the thirteenth century the practice of having towns, ecclesiastical chapters, and rural areas elect proctors began to spread from Italy, where it was probably first employed, to the rest of Europe. The system was used by the Church, kings, feudal magnates, and local royal officials in their supranational, national, provincial, and local assemblies when they desired to commit the inhabitants of their lands to a specific act or policy, though the older type of advisory meetings continued to be used by the French monarchs when the occasion demanded.[8]

The small advisory assemblies present no special difficulties. Those who attended were rarely carefully instructed proctors; they were not obligated to support the policies of the crown nor could they bind their neighbors in the towns and countryside. More difficult is the problem of describing and evaluating the proxy or mandate system that was often employed in the large assemblies. The chancellery never formulated a precise statement of the powers to be given to proctors of communities. Its instructions varied from the request that the deputies be given "good and sufficient power . . . to consent, agree, and conclude on everything that will be advised, counseled and determined" in 1421 to the order that they be entrusted "with ample powers, instructions, and memoirs" in 1649.[9] The form and content of the procurations actually given to the deputies by the electors varied to a still greater degree from locality to locality and from election to election, making generalization even more difficult. But three basic questions may be investigated: First, did the king have trouble getting deputies with full or sufficient powers, that is, the adequate authority to act? Second, could a deputy with full powers resist the authority of the king or did he have to acquiesce to the royal desires? Third, what control, if any, did constituents exercise over a deputy to whom they had given full or sufficient powers?

During the fourteenth century the kings experienced some difficulty in getting jurisdictions to give their deputies full powers, and as late as 1413 the Norman representatives were only authorized "to hear and report."[10] However, resistance to granting adequate powers during the medieval period has probably been exaggerated,[11] and during the Renaissance, rarely occurred. There was difficulty only when the chancellery failed to give sufficient information on the purpose of the assembly or to ask in the letters of convocation that deputies have the necessary powers to treat the matter under consideration. These failures occurred in 1560 and 1575: that they should happen so late comes as a surprise until one remembers that during the three quarters of a century following the Estates General of 1484, most of the assemblies had been held for advisory purposes only, no powers being demanded or needed. In 1560 the letter of convocation failed to say anything about the need of the crown for money or of the deputies for adequate powers except to request that they be "well instructed on the complaints and remonstrances" their constituents wished to make.[12] Some deputies were given adequate powers anyway, but it is not surprising that the estates as a whole claimed to have no authority to vote additional taxes.

The letter of convocation in 1561 made clear that the assembly was to discuss the royal financial difficulties, but nothing was said of giving sufficient powers. The deputies at the estates of August, 1575, refused to vote money on the grounds that they only had powers "to hear what would be proposed in the assembly and report back to those who had elected them...."[13] By 1576 the chancellery had awakened to its faults and required "ample instructions and sufficient powers," though no specific mention was made of the financial problem of the crown in the writs.[14]

If we except the instances when the clerks of the chancellery failed to follow the proper form in the letters of convocation, we find that the few surviving procurations for the fifteenth century and the many for the period of the Wars of Religion indicate that there was no difficulty in getting deputies with adequate powers, although it may be doubted if they conformed to all the prerequisites for procurations in private legal cases. Thus the estates of Brittany empowered its delegation to the national assembly of 1588 to act for the good of the king, the French people, and the province.[15] The naïve assumption that what was good for Brittany was also good for Henry III and the French people was doubtless underlying the grant of powers to many other delegations. Nevertheless, that such powers were regarded as adequate is proven by the failure of the presiding officers at the bailiwick assemblies and the royalist electors to try to have the deputies given greater powers, and by the failure of the clerks at the Estates General to challenge deputies on this score when they examined their procurations. Those whose right to participate was questioned found themselves in difficulty because they had been elected by subordinate jurisdictions, chosen by irregular procedures, or else were unable to produce the proper papers.[16]

Willingness to grant adequate powers during the Renaissance may show a slight growth of national consciousness and a relative weakening of provincialism, but it probably depended more upon a tacit acceptance of the principle that taxes voted in the Estates General would be later acted upon by the provincial estates and privileged towns. Why refuse to give a deputy adequate powers when he attended the national assembly if there were means to check later any over-generous action on his part? Then too, if the giving of full powers to a deputy did not mean that he had to agree to everything that the crown desired at the Estates General or that the electors had lost all control over his actions, there was no reason to avoid doing so. We are thus brought to the questions of whether the deputy with full powers could resist the authority of the king and to what extent his actions were controlled by his constituents?

For some time medievalists have disagreed about what was meant by a grant of "full powers to consent and agree on what will be decided." Was the proctor so empowered bound in advance to acquiesce to the king's desires or did the mandate ensure his capacity for independent action in the assembly? In short, was the mandate system an instrument to further royal power or was it a means to protect provincial rights?[17] In his study of fourteenth century French assemblies, Professor Taylor has shown that a proctor with full powers had the authority to bind his constituents as though they themselves were present, but he did not necessarily have to do anything in particular that the king asked of him.[18] This same situation prevailed in the Renaissance. In 1421 the three deputies from Tours were sent to the estates at Clermont with "full power . . . to hear what the regent (the future Charles VII) and the council will say, expose, and declare, and also to consent and agree . . . to all that the regent and council will counsel, advise, and order to be done for the good, honor and utility of the kingdom . . ."; but apparently joined with representatives from other localities to persuade the crown to moderate its financial demands by 400,000 livres.[19] In 1560 the deputy of the nobility from the seneschalsy of Guyenne was given full powers, but at the Estates General he insisted with others that he could not act until he had referred back to his constituents to learn what course he should take; this was in view of the new circumstances occasioned by the sudden death of the king.[20] The question of the authority of the deputies to act generally came up only in matters of taxation. Professor Post has pointed out that in accordance with Roman law procedure the proctor with full powers was expected to act in the interest of his constituents;[21] these interests were almost invariably interpreted to include lower, not higher taxes. The contents of the cahiers leave no doubts on this score. The French deputies usually had sufficient powers to act for their constituents, but it is obvious that if all the electors could have gone to the Estates General, they would have likewise refused to grant additional aid. In the final anaylsis, it was more the instructions that the deputy received than the powers that he was granted that limited his capacity to act as the king directed.

If the deputy was able to ignore the wishes of the king, was he equally free to consent to things opposed by his constituents, but desired by a majority in the Estates General? In general, the answer to this question is affirmative. For an estate to prepare a cahier to present to the king, it was necessary that the deputies come to an agreement. This meant that those who were in the minority on a particular matter would have to utilize their full powers and abandon the position of their constituents in order for the opinion of the majority to prevail. Often deputies were specifically authorized by their constituents to accept the rule of the majority in the Estates General; nowhere were they explicitly denied this privilege.[22] There was no liberum veto in France as was to develop in Poland.

On the other hand, the giving of sufficient powers did not mean that the electors abandoned all control over their proctor. To guide his actions in the Estates General they usually prepared a cahier listing what they wanted. These local cahiers were submitted to the king as petitions of grievances, but they were also designed to govern the deputy's voting at the Estates General.[23] In addition, deputies frequently wrote local leaders informing them of the developments at the national assembly. These local leaders, in turn, instructed the deputies on the desires of the electors in regard to new matters as they arose.[24] Willful failure to follow instructions might put the deputy in a precarious position. In Switzerland even the death penalty could be imposed for committing this crime, but in France the punishment took a less severe form.[25] Angered constituents could either disavow proctors who disobeyed their instructions or fail to pay them on their return. There was an unsuccessful movement in Burgundy to refuse to compensate a delegate to the Estates General of 1561 on the grounds that he had exceeded his instructions by advocating the surrender of Catholic churches to Protestants.[26] In 1576 an effort was made to disavow Jean Bodin, who, as deputy of the bailiwick of Vermandois, had become one of the leaders of the tolerant party in the Estates General. The move was spearheaded by deputies dispatched to the Estates General for this purpose by the strongly Catholic towns of Reims, Soissons, and Châlons-sur-Marne. Their petition was denied by the king's council on the grounds that only these towns, and not the bailiwick as a whole, had participated in the move to oust the eminent jurist. It is significant that neither Bodin nor the royal council denied the right of a jurisdiction to disavow a deputy who had failed to follow instructions.[27]

One must not, however, exaggerate the dependence of the deputies on their constituents. It must be remembered that those who went to the Estates General were not only proctors, they were also acknowledged leaders of their localities who exercised considerable influence on the thinking of their constituents. A king who knew how to guide the deliberations of the estates could hope that those present would vote as he desired, either after consulting other leaders in their jurisdictions by letter, or on their own authority in the expectation that when they returned home and explained their actions, their constituents would be content. In short, although Renaissance deputies were bound more closely to their electors than modern representatives, the Estates General was far from being a mere congress of ambassadors who could agree on nothing without specific instructions from home.

The Local Officials and the Elections

The control exercised by the bailiwick assemblies over deputies to the Estates General confers considerable importance on these meetings. They were held under the direction of the bailiffs and seneschals or their subordinates. The bailiff and seneschal were very important officials during the late Middle Ages, but during the early Renaissance, their power was greatly reduced. Treasury officials replaced them as collectors of revenue, others took over the administration of the royal domain, the advent of the governors reduced their military duties, and their judicial functions devolved on experts. Often they were absentees and served more as the representative of their bailiwick at court than as the representatives of the king in the bailiwick. Nevertheless, the bailiffs and seneschals were still regarded as men of importance, so much so that the deputies to the Estates General often complained about their absenteeism. The office had usually been held by lawyers during the Middle Ages, but the nobles of the sword gradually usurped it, and under the Renaissance Monarchs the bailiffs were almost always drawn from the more prominent members of that class. This success on the part of the second estate indicates the dynamic nature of the seigneural nobility during the period. True, the duties of the bailiffs had greatly diminished, but they remained the senior representatives of the king in their districts.

The second official of the bailiwick was the lieutenant general, on whom many of the more technical aspects of the bailiff's duties devolved, especially those of a judicial nature. At one time the lieutenant general was appointed by the bailiff and was responsible directly to him, but in 1510 he was removed from the bailiff's control and became responsible directly to the king. The growing complexity of government and the ever present desire of the crown for additional money led to the creation and often the sale of many local offices. Lieutenants criminal and civil were appointed to handle most of the judicial responsibilities and lieutenants particular to assist the lieutenant general and to preside over subordinate seats. Advocates and procureurs of the king were also named in each bailiwick. In 1552 the king created the presidial seat, a judicial court interposed between the bailiwick and the Parlement; thus a host of councilors and other officials, usually under the presidency of the lieutenant general, were added to the local hierarchy. Nearly all of them were trained in law and with a few exceptions had their origin in the third estate, but many became nobles of the robe and purchased fiefs. It would be folly to look on them as reflecting bourgeois ideals or a middle-class spirit. Indeed, they were constantly at odds with the municipal officials, who represented more nearly the interests of the merchant oligarchy.[28]

When the letter of convocation was received in the bailiwick, it was pub-
licly read and registered. The bailiff usually consulted the other officials on
the procedure to be followed. If he were away, the lieutenant general, or in
case of a double absenteeism, the lieutenant civil, criminal, or one of the
lieutenant particulars took the necessary steps for carrying out the orders of
the king. The directives of these officials varied from place to place and
from election to election. The clergymen they summoned to the bailiwick
assembly might in one locality be limited to the local bishop, but in other
places might include every ecclesiastic in the jurisdiction down to the mean-
est parish curé except, of course, those in chapters, monasteries, and other
ecclesiastical communities that sent deputies. Sometimes the senior bailiwick himself would summon the desired ecclesiastics, sometimes he would
direct the officers of the inferior jurisdictions to notify the clergymen in the
area of their responsibility, sometimes he would turn the entire problem of
convoking the clergy over to the local bishop. The resulting confusion was
so great that in 1614 the first estate itself appealed for the establishment of
a more definite system to prevent the disputes that were bringing scandal to
their order.[29]

The local officials might order a handful of the great nobles to attend the
bailiwick estates, summon all nobles with fiefs, or even order nobles without
fiefs to attend. Those who were called were usually permitted to name proctors in lieu of personal attendance. Occasionally, the right of proctors to
vote in the bailiwick assemblies was questioned, and quarrels on this score
inspired a royal order in 1614 forbidding their participation, but it was to no
avail. The crown acquiesced as usual, and in 1651 specifically authorized
the use of proctors by individuals.[30]

Diversity of procedure may also be found in the convocation of the third
estate. In some instances only the towns were directed to name deputies. A
second possibility was for the plat pays or the bourgs and bourgades to be
summoned as well. The exact meaning of these terms is in doubt, but they
probably signified the large, unclosed or non-charted communities; localities
in which the small shopkeeper, important farmer, notary, or judge exercised
considerable influence. A third possibility was for the bailiwick officials to
consult all the heads of families by directing every village or parish to name
deputies. Sometimes these deputies met in castellanies, viscounties, dioceses, or similar jurisdictions to elect representatives to the bailiwick assembly. Sometimes they went directly to the bailiwick estates. Members of
the other two orders likewise made use of subordinate electoral assemblies
when the occasion demanded. Whenever these preparatory elections were
held, the same system of empowering and instructing the deputies was employed as has been described above for the bailiwick assemblies. Often on
the recommendation of the procureur of the king, elaborate steps were taken
to see that news of the approaching Estates General was disseminated. The
information was cried through the various communities, and the relevant documents were posted in market places, town squares, and on church doors.

When orders directing a town to name representatives to the bailiwick or
the national assembly were received, the municipal officials usually held a
meeting to determine the procedure to be followed. Included among these officials was a presiding officer, most often called a mayor or provost of the
merchants, and from four to twelve échevins or consuls. Sometimes there
was also a group of from twelve to thirty-two councilors who were consulted.
These officials formed the governing element in the towns during the Renaissance. Seigneurial influence had largely disappeared and systematic efforts
by the crown to win control were not to begin before the reign of Henry IV.

During the fifteenth century municipal officials often assembled the inhabitants of the towns to elect deputies, but the practice of holding general

assemblies tended to die out during the Renaissance. In their place was substituted consultation with either the leading bourgeois, the deputies from various quarters of the town, the urban parishes, or a few privileged guilds.
Occasionally, the municipal officials acted alone. Thus the towns came more
and more under the control of a bourgeois oligarchy. The guilds as such seldom enjoyed an important place in municipal government, and they rarely
assumed more than an advisory role in the elections to the national assemblies. The only threat to the bourgeois oligarchy came from local royal officials, men who often originated from that very class, but who sought to wrest
control of the towns from their new masters.

The relations between the bourgeois oligarchy and the local royal officials
have not been adequately studied, but it is probable that in most towns they
went through three stages.[31] The first stage was one of friendship. It started
with the establishment of a sovereign court or presidial seat in a town and
was marked by increased prosperity created by the influx of royal officials
and lawyers. The second stage of the relationship was one of conflict. It began when the local royal officials started to interfere in the affairs of the
town either to increase their wealth and power or to protect the lower classes
from the bourgeois oligarchy. In the larger towns where the bourgeoisie was
strong, the resulting struggle endured for generations and greatly influenced
the evolution of electoral procedures. In the smaller localities, the officials
quickly overpowered the townsmen, and the third stage — an era of peace —
was inaugurated with the royal officials in such complete control that no effective opposition was voiced. The kings were far from encouraging this
development and sought to protect the municipalities. In October, 1547, Henry
II issued an ordonnance forbidding crown officials to hold municipal posts,
but he could not enforce his ruling, and the greatest influx of the royal bureaucracy into municipal offices came after that date.

When the rural communities were summoned to the bailiwick estates, they
usually met at the local church under the presidency of a minor royal or a
seigneurial official. All heads of families, including women, were permitted
to participate. Occasionally the priest or even the proctor of the seigneur
took part. Most often it was the presiding official, a prominent farmer, or
the marguiller or syndic of the parish who was elected to go the bailiwick
estates, but there were instances when the priest was chosen. Cahiers were
normally prepared by one or more local leaders and approved by the entire
assembly. The deputies chosen by town or village were empowered to act in
the name of the community as a whole, and the cahiers given them served as
instructions in the bailiwick assembly.[32]

The bailiwick assembly was held in the principal town of the jurisdiction.
The usual procedure was for the three orders to meet together under the
presidency of the bailiff or, in his absence, of the lieutenant general. Royal
orders convoking the Estates General were read, speeches were made, and
the roll of those summoned to attend was called. Then the three orders either
elected their deputies together or else separated and chose them apart. Voting was usually done by voice, but one can find instances where the secret
ballot was employed, especially in southern France. As might be expected,
local magnates sometimes insisted on voting by voice in the hope of being
better able to control the outcome of the election. In 1651 the pro-Mazarin
Bishop of Angers cowed the opposition by insisting that voting be by voice and
not by written ballot. Two years earlier in Languedoc, the diocese of Toulouse complained that the Bishop of Rieux had refused to permit voting by
ballot in accordance with "the ancient and modern usage in this province."[33]

A plurality, rather than a majority of votes, was required for election.
In 1576 the nobility of the duchy of Nevers gave thirty-five votes to the Seigneur of Blanchefort and thirty-eight to six other candidates, but Blanchefort

was declared elected. In 1588 the provost of the merchants received only 139 of the 400 votes cast in the elections of the provostship of Paris, but he was accepted as deputy. No instance has been found where a runoff election was held to secure the backing of a majority of the voters for the chosen deputy. [34]

Sometimes the three estates prepared a joint cahier for their deputies to take to the Estates General. Sometimes each order submitted an individual petition. In either case the actual preparation of a cahier was usually done by an elected committee. The committee or committees of the three estates often had local cahiers made by villages, towns, chapters, and subordinate jurisdictions to guide their efforts. After the cahier was completed, it might or might not be submitted to the assembly for approval. Occasionally no cahier was prepared, but this laxity became rarer as the sixteenth century progressed.

With the framework given above, it is now necessary to study the elections in the individual bailiwicks. Only by this method can an accurate picture be drawn of the diversity of the procedures that were followed, the nature of the quarrels that arose, and the policies of the crown.

2

THE ELECTIONS IN PICARDY

General Considerations

The procedure used in the Estates General determines the method that must be followed in a study of the elections. In 1560 and thereafter it was customary for the members of each estate at the national assembly to be subdivided into governments. The deputies in each government held their own deliberations, kept their own journal, elected their own president and clerk; indeed they behaved as though they were in a separate chamber. When voting was done, the deputies of a particular estate in a bailiwick got together and determined how the bailiwick would vote, then the bailiwicks of each government were polled to determine how the government voted, and the governments were polled to determine the vote of the estate as a whole. It is therefore necessary to approach the elections from the standpoint of the bailiwicks and governments. If it can be determined whether the suffrage in a majority of the bailiwicks of a particular government was broad or narrow, whether the three orders elected their deputies together or apart, whether there were quarrels in the bailiwick assemblies, the stand taken by the estates in the national assembly can be better explained.

We begin the investigation with the government of Picardy, a territory situated in the northwest corner of France. Its boundaries were far from precise, being delineated neither by natural geographical features, save on the sea, nor by long historical development. Indeed, the very name of Picardy cannot be said to have been much more than a geographical expression until the creation of a government by that name early in the sixteenth century. This government, for the purposes of the Estates General at least, was composed of the bailiwick of Amiens, the seneschalsies of Ponthieu and Boulonnais, the small associated provostships and governments of Montdidier, Péronne, and Roye, and the town of Calais.

The fact that Picardy was never a feudal duchy and had to wait so long before it became an administrative unit of the kingdom prevents one from being surprised to find that it possessed no regularly convoked provincial assembly during the Middle Ages. The creation of the government followed by the vicissitudes of the Wars of Religion could possibly have led to the formation of provincial estates, and a few steps were taken in this direction. There were assemblies of the three estates of Picardy in 1544 at Péronne, in 1561 at Amiens, in 1573 at Compiègne, and the bailiwicks met individually in 1583, but the real drive to turn the province into a pays d'état came between 1589 and 1593 under the auspices of the Catholic League. This last fact hardly recommended the experiment to Henry IV, and the matter was allowed to drop when he was finally in a position to assert his authority.[1] The estates of the bailiwicks and comparable jurisdictions met less frequently in Picardy than in many other provinces, but the numerous deputations of the important towns to court and the hardly less frequent delegations sent by ecclesiastical corporations to handle their various affairs provided valuable experience to the

13

local leaders of these two orders in the use of representatives. The problem of electing deputies in Picardy was therefore little worse than in many places with estates.

Amiens

Amiens was the largest town in Picardy and the seat of a bailiwick of that name. Her rich archives provide the best opportunity to study the evolution of electoral procedure in that part of France.[2] Documents have survived for five assemblies of the three estates of the bailiwick between 1483 and 1529, and collectively they reveal who was convoked at this time. In 1483 the writs of summons were sent to "the clergy, nobility, good towns, and others of the third and common estate"[3] of Amiens to meet and approve the Treaty of Arras. Near the end of 1483 the three estates of the bailiwick again met, this time to name deputies to the Estates General of Tours. The fact that only six towns were asked to contribute towards the payment of the deputy of the third estate indicates that only these localities participated in his election.[4] In 1496 the abbots, deans, priors, chapters, seigneurs, and good towns met to ratify the Treaty of Étaples. Much the same elements participated in the assemblies to codify the custom in 1507 and to ratify the Treaties of Cambrai and Madrid in 1529 except for the greater influx of lawyers and officials on the former occasion.[5] It is clear that neither the curés nor the inhabitants of the countryside were regarded as spokesmen for the community of the bailiwick at this time.

The three estates met and voted as a unit. In December, 1483, they elected together their deputies to attend the Estates General at Tours the following January. In 1507 they chose a committee to prepare a draft of the custom, and this draft was later approved by the bailiwick assembly as a whole. In 1529 the estates permitted a slight breach in their unity by deciding to separate and choose those who would swear to uphold the terms of the Treaties of Cambrai and Madrid. However, the men selected sent a joint declaration of their acceptance of this responsibility to Paris.[6]

Meanwhile, municipal elections in Amiens had become less democratic. The guilds were excluded in 1383, and thereafter the upper bourgeois were challenged in their control of the town only by royal officials. This development was naturally felt in elections to the national assemblies. The mayor, échevins, a group of bourgeois, and an undisclosed number of other persons named the deputation of the town to the estates at Paris in 1420. A similar group heard the report of the town representatives who had taken part in an assembly at Arras in 1435, but in 1483 the municipal deputies to an assembly of towns reported only to the échevins.[7] The échevins sufficed to elect the deputies of the town to the estates at Tours in 1506 to ask the king to marry his daughter to the Duke of Angoulême, but no doubt as a result of royal prompting, a larger assembly was held to ratify and approve the alliance. The following year the town of Amiens prepared its local custom. This work was done by the échevins, but was approved by a somewhat larger assembly.[8] Finally, in December, 1557, the mayor received a royal summons to attend the estates at Paris. Upon his recommendation the échevins named a second deputy to accompany him to give advice, for the mayor did not know the purpose of the assembly.[9] Thus, when the Estates General was called in 1560, a tradition had been established that involved limited suffrage for the first and third estates, unified action by the three orders in the bailiwick meetings, and the control of the échevins over the choice of representatives for the town. In less than two decades much of this was to change.

When the bailiff received letters in 1560 ordering a meeting of the Estates

General, he instructed the officials of the subordinate jurisdictions to have all
prelates, abbots, priors, chapters, counts, barons, and temporal lords, and
one or two instructed deputies for each town, bourg, and bourgade attend the
electoral assembly of the bailiwick at Amiens on October 15. To carry out
these instructions the échevinage at Amiens convoked representatives of the
privileged guilds to make any suggestions they desired to be included in the
cahier. A week later, the mayor and about a dozen échevins elected the deputies of the town to the bailiwick assembly. The guilds and corporations had
been consulted concerning the contents of the cahier, but the town officials
actually prepared it and named the deputies to the bailiwick assembly as well.
Probably a similar procedure characterized the elections in the other jurisdictions, and certainly there was no general convocation of the villages, although the inclusion of the terms bourg and bourgade in the bailiff's summons
indicates some increase in suffrage. Unfortunately, almost nothing is known
of the bailiwick assembly held on October 15 except that a quarrel developed
between the crown and town officials concerning precedence and that deputies
were named to the Estates General. Two days later the échevins of Amiens,
reminiscent of the days when the town alone was convoked, proceeded to elect
two deputies to go directly to the Estates General. They did have the tact to
repeat one or both of the nominations made for the third estate of the bailiwick. As a further sign of its independence, the town refused to send a copy
of its cahier to the local bishop.[10]

The bailiwick estates met on March 10, 1561, to name deputies to the estates of the government of Picardy where in turn deputies were to be elected
to attend a national assembly. However, the postponement of the Estates
General made new deliberations necessary, and the bailiwick estates again
assembled on May 26 for this purpose. The clergy met early in the episcopal
palace. Present were the bishop, abbots, priors, and deputies of the chapters
and other religious communities of the diocese of Amiens. The first estate
may have been convoked in the same manner in 1560 since a copy of the
instructions sent to the deputy of the clergy of "the diocese of Amiens" has
survived, but unfortunately no precise information has been found to show
why the clergy separated from the other estates. We can only surmise that
it was the result of the anticlerical attitude of the third estate if not of both
the lay orders. The town of Amiens may well have had good reason to refuse
to show its cahier to the bishop in 1560 because the attitude of the échevins
towards the clergy was revealed by their willingness to discuss the partial
confiscation of church property the following year. Otherwise, there had been
no break with tradition. The same elements that stood for the first estate in
1507 had been convoked, and the curés were still excluded. The clergy of the
diocese did send a deputy to the bailiwick assembly, as well as to the meeting
of the government, perhaps as much to spy on the secular orders as to co-
operate with them. The events that took place in the estates of the bailiwick
are unknown. The town of Amiens had made preparations in a manner similar to those in 1560, but a bitter quarrel had developed between the municipality and the bailiff, apparently over an ordonnance issued by the latter
directing that a municipal assembly be held, this in violation of the town's
privileges. Could the bailiff have attempted to extend the suffrage? There
is insufficient evidence to say yes or no on this occasion.[11]

The crown and municipal officials restrained themselves when the bailiwick assembled to reform the custom in 1567. No doubt the presence of
Christofle de Thou, first president of the Parlement of Paris, had much to do
with the unusual spirit of co-operation. The upper clergy and the deputies of
the towns did not even raise objections when the curés and village proctors
were admitted to the assembly. Those present deliberated together, a virtual
necessity if a single code was to emerge for the bailiwick.[12] A large meeting

of the three estates of the area was held at Compiègne in 1573 where the feud within the third estate was renewed. Only the town of Amiens was directed to name deputies to the meeting of the three estates at Paris in July, 1575, leaving no excuse for the bailiwick officials to interfere.[13]

It was not until the elections to the Estates General of 1576 that the breaking point was reached. Unfortunately, our information is based almost entirely on the complaints of the town of Amiens. Several weeks after the delegates of the bailiwick had been chosen, the échevinage itself determined to send proctors to the king and Estates General to protest against what it considered the illegal electoral procedure permitted by the bailiff. It charged that twelve or fifteen interested persons had gone to the various villages and had persuaded certain individual inhabitants to give them procurations without formal assemblies being held or cahiers being prepared. These uninstructed proctors had not only been seated in the bailiwick assembly, but the vote they cast for each village had been given the same weight as that of the town of Amiens. It is not difficult to see who were the masterminds of this electoral fraud when one notes that the two deputies chosen to represent the third estate were both royal officials and that the cahier they took to the Estates General contained four articles designed to give the officers of the presidial seat places in the council of the town. Here we clearly meet the struggle for power between the town and crown officials that characterized elections of the period.

By the time the town managed to get its deputies to Blois, the king's delegates from the bailiwick had already been seated. Nevertheless, the privy council ordered that the municipal cahier be considered along side that of the bailiwick. It also directed that in the future preparatory elections be held in the provostships and that each of the deputations chosen there be given one vote in the bailiwick estates which followed. No mention was made of whether or not the villages were to participate in the assemblies of the provostships.[14] Indeed, as was so often the case, the royal directives may have been ignored. In 1583 when the estates of the bailiwick were next assembled, the deputies of the villages were instructed to go directly to Amiens to meet with the representatives of the towns and larger communities. At no time was the provostship of Amiens convoked, the town always acting for the surrounding area. Furthermore, in 1614 the échevins of Saint-Valery alone named a deputy to the bailiwick assembly, no mention being made of a preparatory assembly of the provostship of which it was a part.[15]

Unfortunately, little is known of the elections in the bailiwick of Amiens after 1576 beyond that the municipal oligarchy remained discontented. In 1588 the town sent its own deputy with a cahier to the Estates General. He was not, however, given a seat in that assembly. In 1591 and 1593 the échevinage took advantage of the weakened position of the royal officials to name deputies to the revolutionary assembly ordered by the leaders of the League. We have no evidence that the rest of the third estate of the bailiwick was ever convoked. The bailiwick nobility also had their difficulties. In 1588 the royalist faction accused the Duke of Aumale and his League followers of failing to summon all their order to the bailiwick assembly. Their charge is given some credence by the fact that only twenty nobles appeared to elect a deputy to the Estates General of Paris a few years later.[16]

The mayor of Amiens was summoned in 1596 to attend an assembly at Compiègne the last of August in which memoirs were to be submitted. The town received no word of the change in the location of the meeting to Rouen, but on October 30 the échevins decided to send a former mayor to court to attend to other affairs. The envoy found the king at Rouen on the verge of opening the estates. He was invited to attend for his municipality, and the échevinage was ordered to send instructions to him. In this accidental manner, Amiens was represented in the national assembly. The haphazard government of the era is abundantly clear.[17]

In the elections to the Estates General of 1614, the old quarrel between the crown and the town officials was renewed, this time over the question raised in 1560, whether the officers at the presidial seat or the échevins should have precedence in the third estate. When the lieutenant general sided with the former during the bailiwick assembly, the échevins walked out, protesting that the proceedings were null and void. A few weeks later the governor of Picardy tried to bring about a reconciliation, but it was to no avail. The town, charging that "the officers of the king at the bailiwick of Amiens had deputed themselves to prepare cahiers to the prejudice of the third estate and especially to this town," proceeded to prepare its own cahier and to name a deputy to the Estates General. Again it was the royal official, and not the deputy of the échevinage, who was seated in the national assembly. Insult was later added to injury when the town was ordered to pay fifty livres towards the expenses of its rival delegate.[18] In 1651 after studying the procès-verbal of 1614, the échevins again determined to win first place among the third estate. This time the presidial seat, cognizant of the precarious position of the crown at that time, offered no objection. The town had finally won, but the victory was of little significance for the Estates General was never held.[19]

It is well to pause at this moment to indicate some of the issues presented by the electoral history of the third estate of Amiens. No problems arose when only the town was summoned to the assemblies of the estates. The mayor, échevins, and other officials simply named the deputation they desired. Even the rare use of bailiwick elections prior to the middle of the sixteenth century brought no difficulties, for these meetings involved only the addition of the selected magistrates of a handful of towns who recognized the predominant position of the capital city. The growth in the number of the royal officials during the sixteenth century completely changed the picture. Many settled in Amiens where they followed the lead of the lieutenant general, who was no longer the appointee of the bailiff, but in fact, if not in name, the leading local representative of the king. Lawyers by training, ambitious, and often able, these officials were not content to see so much power wielded by the local oligarchy. A vigorous competition ensued in which rivalry in elections was but one manifestation. Town officials in places the size of Amiens were often able to maintain their position, but the smaller, weaker places in the bailiwicks usually succumbed to the lieutenant particulars and inferior judges. By adding these little towns and villages to the list of places convoked to the bailiwick assemblies, the new office-holding aristocracy could hope to impose its will during the elections, and if successful as in Amiens in 1576, to use its power to petition the king to change the municipal constitution to its advantage. The deputies of the nobility of Amiens sided with the delegate of the échevinage in preference to those elected by the bailiwick assembly.[20] One is only surprised to see the bailiff of Amiens adopting a policy in that year favorable to the new officer class. The best explanation for his action lies in his preliminary conference with other royal officials to determine how the elections were to be held. He was probably ignorant of the correct procedure and relied on the arguments of his subordinates.[21]

The increase in suffrage created a major procedural problem. If bailiwick assemblies were to be composed of great cities, small towns, and even villages, how was voting to be done? To give each locality one vote regardless of its size was clearly unjust; but to allow the leaders of the principal city to flock to the bailiwick assembly and each cast a vote equal in value to that of entire towns and villages was almost as bad. The king's suggestion in 1576 that preparatory assemblies be held in the provostships, and that in the bailiwick assembly each provostship, including that of the capital city, be given one vote, was designed to protect the municipalities from his own officials. Unfortunately, no definite policy was ever established for France as a whole, and where royal directives were issued, they were frequently ignored. As a result, a different answer was apt to be given for each locality when the problem arose.

The increasing number of those who attended the bailiwick assemblies for the third estate may have caused the clergy and nobility to withdraw from the common meetings of the three orders so as not to be outvoted. The anticlerical attitude of the secular orders in 1560 and 1561 also may have had its effect, but more likely, it was the royal officials who sparked the separation of the estates. It was they who established the procedure to be followed, and it was easier for them to find means to outvote the remainder of the third estate than to manipulate an election in which the other orders also participated.

Montdidier, Péronne, and Roye

The small but associated towns and provostships of Montdidier, Péronne, and Roye lay to the southeast of Amiens. The three towns had sent deputies to Laon near the close of 1482 to attend the assembly of the bailiwick of Vermandois to approve the Treaty of Arras, but they acted together as a separate electoral jurisdiction when they chose deputies to the Estates General of 1484. Little is known of the procedure followed, but the assembly was held at Montdidier and one delegate was elected from each estate.[22]

For some reason, the three provostships separated, and in 1507 the three estates of Péronne met alone to codify their custom. Present was the usual group of prelates, deputies of the ecclesiastical corporations, seigneurs, royal and municipal officials, and surprisingly enough, several curés.[23] The provostships continued to act apart in 1560, and each of them sent a delegation to Orléans.[24] In March, 1561, the town of Roye directed its deputies to go directly to the estates of the government of Picardy which met at Amiens to name deputies to the Estates General at Pontoise.[25]

By 1567 when the custom was reformed, the three provostships had once more been combined into a single government. There was some difficulty over whether the assembly should be held at Péronne or Montdidier, with the former emerging as the victor in the municipal rivalry. Otherwise, there were no difficulties, and the three jurisdictions prepared a single custom. Present were the curés and deputies of the villages as well as the upper clergy, seigneurs, officials, and representatives of the towns.[26]

Co-operation proved more difficult in the elections of 1576. The governor, Jacques d'Humières, assembled the three estates of Montdidier on September 13. Even the parish curés and the representatives of the villages were present along with the more important members of the three estates. After the roll call, the governor instructed each order to separate to elect its deputies. Near the end of October a meeting was held in which each estate prepared its cahier.[27]

Péronne and Roye had not been summoned to these meetings at Montdidier, and the two localities held separate elections to choose delegations to go to Blois. At some later date the first two estates of the provostships decided to co-operate with Montdidier, probably to save expense. Jean de Rivery, Seigneur of Pothonville, who had been elected at Montdidier, represented the nobility of the other localities at Blois as well. On the other hand, Adrien de Mailly, Abbot of Saint-Just, who had been elected by the clergy of Montdidier, was dropped and C. Chanleu, Canon of Péronne, stood for all the clergy. How these changes came about is not known, but co-operation between the three jurisdictions was undoubtedly facilitated because in Jacques d'Humières they had the same governor.[28]

The elections in 1588 saw still another change. The clergy of the town of Roye accepted the deputy of the provostship of Péronne, but the clergy of the remainder of the jurisdiction was charged with the support of the deputy from the provostship of Montdidier. The nobility of the three jurisdictions had a single representative, but the third estate of each elected its own deputation to attend the national assembly just as it had done in 1576.[29]

The three estates of Montdidier met in February, 1593, and twelve nobles sufficed to name their deputy to the Estates General. When the nominee of the third estate refused to attend, that order sent a blank procuration to the governor asking him to fill in the name of someone he thought suited for the post. One is struck by the third estate's lack of interest and by its complete trust in the governor who was a nobleman. The affair had no practical significance, for no deputies reported to Paris from Montdidier or the other two provostships.[30]

The elections in 1614 produced further variations. An unsuccessful effort was made to have the three provostships choose a common delegation, but the third estate refused, and each provostship sent a deputation to Paris. The national assembly was unwilling to recognize that the three jurisdictions were comparable to bailiwicks and made them share the same vote. Roye named Péronne's deputy of the clergy as its representative, and Montdidier was content to repeat the nomination of the delegate named by the clergy of Amiens. The nobility of the three provostships shared the same deputy.[31]

During the Fronde the officials of the town of Péronne decided on the delegate for the third estate, and then informed the representatives of the villages of their action when they later assembled.[32]

Ponthieu

The seneschalsy of Ponthieu with its capital of Abbeville was situated to the northwest of Amiens. Unfortunately, the archives of the town were destroyed during World War II, and little remains on which to base a study of the elections except a few printed documents and secondary materials. The seneschalsy participated in the Estates General of 1484. Eleven years later when its custom was codified, the five royal bailiffs of the subordinate jurisdictions were ordered to hold preparatory assemblies to name deputies to the estates of the seneschalsy. In 1529 the seneschalsy ratified the Treaties of Cambrai and Madrid. Little is known of the composition of these assemblies beyond that they were dominated by the same aristocratic elements found in the estates of Amiens during that period.[33]

Also, little is known as to the procedure followed by the estates of Ponthieu during the early stages of the Wars of Religion. Only the cahier of the town of Abbeville survives for the Estates General of 1560. In the elections held in March, 1561, to name deputies to the estates of the government, the third estate deliberated apart from the other two orders. Present in addition to the royal officials were the mayors and échevins of Abbeville and the communities of the plat pays. Less is known of the elections in 1576, although in that year it is at least possible that the secular estates named their deputies together.[34]

Only in 1588 do we get a fair idea of the procedure followed. In the opening assembly of the estates a quarrel occurred between the mayor of Abbeville and the lieutenant criminal of the seneschalsy on the matter of precedence; each claimed to be the chief person in the third estate. The seneschal called on the nobility for advice, and they sided with the mayor against the royal official. The three estates met in the same chamber, but it is not certain how they chose their deputies or prepared the cahiers. Mention is made of the villages being present.[35]

Small importance seems to have been attached at Abbeville to the estates of 1593, for no action was taken until it was learned that a former mayor was going to Paris anyway on his own business. The town officials hastily named him deputy and proceeded to prepare a cahier. More than two months later, long after the estates of Paris had begun to deliberate, some prodding by the Duke of Mayenne led the three estates of Ponthieu to assemble. The third estate, comprising the entire "body and community" of the town and some representatives of the plat pays, unanimously named the former mayor as deputy. Evidently the earlier election in which only the town had participated was not regarded as valid. Nothing is known of the activity of the other orders except that the Bishop of Amiens served as the deputy of the clergy of Ponthieu as well as of Boulonnais and Amiens and that no representative from the nobility attended the estates.[36]

On the morning of July 30, 1614, an assembly of the third estate was held which included those inhabitants of Abbeville who desired to attend and the deputies of the other towns and villages of Ponthieu. After the usual quarrel concerning precedence, a delegate was named to attend the Estates General. That afternoon the nobility and ecclesiastics met in the same chamber and elected one deputy from each order.[37] In 1649 the quarrel over the relative position of the officials of Abbeville and those of the crown was renewed.[38]

In general, our knowledge of the elections in Ponthieu is far from complete. It is not known whether all of the lesser clergy were invited to participate. Though the documentation is by no means precise, the substitution of such vague phrases as "the plat pays" in the assembly of 1561 by "the deputies of the towns, bourgs, and villages" in 1588 and 1614 would seem to indicate the increased attendance of the rural areas. Sometimes two or more orders named their deputies in a single chamber, sometimes they did not. When they did meet in the same room, it is not said whether one order participated in the voting for the deputies of the other. No friction was apparent between the nobility and third estate, but a constant quarrel existed between the échevins of Abbeville, supported by the nobility, and the royal officials of the seneschalsy.

Boulonnais

The seneschalsy of Boulonnais, like that of Ponthieu just to the south, sent deputies to the Estates General of 1484, codified its custom near the end of the fifteenth century, and ratified the Treaty of Étaples in 1496 and the Treaties of Cambrai and Madrid in 1529. What little is known of the procedure followed in these meetings indicates that the composition of the three estates was restricted and that the orders deliberated together.[39] The records are more complete for the meeting of the estates to reform the custom in 1550. Only a handful of the upper clergy attended, a fact which did not prevent a dispute over precedence among them. Lawyers, officials, and the deputies of a few towns stood for the third estate.[40]

With this background one is surprised to find that both the curés and the deputies of the rural parishes were present ten years later when the estates of the seneschalsy met to name deputies to the Estates General of Orléans. After a preliminary meeting together, the three orders separated to prepare their cahiers. When they reassembled, each order was invited to read its remonstrances. Those of the secular estates strongly attacked the clergy, and the spokesman of that order made a vigorous reply. Thereafter, deputies were elected in the presence of the three estates to go to the Estates General. On March 6, 1561, the estates of Boulonnais again assembled, this time to choose deputies to a meeting of the government at Amiens, where in turn deputies were to be named to the Estates General at Pontoise. The electoral procedure of 1560 was repeated in 1576.[41]

The elections in Boulonnais in 1588 were held under the most difficult circumstances. The town of Boulogne was almost alone in Boulonnais, and for that matter in Picardy, in not accepting the League. It had just successfully withstood a siege and was hardly regarded as a safe spot for the partisans of the League. As a result, the meeting of the estates of Boulonnais on August 10 was not well attended. Several of the upper clergy, including the Bishop of Boulogne, thought it better to absent themselves whereas the parish priests were probably not summoned. Only forty-five nobles attended in person, but nineteen more sent proctors. The third estate was more dutiful, and in addition to the royal officials, five towns and eighty-one villages were represented. During the introductory meeting, both the clergy and the nobility moved that the assembly be adjourned because of the many absentees. The royalist lieutenant general refused on the grounds that the absentees had been summoned and that there was insufficient time before the opening of the Estates General to permit postponement. He then suggested that the three orders separate to name their deputies. The clergy chose a deputy, but the nobility was not so obliging. After a stormy meeting in which the partisans of the royal cause were unable to get a majority for their candidate, the second estate disbanded. For some reason the third estate delegated to the mayor and échevins of the town of Boulogne the authority to name the deputies of the order.

Hardly had the assembly disbanded when the lieutenant general received a directive from the king ordering that the estates be held at some place other than Boulogne because access to that town was not as free as he desired; that is, many Leaguers did not dare go there and place themselves in the hands of the royalist governor and the lieutenant general. This strange action by Henry III reflected both the strong sense of justice so characteristic of the Renaissance Monarchs and the royal desire not to further alienate the Guises. Nevertheless, with their usual independence, the local crown officials ordered the nobility to assemble at Boulogne on August 20 to complete the anti-League ticket. Only thirty-three nobles came in person, but thirty-five others sent their procurations. Those present gave nineteen votes to the royalist candidate and twelve to that of the League, but when the votes of the proctors were added, the total for the League candidate was thirty-two, and that of the royalist remained at nineteen. The crown officials were not to be easily defeated. They ruled that the king had ordered everyone whose name was inscribed in the electoral registers to confer together, and that this condition had not been filled by those represented by proctors. Hence they declared their candidate elected, and Boulonnais sent royalist deputies from each estate to Blois.

Again the king intervened against his own supporters. He annulled the election that had been held at Boulogne on grounds that many persons did not have safe access to the town, and he ordered a new assembly. These elections were held under the leadership of the League at Étaples, and the deputies chosen were later given seats at Blois, in preference to those selected at Boulogne. Unfortunately, little is known of the elections in 1593 and 1614 other than, in the latter, a dispute arose between two nobles each claiming to be the deputy of his order. In the end both were seated.[42]

Calais

Calais with its surrounding area known as the pays reconquis was located farther north along the coast. After a long period of English domination, the territory was retaken by the French in 1558. The area named three deputies to the Estates General in 1576, at least one in 1588, and two in 1614. We are unable to ascertain the electoral procedure used except that both the curés and the deputies of the villages were included in the assembly that codified the custom in 1583.[43]

Summary

Even for a government as small as Picardy, it is difficult to make generalizations on electoral procedure, yet certain trends can be ascertained. After the middle of the sixteenth century the curés and deputies of the villages or parishes began to be added to those who were convoked to the bailiwick assemblies. In Amiens, Montdidier, Péronne, and Roye, their presence can first be documented in assemblies to codify or reform the custom. This suggests that the desire to give everyone a voice in so important a matter led to the addition of these elements to the bailiwick assemblies, and that after the precedent had been established, it was continued. However, in Ponthieu the curés and villages were convoked without the benefit of being included in a prior meeting to codify the custom, and in Boulonnais they were actually excluded from the codification in 1550, but were summoned to name deputies to the Estates General ten years later. Clearly other factors must have been involved. One possibility lies in the desire of the royal officials to increase the suffrage in the hope of defeating the municipal bureaucracy in the bailiwick elections. The case seems clear in Amiens, and it is worthy of note that the suffrage was more restricted in several places during the elections in 1588 and 1593 when royal officials were weak.

The attendance of the proctors of the villages immediately raised the question of how voting should be done, whether the village ballot should be given equal weight to that of the town. The same problem arose elsewhere in regard to the vote of a curé who attended in person and the deputy of a cathedral chapter or monastery. Likewise, there was the matter of whether the vote of the proctors of nobles should be counted or whether only the ballot of those who attended in person ought to be included.

The custom of the three estates of meeting together and voting by head was replaced near the end of the sixteenth century by the practice of voting by order. Only circumstantial evidence can be offered to explain this change. Perhaps, the royal officials separated the orders so as to have a freer hand in the third estate, perhaps the inclusion of many curés and village proctors led the clergy and nobles to withdraw to avoid being swamped, or perhaps the anticlerical attitude of the secular estates in 1560 and 1561 caused the withdrawal of the clergy. Problems such as these must be considered in the following chapters. It can only be said that no ill-feeling between the nobility and third estate can be found in the electoral assemblies. Indeed, the nobility supported the bourgeoisie in Amiens and Ponthieu when they became involved in a bitter quarrel with the royal officials. Another characteristic of the elections was the tendency of the crown to protect the privileges of the municipalities against its own officials whereas these same officials were willing to disobey the directives of the crown.

3

THE ELECTIONS IN THE ÎLE-DE-FRANCE

The Government

South of the broad plains and low rolling hills of Picardy extends the fertile land of the Île-de-France — a vast ill-defined territory whose long subservience to the crown had led to an unusual amount of administrative confusion. In no other area of equal size in France was there a greater multiplicity of tiny bailiwicks and overlapping and confused jurisdictions. As with Picardy, the Île-de-France had no long history as a feudal duchy or as an administrative division of the kingdom to give it important provincial institutions. The first governors appeared only at the close of the Middle Ages, and in 1561 in the one known meeting of the estates of the government, half the bailiwicks did not participate. The officials of the government frequently had boundary disputes with those of Champagne and Picardy, and in the Estates General some confusion existed over where the Île-de-France ended and Normandy began.[1]

Vermandois

Most of the jurisdictions of the Île-de-France were small, but there were several notable exceptions. Among them was the bailiwick of Vermandois which contained in 1483 such towns as Soissons, Reims, Laon, Châlons-sur-Marne, and Saint-Quentin that had sent deputies to the assemblies of the medieval kings. Indeed, the very size of the bailiwick presented a problem because some of the inhabitants had to travel long distances to attend meetings of the local estates. Perhaps for this reason, Vermandois was one of the first jurisdictions to use provostship assemblies to choose deputies to go to the seat of the bailiwick. To our knowledge the issue first arose in 1482 when the various bailiwicks of the kingdom were ordered to assemble to ratify the Treaty of Arras. The initial instructions the lieutenant general sent to the provostship of Châlons-sur-Marne were for the clergy, nobles, and people of the third estate who were customarily summoned to attend the estates at Laon. Since Châlons and Laon were more than fifty-five miles apart, it is very doubtful if many persons were anxious to answer the summons. It was probably for this reason that a royal directive was later issued ordering that an assembly of the provostship of Châlons be held to elect deputies from the clergy, nobility, and towns to go to the bailiwick estates. The fact that the deputies from the third estate were to be chosen from the towns indicates that the plat pays was not consulted.[2]

When the time came to choose deputies to the Estates General at Tours the following year, provostship elections were once more held at Châlons to name deputies to go to the bailiwick assembly at Laon. Unfortunately, we are unable to ascertain whether the other subordinate jurisdictions followed a similar practice.[3]

The document on the ratification of the Treaties of Cambrai and Madrid in 1529 gives no indication of how the bailiwick assembly was held, but the meeting to codify the custom in 1556 is of interest. Those summoned went directly to the bailiwick meeting at Reims. Included were the curés and deputies of the villages, as well as the more important members of the estates. Many villages, presumably to save expense, combined to name a single deputy. Possibly it was to reduce costs that the royal officials returned to the earlier practice of holding provostship elections in 1560.[4] Our data are limited to documents on the expenses of holding the electoral assemblies and of paying the deputies, but this material indicates the amount given the messengers who carried the orders of the bailiff "to convoke the deputies of each provostship." Laon and Soissons also claimed reimbursement for the cost of sending four hundred letters to the villages of their jurisdictions; probably these letters were for summoning the villagers to the local elections. The failure of the other subordinate jurisdictions to make a similar request indicated that they did not summon or even inform rural areas. The bailiwick estates prepared separate cahiers, but it is not known how the deputies were elected. The only clue is that in the provostship assemblies held in 1562 for another meeting of the bailiwick estates, two or more orders voted together in several cases.[5]

Some of the confusion over the boundaries of the various bailiwicks was brought to light in the elections in 1576. The provostship of Saint-Quentin was ordered to send deputies both to an assembly at Amiens on the grounds that it was in Picardy and to one at Laon on the theory that it was part of the bailiwick of Vermandois. Although protesting against the double summons, the three estates of the provostship prepared to honor both. One deputy for the clergy was sent to Laon, along with one for the Catholic nobility, one for the Protestant nobility, and one for the towns and villages. At Laon the third estate of Saint-Quentin won a reprieve from delegating to Amiens and accepted Jean Bodin as deputy of the bailiwick, but at the same time reserved the right to send someone with Bodin to make remonstrances for the town. Later, when Bodin became a leader of the tolerant party in the Estates General, strongly Catholic Saint-Quentin sought to disavow him, charging that he had been elected by a plurality of the votes of the officers of the presidial seat of Laon only and not by the greater number of those present. Saint-Quentin, assisted by Reims, Soissons, and Châlons, failed in the attempt to unseat Bodin because the eminent jurist was able to show that the four municipalities had not consulted the inhabitants of the plat pays who, he implied, had participated in his own election. Disappointed, Saint-Quentin availed itself of the right it had reserved of sending a deputy directly to Blois, and he was given a seat under the bailiwick of Vermandois. It would be desirable to know more of the elections at Laon, but this much appears evident. The local royal officials had acted in a high-handed fashion and had imposed their candidate on the deputies from the provostship.[6]

In the same year Châlons wrote the king saying that the disorders in the area were so great that the provostship could not be assembled in time to elect deputies to go to the meeting of the estates of the bailiwick. Permission was requested to delegate directly to the Estates General. The king refused and ordered the deputies to take the cahier to Laon for comparison with the one that had already been made for the bailiwick. The townsmen must have been dismayed at the tolerant directives given Bodin, for on September 16 they assembled to name deputies to the Estates General in spite of the royal order, but no representatives of the municipality appeared at Blois except to disavow Bodin. Reims also dispatched deputies for the clergy and the third estate to the national assembly, but they were not given seats. There was certainly a pronounced tendency for the important towns and provostships to seek independent representation in the Estates General in spite of the rule for bailiwick elections.[7]

The elections in 1588 in Vermandois remain in oblivion, but the provost-ships came into their own during the estates of the League. The Duke of May-enne bypassed the bailiwick assembly, and in 1590 ordered the provostships to send deputies directly to the Estates General. The national assembly was not held during that year, but the provostships of Reims, Laon, and Soissons had deputies present when the meeting finally took place at Paris in 1593.[8] The action of Mayenne is easily explained. He controlled most of that part of France, and election by bailiwick gave him only one vote at Paris, but election by provostship gave him several more. He was therefore not unwilling to profit by the particularistic tendencies of the inferior jurisdictions.

The towns of Reims and Châlons were both asked to send a deputy to the assembly of the estates at Rouen in 1596. About twelve officials sufficed to name the representative of the latter.[9]

The Estates General of 1614 saw a return to the traditional procedure. An assembly of the provostship of Laon was ordered for July 26 to name deputies to the bailiwick assembly on the first of the following month. The nobility and clergy were directed to attend, and the towns and villages were to send proctors. A similar preparatory assembly took place at Châlons where two meetings were held that were composed of the clergy, nobility, royal officials, and deputies of the towns and villages. In the first, deputies were elected to prepare cahiers. In the second, the cahiers were approved, and each estate named one deputy to the bailiwick assembly at Laon. In Reims, the cahier of the town was prepared by the council, but approved by an assembly of the inhabitants.

The deputies of the three estates from the eight provostships assembled at Laon on August 1, and each order named its deputies separately. The town of Reims expressed a desire to send deputies directly to the Estates General, but no one appeared under its banner at Paris. Soissons was more fortunate having become an independant bailiwick by that time, but the deputy of the third estate from Soissons was to be unsuccessfully challenged by Vermandois in the Estates General. The parishes were told to pay part of the salary of this deputy so it is possible, though not certain, that the rural areas were consulted during the elections.[10]

The elections of 1651 added to the confusion already created by the Fronde. The lieutenant general at Laon took it upon himself to draw up the cahier for the third estate and then asked the municipal officials to give their approval. The municipal officials protested violently against this intrusion by the royal official on one of their fundamental rights.[11]

Far more serious were events in Châlons during the same election. The provostship had become a bailiwick in 1637, and with this elevation came the privilege of naming deputies directly to the Estates General. In the absence of the lieutenant general, the lieutenant criminal convoked the three estates of the bailiwick, but two days before the elections were held his superior returned and issued different orders. A quarrel ensued with the lieutenant general and the officials of the treasury and the presidial seat on one side, and the lieutenant criminal, supported by the provost, the mayor of Châlons who was his uncle, and the council of the town on the other. When the lieutenant general attempted to preside over the meeting of the third estate ordered by his rival, the lieutenant criminal entered with forty or fifty armed men and forced the crown officials to retire, after their robes had been torn from them and several persons had been wounded. He then assumed the presidency of the assembly and was elected deputy along with the provost. The lieutenant general later held another assembly in which deputies were also elected, and the royal officials appealed to the Parlement of Paris for protection. It was to no avail, for the king's council sided with the lieutenant criminal, and his election stood. The episode marked one of the most violent quarrels between the town and crown officials, for the lieutenant criminal, though also a royal official, was the nephew of the mayor and drew his support from the town. Once again the king's council had defended the municipality. The royal officials did get partial revenge by persuading the bakers to complain to the king's council about a municipal tax on wheat that had been levied in 1639 to pay soldiers but was serving only to enrich the town officials.

A less violent but more interesting dispute arose in the chamber of the clergy in the same elections. The lieutenant general convoked the parish clergy, and they came in such numbers that they overwhelmed the deputies of the chapters. The latter protested and boycotted one of the assemblies, for which they were fined by the lieutenant general. The chapters appealed to the Parlement of Paris to remit the fine and to order that in the future the curés not be summoned. Only the rural deans were to share with them the responsibility of speaking for the first estate. They based their argument on grounds that the procedure ordered by the lieutenant general violated the custom of the whole of France, the province of Champagne, and the town of Châlons. Furthermore, it was contrary to reason to give the curés, who were only "cadets," individual votes when the canons of the cathedral church, who were the principal priests of the diocese, could only deputize one or two of their number. If this procedure was continued, the curés would become the "absolute masters."

A spokesman for the curés denied that it was not customary for them to be convoked. Curés voted in the diocese of Paris, "which as capital of the kingdom ought to give the law to the other towns," and also in the bailiwicks of Meaux, Senlis, Vitry-le-François, Beauvais, Étampes, and other places.

A substitute for the procureur of the king pointed out that there was no regular, uniform electoral procedure for France, but that it varied from place to place and for that matter from time to time in the same place, depending on the circumstances. Hence the argument of neither side should be accepted on this point. However, since the curés' interests were involved in the elections to the Estates General, it would be unjust to exclude them and permit the seigneurs and deputies of the parishes to participate. On this recommendation the case was dismissed and the fine allowed. [12]

The most interesting feature of the electoral procedure in Vermandois was the use of preparatory elections in each provostship for the nobility and the clergy, as well as for the third estate. This procedure was probably introduced in 1482 because the bailiwick was too big to permit a large number of people to attend the estates in person. The earlier method must have created real hardship for those who obeyed the summons, and was no doubt changed for this reason. Villages began to appear in the bailiwick assembly in 1556 and in the provostship assemblies four years later, but as late as 1614 the rural areas were not consulted in several jurisdictions, including Reims. It is not known whether the nobility without fiefs or the parish clergy attended the provostship assemblies prior to the Fronde. The three orders sometimes voted together in the provostships during the early stages of the Wars of Religion, but they nearly always voted separately in the bailiwick assemblies. The quarrel between the royal and municipal officials was as bitter as in Picardy.

Senlis

Senlis was the second largest bailiwick in the Île-de-France at the close of the Middle Ages. The jurisdiction included some important towns, but there was a tendency for them to break away and, with the surrounding countryside, form new jurisdictions; both Clermont-en-Beauvaisis and Beauvais became independent bailiwicks during the sixteenth century. By 1614, Compiègne and Senlis itself were the only important towns undisputedly in the jurisdiction.

Voting in the town of Senlis during the fifteenth century was still done in general assemblies of the inhabitants. In 1468, one hundred ten persons from both the clergy and the laity met together to name deputies to the Estates General. Compiègne and Beauvais also sent delegations to Tours that year, but their voting procedure is unknown. In 1483 when the electoral system was changed, the town of Senlis chose ten persons to attend the estates of the bailiwick. Compiègne named three. Little else is known beyond that the deputy who attended the Estates General was said to represent "the towns and pays of the bailiwick" — a vague expression. His constituents are perhaps better indicated by a letter concerning him addressed only to the bourgeois of Senlis, Beauvais, Compiègne, and Clermont-en-Beauvaisis. The activities of the other orders remain a mystery.[13]

The meetings of the bailiwick to ratify the Treaties of Cambrai and Madrid in 1529 and to codify the custom ten years later provide a better opportunity to study the composition of the estates. Here one notes that there were preparatory assemblies in some of the subordinate castellanies to name deputies from the three orders to the local capital, thereby saving many people from making the journey. In 1529 only the summoned inhabitants of the castellany of Senlis preferred to come in person, but in 1539 those in neighboring Compiègne and Pontoise did likewise. The people who attended the bailiwick estates from these jurisdictions were the usual members of the upper clergy, seigneurs, royal officials, lawyers, or deputies of the towns, the one exception to this rule being the curés of Pontoise who attended in 1539. The composition of the preparatory meetings remains in doubt, but since curés were occasionally chosen as deputies for the clergy, they were probably present. On the other hand, the fact that the representatives of the third estate who attended the bailiwick assembly were described either as the deputies of a town or, at best, of a town and castellany, suggests that the rural villages had little or no role.[14]

The bailiwick of Senlis sent deputies to the Estates Generals of 1560, 1576, 1588, and 1614, but the destruction of the communal archives leaves much in doubt concerning the procedure followed during the elections. Scattered references in local chronicles indicate that in 1560 the town of Senlis named two deputies to meet with "other delegates of the towns" at the bailiwick estates. Such statements suggest that the rural population was still excluded, but chroniclers are notoriously inaccurate in these matters.[15]

The bailiwick of Senlis was as troubled as Vermandois by disputed boundaries and by a tendency of subordinate jurisdictions to break away and become independent. The castellany of Pontoise, for example, was also claimed by the Norman bailiwick of Gisors. In 1529 the inhabitants of Pontoise protested against being summoned to Senlis, in 1560 her clergy sent a deputy directly to the Estates General, but the third estate acted with Gisors. In 1614 the third estate of Pontoise voted with Senlis, but when her lieutenant civil was chosen, the échevins of Senlis tried to reverse the election. They were unsuccessful, but Senlis sent a second deputy for the third estate and he was seated.[16]

Beauvais was another subordinate jurisdiction that was for a long time dependent on Senlis. In 1560 and 1576 the various guilds of the town assisted in the preparation of the municipal cahier which was taken on both occasions by two deputies to the bailiwick assembly at Senlis.[17] A few years later, Beauvais and the surrounding territory were made into an independent bailiwick and were therefore authorized to send a separate delegation to the Estates General of 1588. The municipality named one deputy from each of the three estates to the bailiwick assembly in that year. The nobility and clergy took offense at this action and saw to it that a representative unacceptable to the town was elected to go to Blois for the third estate. Whether or not this was accomplished by the three estates voting together is not known. It is only certain that the nobility prepared a separate cahier. In any case, the town of Beauvais took the usual recourse on such occasions and named two deputies directly to the national assembly. They were both seated without difficulty, but the representative named for the third estate by the bailiwick was challenged by the deputy from Senlis on the grounds that the conditions justifying the creation of the bailiwick of Beauvais had not been fulfilled. As an additional point, it was charged that the seven castellanies which made up the new bailiwick had not been consulted in the elections. Nevertheless, with assistance of the king's council, the deputy from Beauvais was given his seat. This did not prevent Senlis from renewing the quarrel in 1614.[18]

In 1591 the municipality again elected a deputy to go directly to the Estates General, and he appeared at Paris when the assembly of the League was finally held in 1593.[19]

Our knowledge of the elections in 1614 is more complete. The three estates met in July and elected their deputies separately. Unfortunately, the brief procès-verbal does not indicate who attended.[20] Just four days before the local estates were to open, the mayor of Beauvais assembled the town's guilds to name three persons to receive suggestions and to prepare a cahier. It was not until October 17 that the committee made its report, and the cahier was accepted by the town. The bailiwick officials also prepared a cahier to send to Blois. The bourgeois oligarchy felt its interests threatened by this move and decided to attach this second cahier to that of the town. Apparently the other communities in the jurisdiction were not consulted anymore than they had been in 1588, and a bailiwick cahier was never prepared.[21]

During the Fronde the municipality continued its practice of naming the bailiwick's deputy of the third estate to the Estates General.[22] At no point in the electoral history of the jurisdiction is there evidence that any other community was ever consulted. The usual quarrel between the town and royal officials was clearly in evidence by 1614 and may have existed during the elections of 1588. Little is known of the composition of the first two orders except that the attendance of the nobility is suggested by an average of twenty-four signatures on their cahiers in 1588 and 1614. The three estates voted apart in 1614, but may have acted together in 1588.[23]

There were three other bailiwicks north of the Seine River in the Île-de-France that had at one time or another been claimed by Senlis. Very little is known of the electoral procedure followed in these localities except that in 1539 the curés and deputies or inhabitants of the villages were allowed to attend in Clermont-en-Beauvaisis and Valois. For the Estates General, it can only be added that in 1614 the three estates voted apart in Clermont and that there was a disputed election that was carried to the king's council for settlement. The data presented here prove that so many persons voted in the first estate that the curés must have been present.[24]

Information is more abundant for the third bailiwick. Chaumont-en-Vexin and the associated jurisdiction of Magny were claimed by the bailiwicks of Senlis and Gisors. In 1539, Chaumont and Magny participated in the codification of the custom of Senlis. The tie was continued in 1576 when Chaumont shared her deputies for the secular estates with Senlis and in 1588 when a single delegate represented the third estate of the two bailiwicks. By 1614, Chaumont felt itself to be in a financial and legal position to act independently and named a complete delegation to the Estates General.[25]

While Chaumont was seeking its independence from Senlis, Magny was doing likewise in regard to Chaumont. The area chose deputies for the three estates in 1588 and 1614, but no trace of them can be found at Blois in the former year. Perhaps the explanation is to be found in a decree of the king's council in November, 1614, in which Magny's status as an independent bailiwick was not recognized, and her deputy for the third estate was given a status inferior to the representative of Chaumont. The deputy of the nobility of Magny was also successfully challenged by Chaumont. Only the representative of the clergy was able to hold his seat. Little is known of the electoral procedure except that in 1614 both the curés and deputies of the villages were among those who attended and the three orders met together, but possibly voted apart.[26]

The Town and Provostship of Paris

South of Vermandois and Senlis, there were several jurisdictions which straddled the Seine River. The most important of these was the provostship of Paris. Not only did the provostship have the privilege of electing deputies from the three estates to the Estates General just as if it were a bailiwick, but the town of Paris was also permitted to send a separate delegation which sat with the third estate. As one might expect, a bitter rivalry developed between the two jurisdictions and was often in evidence during the elections.

The provostship of Paris, which included the capital and the surrounding towns and villages, was administered by a provost, who was generally a noble of the robe, and a host of subordinate officials comparable to those found in any bailiwick. Executive power in the town was vested in a provost of the merchants and four échevins who were elected for two years by a complex system of indirect suffrage which gave control to a small patrician oligarchy. These five men were assisted by twenty-four councilors who served indefinitely and were replaced on death or resignation by the provost of the merchants, échevins, and other councilors. The town was subdivided into sixteen quarters each under the charge of a quartenier who was likewise chosen by a very limited and carefully selected suffrage. Under the quartenier there were cinquanteniers and dixainiers.[27]

When it was necessary for the town to take action on important matters, the provost of the merchants and échevins might be content to summon the councilors, but sometimes they called a larger assembly. The quarteniers, cinquanteniers, dixainiers, a limited number notables from each quarter, the clergy, members of the sovereign courts, and representatives from a few privileged guilds were all asked to participate at one time or another.

Little survives of the register of the town of Paris prior to 1500, but we have some knowledge of the elections in the provostship to the Estates General of 1484. The three estates assembled with the intention of naming their deputies together, but the clergy preferred to act alone and withdrew to choose its delegation. The two lay orders argued that this violated the traditional practice of the three estates voting together, and they elected two deputies for the clergy along with their own representatives. The clergy complained of this threat to the "authority and liberty of the church," and retaliated by refusing to give powers to the lay delegates named by the other estates. Nothing is known of the composition of the assembly except that the curés were not consulted. Each order prepared its own cahier, but showed it to the other estates before departing for Tours.

The cause of the disagreement between the clergy and the lay orders is difficult to determine. Our only clue lies in an article in the cahier of the third estate against the frequent nonresidence of the clergy. This brought forth protests from the first estate whose three leaders were of necessity absentees because they held two or more benefices.[28] Thus the critical attitude of the secular estates toward the clergy possibly led to the division of the three estates.

The composition of the provostship estates in the early part of the sixteenth century may be obtained from a meeting held in 1510 to codify the custom. Present were 45 clergymen, 45 nobles, and 65 royal officials, lawyers, and bourgeois of Paris. Excluded were the lesser clergy and inhabitants of the villages. The full extent of those who were not summoned is best realized by the hundreds of persons from each estate who attended the assembly to reform the custom in 1580; no clergyman, noble, or village was intentionally omitted.[29]

The electoral activities of the town of Paris in 1468 and 1483 remain a mystery, but in 1506 the provost of the merchants, échevins, and councilors chose a large delegation to go to persuade the king to marry his daughter to the Duke of Angoulême. After the estates, a larger assembly was convoked to ratify the proposed marital alliance. Even then only forty persons attended. In 1516 again only the provost of the merchants, échevins, and councilors chose the deputation to the national assembly. The elections of 1558 were also handled with dispatch by the same officials, though the crown seems, in truth, to have given the municipality too little warning to have expected otherwise.[30]

The royal decision in 1560 to have deputies named by bailiwick brought two problems to the fore: could the town of Paris send deputies directly to the Estates General and did the provost of Paris have the authority to convoke elements from the city of Paris to the electoral assembly of the provostship? These two issues, especially the second, were hereafter raised whenever the Estates General was convoked. On receipt of the letters of convocation, the council of the town ordered that an inquiry be made to ascertain the procedure used in 1484 and at the same time took steps to have remonstrances prepared by the masters of all the trades and by eight or ten inhabitants from each quarter. The crown officials moved with almost equal dispatch and ordered an assembly of the estates of the provostship of Paris to meet on November 4 in the episcopal hotel of the Bishop of Paris. Both rural and urban parishes were to name deputies. The provost of the merchants and échevins protested to the king against this summons, and on October 8 a royal order was issued which excused them from attending the provostship assembly and at the same time gave the town permission to name deputies for the third estate directly to the Estates General, a privilege which it had not exercised in 1484. The first round had been won by the municipality. Later, the provost of the merchants and échevins were specifically given the sole right to convoke the third estate of the town, but at the same time they were instructed to have delegates attend the assembly of the provostship on November 4 to explain what actions the municipality had taken. In a general assembly, the town decided to acquiesce, and several persons were elected and given powers "to hear and see what was done" and to say that they had begun to prepare their cahier.

The estates of the provostship opened at 7 o'clock on the morning of August 4 as scheduled. The roll was called and the Bishop of Paris, deputies from the ecclesiastical chapters of Paris, Meaux, and Saint-Denis, and the curés of several villages were present for the first estate. An unspecified number of seigneurs attended for the second estate. While the role of the nobility was being called, the deputies of the town appeared. They were asked to take seats below those of the royal officials, but objected with demands that they be given first place in the third estate. Hardly had this dispute been settled and the roll of the nobility completed, when a new tumult broke out. The deputies of the town had discovered that representatives from the quarters of

Paris had been summoned by the provost. They complained bitterly, saying
that the king had given to their council alone the right to convoke inhabitants
of the town and that the group here represented had already taken part in the
municipal assemblies. The crown officials offered the flimsy excuse that they
had summoned every order in each quarter whereas the king had only acknowledged the right of the provost of the merchants and échevins to convoke
the third estate. A further dispute arose when it was revealed that representatives from the privileged guilds were present. Unfortunately, the remainder of the manuscript is lost, but the estates of the provostship finally
managed to name delegations from each of three orders to the Estates General.

If the town had been defeated in the estates of the provostship, it still held
the right to name deputies directly to the Estates General. In a series of
general assemblies attended by the provost of the merchants, échevins, councilors, quarteniers, representatives from the sovereign courts, six privileged
guilds, and ten persons from each quarter, cahiers were prepared and deputies elected.[31]

On February 14 of the following year the Estates General was again convoked. In a general assembly of the municipality, four deputies were named
to attend the estates of the provostship and give the opinion of the town concerning the proposed new taxes. The deputies were not empowered to participate in any elections, nor was the town authorized to name deputies directly
to the Estates General. After the inevitable quarrel between the crown officials of the provostship and the municipal authorities, the assembly proceeded
to attack the royal government so violently that the elections were postponed.
To prevent a recurrence of this unhappy episode, the king ordered two pres-
idents of the Parlement of Paris to direct the assembly of the provostship
when it met again the latter part of May. This time the municipal officials
attended in mass, but once more they found that the representatives of the
privileged guilds had been summoned and the argument continued. Not until
several days later were the estates able to transact business and then to the
disadvantage of the crown, for the third estate refused financial aid. For
some reason no deputies were elected. Conscious of this omission the town
council named a delegate on August 7 to take the cahier of the third estate to
the Estates General, but he returned after delivering it. Neither the town of
Paris nor the third estate of the provostship had any other contact with the
national assembly.[32]

On August 27, 1576, the provost instructed the Bishop of Paris to appear
with the clergy of his diocese at an assembly of the three estates of the provostship on September 17. He also convoked the nobility, the deputies of the
parishes, and the provost of the merchants and échevins of Paris. As usual
the municipal council protested to the king, saying that it was customary for
it to assemble the third estate of the town. Henry III, as was his wont, supported the council against his own officials and again granted the town a separate delegation to the Estates General. He further freed it from the obliga-
tion of sending deputies to the assembly of the provostship. The échevins
acted quickly and instructed each quartenier to name six notable bourgeois to
attend the municipal assembly on September 6 along with the deputies of the
sovereign courts and corporations, chapters, communities, orders, and estates of the town. A large committee was named to prepare the cahier, but
actually the work was done by Versoris, who was to become the leading ad-
versary of Bodin at Blois. Everyone in the town was invited to submit suggestions, and on order of the king, a box was prepared to receive them. Then,
just as in 1560, the king partly changed his mind and directed that an échevin
and one or two bourgeois of the town attend the assembly of the estates of the
provostship. The delegation was named and made its appearance in the estates where it successfully won precedence over the lieutenant civil and the

procureur of the king, but it refused to take an active part, no doubt to uphold the independence of the town. Indeed, the assembly of the provostship must have been a noisy affair, for an earlier session had been devoted to a quarrel between the provost and the Bishop of Paris over whether the nobility or the clergy should occupy the right side of the chamber. In spite of difficulties, the estates separated into three chambers and named their deputies.

In a series of general assemblies held between the second and eighth of November at the town hall, a draft of the cahier of the town was read and approved, and three deputies were named to the Estates General. These assemblies were attended by the municipal officials, ten persons from each quarter, five of whom were officers of the sovereign courts and five bourgeois and merchants, two of the masters from each of the six privileged guilds, and the deputies of the colleges, chapters, and convents of the town. Later, the merchants of Paris complained to no avail that no one of their number had been elected to go to Blois to defend the "liberties of their estate."[33]

Little is known of the elections in the town of Paris in 1588, but we can study the assemblies of the provostship in some detail. The three estates met on August 13 in the episcopal hall of the Bishop of Paris. After a preliminary discussion which included some bickering on precedence among the clergy and the certain protest by the deputies of the town against the possible presence of any merchants or citizens of the municipality, the three orders separated to name their deputies. The third estate, which was composed of the delegates of more than 380 parishes, elected the provost of the merchants by a plurality of votes. The municipality did not participate. The second estate selected a deputy and nominated a committee to prepare its cahier. We know nothing of the activities of the clergy.[34]

Paris, the stronghold of the League, participated in the various elections ordered by the Duke of Mayenne between 1591 and 1593. Much of the usual procedure was followed except that the clergy did not participate in the assembly to prepare the cahier and name deputies of the town. The clergy of the provostship in 1591 chose its delegation without difficulty, but the second estate presented a problem, for so few nobles supported the League that only two reported to take part in the election. The municipal elections of 1593 saw another interesting innovation. Instead of the quarteniers naming the officers and bourgeois from their quarter to attend the electoral assembly as in the past, it was decreed at the suggestion of the provost of the merchants that since the elections "concerned everyone and were of such consequence, the deputation should be made by everyone and in as large a company as possible." Therefore, the inhabitants of each dizaine were instructed to assemble and name two deputies to attend an assembly of the quarter and there elect four persons to the municipal assembly. Thus the influence of the League made for greater suffrage.[35]

The restoration of royal authority brought to a quick end the movement toward increased municipal suffrage. In 1596 Henry IV simply ordered the provost of the merchants to bring one échevin with him to court to attend an assembly the last of August.[36]

The elections in the town in 1614 were similar to those held during the reigns of Charles IX and Henry III. After some debate it was decided that each quartenier should choose six bourgeois from his quarter to attend the municipal assembly rather than have them elected even by a very restricted suffrage. The Parlement and the Chambre des comptes were invited to send deputies, but they declined on the grounds that "the cahiers which will be decreed in the said estates would be presented to them for registration and verification." The provost of the merchants and the échevins countered by ordering the quarteniers to name ten deputies rather than six. Five were to be from the sovereign courts and five were to be bourgeois or merchants. The

Bishop and chapter of Paris and the convents of the city were also invited to
send deputies. Nine ecclesiastical corporations complied with this request.
On June 25 the general assembly commenced with members of the sovereign
courts convoked by the quarteniers attending as citizens of their quarter
rather than as mandataries of the Parlement and the Chambre des comptes.
Two ecclesiastics, two members from each of the sovereign courts, two bourgeois, and two merchants were elected to meet with the provost of the merchants and the échevins to prepare the cahier. A box was established to receive the suggestions of anyone in town. The members of the committee took
an oath to keep their deliberations secret. They prepared the cahier carefully, the suggestions of the people and past ordonnances of the estates being
considered. No less than thirty-six meetings were required to complete the
task.

The usual difficulties arose between the town and provostship. The municipality refused to answer the summons to the assembly of the provostship,
and the lieutenant civil retaliated by ordering two bourgeois from each quarter to attend. The town immediately complained to the chancellor who directed
that they send deputies to the estates of the provostship, but in return the lieutenant civil was to revoke his convocation of the bourgeois. Unfortunately, we
know little that took place during the estates of the provostship except that the
chancellor's orders were obeyed. [37]

On October 8 a second general assembly of the town was held. The same
persons were convoked as in the earlier meeting on June 25, except that this
time two of the masters from seven rather than the usual six privileged guilds
of the town were ordered to be present. The purpose of the assembly was to
elect deputies to the Estates General, but no action was taken because it was
decided to prepare the cahier first. This left the provost of the merchants in
an embarrassing position, for he had held the assembly in response to prompting by the crown to speed the selection of the town's delegation. When the
Estates General began to assemble on October 14, Paris still had no representatives. On the preceding day, the king had directed that the provost of
the merchants and two échevins attend anyway. In a hurridly called meeting,
the municipal council authorized these officials to participate in the Estates
General, and another general assembly of the town was ordered for the seventeenth to elect a permanent delegation. It was not until the fourth general assembly held on October 30 that the cahier was read and approved. The fourteen masters of the privileged guilds also attended these last two meetings,
bringing the total who participated in the elections and in the approval of the
cahier to about two hundred persons. [38]

The quarrel between the municipal council and the officials of the provostship was continued in 1651. The provost of Paris summoned representatives of the town to the estates of his jurisdiction and refused to listen to the
protests of the two échevins of the municipality who were present. The latter
departed and won an order from the king in council declaring the elections in
the third estate null and directing that a new assembly be held. [39]

A review of the electoral procedure used in the municipality points to
some variation. In the assemblies in which only the towns were convoked for
the third estate, the provost of the merchants, échevins, and councilors sufficed to name the deputation. When elections to the Estates General were
held by bailiwick, the town was a little more democratic. The provost of the
merchants, échevins, councilors, quarteniers, deputies of six or seven privileged guilds, and from six to ten appointed persons from each quarter always
attended. Only in 1593 did a large part of the population have the privilege of
naming the representatives from the quarters. The sovereign courts sent
deputies until 1614, when they refused and sought to place themselves in a
special position above and beyond the municipality. Beginning in 1576 the

clergy of the city was generally represented and voted for the deputies from the third estate. The actual electoral assemblies included few persons, but an effort was made to get all who so desired to submit complaints and in several instances special boxes were established to receive them. Of course, it was the notables again who chose which of these complaints to put in the cahier, so the control of the municipal oligarchy was not effectively challenged by this practice.

Suffrage in the provostship of Paris expanded during the first half of the sixteenth century. In 1560 and thereafter the Bishops of Paris and Meaux were convoked, the former being instructed to bring "the clergymen of his diocese," an order which was interpreted to include the deputies of the chapters and at least a limited number of the curés of the parishes. Nobles with fiefs attended for the second estate. The representatives of the secondary towns and parishes comprised the third estate, the deputies from Paris itself having only the power to hear and report, and not to take part in the elections. Elements in the city were convoked by the provost, but when they attended it was over the protests of the town and contrary to the intentions of the king. Thus only the clergy of Paris habitually took part in the elections of both the town and the provostship. They alone had double representation. After the preliminary meeting, the three estates separated to prepare their cahiers and elect their deputies. Except for the quarrel between the clergy and lay estates in 1484 and between the nobility and the clergy in 1576, no friction appears to have existed between the three orders. It was the struggle between the municipal oligarchy of the town and the crown officials of the provostship that embittered the proceedings.

The provostship of Paris was plagued by another, though less troublesome, subordinate jurisdiction. The little bailiwick of La Ferté-Alais, which consisted only of the municipality and eight parishes, sent a deputy from the third estate to Blois in 1576 with a cahier. He deposited it and departed soon thereafter to save expense. In 1588 deputies from the clergy and nobility, as well as the third estate, tried to get seats in the Estates General, but this time the representatives of the provostship of Paris were successful in getting a decree from the king in council denying their request on the grounds that the bailiwick was subordinate to the provostship. The three estates of the bailiwick prepared cahiers in 1614, but their deputies were again refused seats in the Estates General. [40]

Mantes and Meulan

The associated bailiwicks of Mantes and Meulan were situated down the Seine River from Paris. Here, instead of the usual duel between the municipal oligarchy of the principal town of the bailiwick and the officials of the presidial seat, there was a triangular conflict between the towns of Mantes and Meulan and the royal officials. The usual solution of the trio during the sixteenth century was for each to name a deputy for the third estate. By 1614 the royal officials had apparently gained control of both towns, for the number of deputies was reduced to two: the lieutenant civil and criminal at Mantes and the lieutenant civil and criminal at Meulan. By the time of the Fronde the royal officials seated in the towns had begun to quarrel bitterly over the question of who should have precedence in the electoral assembly of the bailiwick. The suffrage was probably extended, for both the curés and the deputies of the villages participated in the codification of the custom in 1556. [41]

Melun

The bailiwick of Melun was up the Seine River from Paris. Here the same extension of the suffrage to include the curés and deputies of the parishes that has been noted elsewhere took place between the codification of the custom in 1507 and its reformation in 1560. Unfortunately, it is only for 1614 that sufficient documents have survived to enable one to form some idea of how the deputies to the Estates General were elected. In that year notices of the coming elections were posted in the towns and bourgades, and curés were instructed to make announcements on Sunday. All ecclesiastics, including the curés, nobles, and parishes were to attend or send deputies to the bailiwick assembly. Even the three parishes of Melun were to be represented rather than the municipality itself. Certainly the suffrage was as complete as could be desired.

We can only guess how well the people responded in the rural parishes. In the town of Melun only sixty-nine persons attended the assembly of the parish of Saint-Aspais, but they were nevertheless described in the procès-verbal as being "the larger and wiser part" of the inhabitants. The combined vote of the members of the other two parishes came to only fifty-two. Merchants and artisans rarely attended, and the three parish assemblies were dominated by lawyers and officials. It is not surprising that they agreed in their separate assemblies that the lieutenant general of the bailiwick should be elected to attend the Estates General and that he should be nominated in the bailiwick assembly by the mayor. Prior planning by a few officials was certainly in evidence here.

The bailiwick assembly took place the following day. The advocate of the king delivered a long speech so full of historical and biblical illusions that he almost neglected to explain the object of the assembly. The roll of the estates was called and the voting took place. Although the three estates sat in the same chamber, each order elected its own deputies. About seventy-five persons from the first estate were present, many abbots sending proctors. The nobles were less numerous, and again frequent use was made of procurations. Women holding fiefs invariably sent proctors. Deputies from about one hundred parishes represented the third estate. On the whole, the procedure followed was less democratic than the suffrage. The clergy and third estate of the town of Melun announced their candidate before the vote was taken, and enough curés and deputies from the rural parishes followed the lead of the capital to ensure the desired results. No cahiers were made at the assembly, but the bailiff instructed the deputies to present at the Estates General complaints given them by the three orders. It is not known how or when these complaints were prepared. The most unusual features about the elections were the convocation of the parishes of the town of Melun coupled with the absence of a special deputation from the municipality, and the lack of strife between the officials of the town and crown.[42]

Montfort-l'Amaury, Dourdan, Nemours, and Dreux

South of the Seine River were four tiny bailiwicks about which very little is known. Probably the suffrage was generous, judging by the fact that both the curés and the representatives of the villages were admitted to assemblies which codified the customs of Montfort-l'Amaury and Dourdan in 1556. The third estate of Dourdan prepared a separate cahier in 1560, and the nobles of Nemours, a third jurisdiction, did likewise in 1651. Small as Nemours was, the nobles of one subordinate locality held a preparatory assembly to name a deputy to the bailiwick estates in 1614. These facts suggest that the three

orders normally acted apart. Nothing at all is know of the elections in the
fourth bailiwick, Dreux. [43]

Summary

Perhaps the most striking feature about the elections in the Île-de-France
was the conflict that almost invariably existed between the king's magistrates
and the municipal officials. This ill-feeling exerted itself constantly in Paris
and flared up at Saint-Quentin, Laon, Châlons, Senlis, Beauvais, Mantes,
Meulan, and elsewhere. An election as at Melun in 1614 for which there is
adequate information, but which had no apparent conflict, is indeed rare. On
the other hand, though the three estates generally voted for their deputies
separately throughout the sixteenth and seventeenth centuries, ill-feeling
between the orders can rarely be discerned.

Another problem which emerges is that of the inferior jurisdictions seeking independent representation. Vermandois was especially beset by this difficulty; by the time of the Fronde, Soissons and Châlons had won seats in the
Estates General, and Saint-Quentin and Reims had tried on one or more occasions. Perhaps the use of preparatory elections for the three orders in
these jurisdictions provided too great a temptation to depute directly to the
Estates General rather than merely to bailiwick estates as ordered. Beauvais, Clermont-en-Beauvaisis, and Chaumont-en-Vexin also won independence
in the post-Medieval period, while Magny and La Ferté-Alais tried without
success.

Suffrage increased during the course of the sixteenth century. The curés
and deputies of the villages did not attend the assemblies of the provostship
of Paris in 1484 and in 1510, but were present in 1560 and thereafter. At
Melun these two groups were excluded from the codification of the custom in
1507, but participated in its reformation in 1560 and in the elections to the
Estates General in 1614. The belief that the suffrage was widespread elsewhere is substantiated by the convocation of the curés and villages when the
customs of Clermont-en-Beauvaisis and Valois were codified in 1539 and in
many other places thereafter. This points to their participation in the elections to the Estates General as well. On the other hand, the curés, villages,
or both, were probably ignored in some of the subordinate jurisdictions in
Vermandois and Senlis and in all of Beauvais until the Revolution.

4

THE ELECTIONS IN CHAMPAGNE AND BRIE

The Government

The rolling plains of northern France that so characterize Picardy and the Île-de-France extend eastward into Champagne and Brie, and with them went the lack of well-defined political subdivisions. Champagne had once had a feudal count, but the area had been under the control of the crown for so long that the institutions there were quite similar to those of the regions already discussed, and there were no regularly convoked provincial or bailiwick estates during the Renaissance.

Meaux, Sézannes, and Provins

The bailiwicks near Paris were small, but that of Meaux nevertheless managed to give birth to the bailiwicks of Sézannes and Provins at the beginning of the Renaissance. Very little is known of the electoral procedure. The assembly of the estates of Meaux in 1496 to ratify the Treaty of Étaples reveals the use of preparatory elections. One or more deputies from each estate were named by the castellanies. The suffrage may have been quite broad for such an early date. The curés of the urban, but not the rural, parishes attended with the deputies of the chapters. At Provins, then a subordinate jurisdiction, a large number of nobles were present, not over a third of whom were listed as having seigneuries, the remainder merely being described as écuyers. The third estate included many people from villages. Since they were called farmers or marguilliers and not deputies, it is not certain that they had been elected at village meetings. Possibly there had been a general convocation of the inhabitants of the jurisdiction and these were the people who had been prevailed upon to respond. This interpretation is supported by the fact that four or five persons often came from the same locality when one or two were all that any village was likely to elect. On the other hand, it is more than probable the parishes in the castellany of Montereau-faut-Yonne elected deputies to the preparatory assembly.[1]

A different method was used to convoke the bailiwick of Meaux in 1509 to codify the custom. The castellanies did not elect deputies, and only the upper clergy, counts, barons, castellans, seigneurs with high justice, officials, lawyers, and notable bourgeois were summoned.[2] Unfortunately, it is not known how Meaux selected her deputies to the Estates General. The same must be said of the castellany of Sézannes, a jurisdiction that broke away from Meaux to become an independent bailiwick before the sixteenth century meetings of the Estates General.

There is a little more information on the elections in Provins. The three estates of the bailiwick met together in 1560 to elect their deputies. It is not known whether voting was done by head or by order, but the estates drew up their cahiers separately. The procedure followed by the third estate was for

the municipal council and a few notables to prepare the cahier for presenta-
tion to a general assembly of the inhabitants for approval. The inhabitants
had not been previously informed of the Estates General nor had they taken
part in the elections. However, in the general assembly of the town, those
present did not hesitate to alter the proposed articles in the cahier when they
desired. Preparatory assemblies for the bailiwick estates were apparently
not held, for in 1614 the bailiff of Provins ordered the marguilliers of the
parish of Saint-Maurice in the castellany of Montereau-faut-Yonne to have
one person elected to attend the meeting of the bailiwick estates at Provins.[3]

Sens

The activities of the bailiwick estates of Sens are better known. The assembly to codify the custom near the close of the fifteenth century did not include the lower clergy or the bourgeoisie of any town save Sens. Needless to
say, the rural population was not there. In 1529 the bailiwick estates that
ratified the Treaties of Cambrai and Madrid consisted of the deputies of the
chapters and castellanies. Some of the castellanies chose members of all
three orders to attend the bailiwick estates, but others sent only a deputy
from the third estate. In 1555 when the custom of Sens was reformed, the
bailiff employed still another method of convoking the bailiwick. Not only
were the upper clergy and the nobility told to be present, but also deputies
representing the "cures, men, and inhabitants" of the small towns and villages.[4]
The readiness of the bailiff to change the procedure for holding the estates brought him into conflict with at least one subordinate jurisdiction. In
1576 he ordered every town and village to send deputies to Sens. Both the
countess and the town of Tonnerre protested, pointing out that in the past,
preparatory assemblies had been held in which the inhabitants of the county
had named deputies to the bailiwick, thereby saving the poor people the expense of supporting representatives from each tiny locality. After the protest, the bailiff of Tonnerre convoked the three estates of the town and invited
the villages to send complaints and remonstrances, an invitation which they
did not accept. The three orders acted together in naming deputies to go to
Sens.[5] In 1614 the bailiff of Sens again instructed the villages to send their
proctors direct to the seat of the bailiwick where he divided the assembly into
two chambers, one for the clergy and nobility and one for the third estate.
Unfortunately, the reaction of Tonnerre on this occasion is unknown.[6]
The subordinate bailiwick of Langres, situated far to the east of Sens on
the borders of Burgundy and the Empire, caused the bailiff of Sens still more
trouble. In 1555 the leading inhabitants protested against being summoned to
the assembly to reform the custom, and in 1576 and thereafter they sought
direct representation in the Estates General. The Bishop of Langres as a
peer of France had the privilege of attending the national assembly without
election, and since his large diocese extended into the neighboring bailiwicks
of Chaumont-en-Bassigny and Bar-sur-Seine, a dean or canon of the cathedral chapter was nearly always elected by one bailiwick or the other. The
nobility displayed little desire to change the existing situation, and it remained
for the municipal officials of the town of Langres to spearhead the movement
for separate representation. In 1576 the municipal council proceeded to summon from 100 to 120 notable bourgeois to elect a delegation. As an insufficient number appeared on the appointed date, it was decided to have the diz-
ainiers collect the votes desired from their jurisdictions and report to the
council. This was done and two deputies were elected to go to Blois. About
one hundred persons attended a meeting in which the cahier was read and
approved. When the delegation arrived at Blois, it was challenged by the

deputies of Sens, and the king in his council ruled that their cahier must be turned over to their attackers, but the two deputies of the third estate remained at Blois in a subordinate capacity. The representative of the clergy apparently had little difficulty, being armed with procurations from the bailiwicks of Chaumont and Bar-sur-Seine as well as Langres.[7]

Undaunted, the municipality made a second attempt in 1588 to win a seat in the chamber of the third estate. This time less effort was given to get the approval of a large number of the inhabitants of Langres, but the quarrel with the deputies of Sens was repeated at Blois. The royal council, quoting its decision of 1576, ordered that the cahier of Langres be turned over to the deputies of Sens, and none of the representatives of the subordinate bailiwick were listed as deputies at the Estates General.[8] In 1614, 1649, and 1651, Langres also named delegations, but without success either because of the activities of Sens or the cancellation of the Estates General. One sees here the persistent hope of a proud, old municipality to gain a seat in the Estates General, a hope undimmed by frequent adverse rulings by the king's council. One would think that the crown would be impatient at such determination, but in fact Langres was only one of many.[9]

Troyes

The most detailed information of the elections in Champagne is to be found for the town and bailiwick of Troyes. The procedure followed at the close of the Middle Ages varied with the situation. In 1506 the two assemblies of the town, to elect deputies to the estates of Tours and to ratify the marriage treaty between Claude of France and the Duke of Angoulême, were widely attended. One hundred sixty-six persons, including the bishop and other clergymen, were specifically named as being present at the earlier assembly and 435 at the latter. In addition, we are informed that at both assemblies others were there "in great numbers." On the other hand, in 1516, 1517, and again in 1558, the mayor, échevins, and councilors sufficed to name the deputations.[10]

The bailiwick assemblies also varied. In the meeting to choose a delegation to the Estates General of 1484 and to codify the custom in 1494, deputies were elected in the subordinate jurisdictions, but when the custom was reformed in 1509, Louis XII directed the upper clergy, important nobles, officials, lawyers, and other notable bourgeois to attend in person. Apparently this injunction was obeyed, the lesser clergy and nobility were ignored, and the preparatory elections in the subordinate jurisdictions were abandoned. The three estates named together their representatives to the Estates General of 1484 and acted as a single chamber when they considered the custom.[11]

The absence of specific directives from the king in 1560 on how the bailiwick should be consulted left the local officials free to issue what directions they pleased, and a return was made to the use of preparatory elections in the subordinate bailiwicks. Unfortunately, no information has been found concerning the activities in these jurisdictions, and it is impossible to tell whether the inhabitants of the villages or only those in the principal locality were consulted for the third estate, but there is no doubt that the curés were present. Even if the villages were ignored, the fact that forty-one subordinate bailiwicks or comparable jurisdictions, exclusive of the town of Troyes, sent deputies and nine more failed to honor the summons shows that at the worst the petty bourgeoisie and some of the well-to-do farmers were given the opportunity of participating. The same extended suffrage was found in the elections in the town of Troyes. Here the officials, deputies of the individual chapters, guilds, and other groups, such as the nobles and advocates, were called in turn to ballot. Each individual or deputy voted for at least one and generally two persons to represent each estate in the bailiwick assembly.

A similar procedure was employed in the bailiwick estates soon thereafter. The eighteen deputies of the three estates of the town of Troyes were asked to express their individual preferences for those who would attend the Estates General for the three orders. Then the subordinate bailiwicks were called upon, and the deputies of the clergy, nobility, and third estate of this or that jurisdiction cast their ballot collectively for one or more members of each order to go to the national assembly. The intermixing of the three orders was complete and there was no evidence of any difficulties resulting. The task of preparing the cahier of the bailiwick was accomplished by reading the one prepared by the municipal officials of Troyes and amending it in open assembly with those submitted by many of the subordinate jurisdictions. The clergy of the chapters of Troyes was unhappy with the results and added a separate petition. [12]

A few months later the Estates General was again convoked, and on March 13, 1561, the municipal council of Troyes consulted the guilds on the contents of the cahier. Four days later the bailiwick assembly was held to elect deputies to the estates of Champagne, and on March 20 the governmental meeting opened at Troyes. Unfortunately, nothing is known of the procedure followed in the elections to the bailiwick estates or what actually happened at either the bailiwick or governmental assemblies except that on March 22 the clergy of Champagne prepared a separate cahier. The separation of the orders may have been provoked by the anticlerical attitude of the lay estates, but no certain proof is available. Later, new elections were ordered, and on May 10 the nobility and third estate of the town of Troyes prepared a common cahier, but in a meeting of the estates of the government in June the clergy once more acted alone. [13]

The lieutenant general changed the electoral procedure in 1576. The clergy and nobility were directed to come to the bailiwick estates rather than go to assemblies in the subordinate jurisdictions to elect deputies as they had done in 1560. The members of the third estate in the lesser towns and rural areas were thus left to prepare their cahiers and elect their deputies alone. This was to be done by having each village or parish prepare a cahier and elect one or two deputies to take it to a meeting composed of the representatives of the other inhabitants of the same castellany. In the castellanies and comparable subordinate jurisdictions, cahiers were to be prepared and deputies elected to the bailiwick estates. These directives of the lieutenant general were usually followed, although there were the inevitable exceptions. The three estates deliberated together at Garchy and Isle-sous-Montréal, they prepared a common cahier at Jaucourt, and the secular orders submitted a single petition from Méry-sur-Seine. At Neuvy-Sautour and La Coudre, clergymen were elected as deputies. Occasionally all the inhabitants of a jurisdiction were told to attend instead of each locality naming representatives. From sixty to eighty inhabitants of Chassenay and five other villages joined together to send a deputation to Troyes. The number of persons who attended these rural meetings was usually not large, although we are almost invariably told that "the larger and wiser part" of the inhabitants was present. Once more there are exceptions. At Garchy, 193 persons including 32 widows participated, the latter taking part as heads of families. There was a tendency for the seat of the subordinate jurisdictions to dominate the proceedings as was so often true at the bailiwick level. The deputies of eleven dependent villages found it necessary to compete with one hundred inhabitants of Chaource who attended in person. Yet when all is said, the suffrage was generous and the procedures relatively democratic for the age. The exclusion of the first two orders that had characterized the elections in most of the subordinate jurisdictions must also be marked in the town of Troyes. Otherwise, the municipal electoral assembly was composed of the same elements as in 1560.

Only two deputies — both for the third estate — were selected to attend the bailiwick assembly. Here the three estates prepared individual cahiers and presumably elected their deputies to the Estates General separately, although the older practice of voting by head died with difficulty. The cathedral chapter did not hesitate to name its choice for representatives for all three orders.[14]

Almost nothing is known of the electoral procedure followed in 1588. The lack of documents has led one historian to suggest that they were destroyed along with other papers of the League after the triumph of Henry IV, but whether this be true, as seems probable, or whether the scarcity of material results from the failure to convoke the subordinate jurisdictions, cannot be said. It is only known that the clergy once more prepared a separate cahier.[15] The growing predominance of the town and its municipal oligarchy becomes more clear when one considers the various elections ordered by the League. There is no evidence that the subordinate jurisdictions were consulted; the guilds in Troyes were likewise forgotten, and the right to name the deputation was left to the municipal council.[16] The council and some bourgeois also sufficed to elect two échevins to attend the estates at Rouen in 1596.[17]

The restoration of royal authority brought about a partial return to the practices of 1576. In 1614 the bailiff told the bishop to summon the benefice holders in his diocese, and he himself took measures to contact the clergy of the other dioceses who inhabited his jurisdiction. The officials of the castellanies were instructed to send the nobility to the bailiwick estates and to have the villages elect deputies to preparatory assemblies, where in turn deputies were to be chosen to meet at Troyes with the other estates. On the whole, the castellanies followed the procedures they had used in 1576, those who deviated from the bailiff's instructions on the first occasion very likely doing so in the same manner again. Two changes may be noted, however. The first two estates now almost never attended, and here and there the part played by the village deputies was reduced. At Joigny the judges of the villages predominated, while at Saint-Florentin the villagers were not consulted at all. On the other hand, this antidemocratic tendency was not universal as is shown by the unusually large number of documents that survive concerning the activities of the rural inhabitants of Jaucourt, a jurisdiction that had been convoked by the bailiff of its seigneur, the Duke of Vendôme.[18]

Little is known about the procedure followed in the town of Troyes in 1614, but the powerful position that the municipal oligarchy had achieved during the Wars of Religion at the expense of the guilds and the deputies of the subordinate jurisdictions was maintained. The patrician class found itself challenged only by the royal officials. For the first time quarrels ensued between the two groups who were less closely related than in the past when, for example, Pierre Belin was mayor and Philippe Belin was lieutenant particular during the elections of 1576. The natural rivalry between the royal and municipal officials was furthered by the support that Henry IV gave to the pretension of the lieutenant general to preside over assemblies of the council of the town. The king had bitter memories of the League and was the first ruler to impair seriously the privileges of the municipalities in the hope of maintaining order. One is therefore not surprised to find quarrels over precedence appearing between the two groups of officials in the elections in 1614, but the town leaders were more fortunate in their dealings with the guilds and the subordinate jurisdictions. The former were consulted in an advisory capacity, but were not present when the municipal council elected two deputies to go directly to the Estates General and a committee of six to prepare the cahier. In the bailiwick estates the deputies of the castellanies did no more than confirm the town's choice of representatives to attend the Estates General and to ask the same committee of six to draft the bailiwick cahier. The clergy voted separately and committed the task of preparing its cahier to a group of eight.[19]

The elections of 1649 began with another brush between the crown and municipal officials. The lieutenant general had availed himself of the printing press to prepare the instructions for the bailiwick assembly; they were distributed to the various towns, villages, and other jurisdictions. The mayor of Troyes had little sympathy for this economy of effort and argued that the lieutenant general ought to appear in person before the municipal council to read the letters of the king as had been done in 1614. He appealed to Marshal l'Hôpital, lieutenant general of the king in Champagne, against the actions of the bailiwick official and the marshal appeased his anger by giving him original letters from the king and queen-regent.

The municipal councilors then turned to the problem of the elections and decided that they would follow the form used in the past. A few days later when a meeting of the council and some bailiwick officials was held, it was revealed by the mayor that the register of the town was not clear as to what had happened in 1614, but that he thought the guilds ought to be consulted. The lieutenant general said that the bailiwick records showed that the procedure in 1576, 1588, and 1614 had varied from election to election. He suggested that they proceed with prudence; if it was desired they could summon a few more persons, but a general assembly of the town was unnecessary. "The people do not have the knowledge and ability of those who could and ought to be employed to make the cahiers and take them to Orléans" where the estates were to meet.[20]

Several more meetings of the council were held, which some bailiwick officials and eight former échevins also attended. This group elected deputies to the bailiwick estates and a committee of six to prepare the cahier of the town.

The bailiwick estates saw the procureur of the king protest against the exclusion of the advocates and the guilds, but without success. The three estates separated and each order elected its own deputies and committee to prepare its cahier. The third estate repeated the nominations of those selected by the town to draft its remonstrances, but plans were made to receive the suggestions of the subordinate jurisdictions and the guilds. [21]

When letters convoking the Estates General reached Troyes in 1651, the lieutenant general informed the town council in person, and it was decided to follow the procedure used in 1649. Thus it was hoped to avoid the quarrels that had colored the earlier elections. The advocates, who were present this time, protested against the exclusion of the guilds, but they could win the support of only the provost of the merchants who marvelled at the right of the peasants of the villages to be consulted while the guilds of the town were ignored. The lieutenant general did not even trouble himself to answer these arguments, and the town and bailiwick elections were held as before.[22]

Thus in 1484 and 1560 the three estates voted together, but in 1561 the clergy acted apart to protect its interests. The complete separation of the orders in 1576 was marked by the abandonment of preparatory elections for the clergy and the nobility and the presence of a large number of the proctors of the villages in the local assemblies. Such changes appear to have been initiated by the lieutenant general and not by the three estates themselves. The possible limiting of the suffrage in the bailiwick in 1588 and its more certain curtailment in 1593 resulted from the activities of the municipal council who, when freed from royal control, seized full authority for the town. On the other hand, the refusal to permit the guilds to participate in the elections during the Fronde must be charged against the lieutenant general.

Vitry

The bailiwick of Vitry-en-Perthos was situated east of Troyes on the border of France and the Empire. Here only the prelates, abbots, deputies of the chapters, counts, castellans, seigneurs with high justice, royal officials, lawyers, and other notable bourgeois were ordered to participate in the codification of the custom in 1509. Two decades later in the assembly to ratify the Treaties of Cambrai and Madrid, the priors and lesser seigneurs were included and more of an effort was made to get the towns to name delegations. The curés and villages continued to be ignored, and there is no evidence of preparatory elections in the subordinate jurisdictions.[23]

In 1544 the imperial forces of Charles V captured and burned Vitry. To prevent a recurrence of this misfortune, Francis I ordered that the town be moved to a more easily defended position, and the new municipality and bailiwick was called Vitry-le-François. This change in name was paralleled by a more gradual change in electoral procedure.

The limited data available suggest that the assembly in 1560 differed little from those that had been held before. The towns continued to deputize directly to the bailiwick estates. Épernay held an assembly attended by the captain of the town, several clergymen, and a large number of inhabitants in which the deputies were named to go to the bailiwick assembly at Vitry. Rethel and presumably the other municipalities did likewise. At Vitry the three estates prepared a common cahier and elected representatives to go to Orléans. Again, in March, 1561, Rethel and probably the other towns sent deputies directly to the bailiwick. Then in the elections of May, 1561, a change in procedure may be noted. Rethel dispatched her representative to Sainte-Menehould where the nobility and the deputies of the other towns and villages of the provostship assembled to name deputies to go to Vitry and to prepare separate cahiers for each order. The first evidence of the introduction of the villages had been marked by preparatory elections in the provostships and a separation of the estates.[24]

The lieutenant general took no notice of the new procedure when he convoked the bailiwick in 1576. All ecclesiastics, including curés, seigneurs, lawyers, bourgeois, and inhabitants of the towns and villages were told to come to the assembly at Vitry. No mention was made of preparatory elections in the provostships or even of the towns and villages electing deputies. The results were foredoomed. Each individual or locality did as it pleased. Some of those who attended the bailiwick assembly for the clergy stood for deaneries, but several had been elected by provostships. Many nobles came in person, but several subordinate jurisdictions such as Épernay and Fismes sent deputies for the second estate. Some of those who attended for the third estate had been elected by provostships, some by groups of towns and villages, and some by individual communities. The variations in the electoral procedure were certain to provoke confusion at the bailiwick assembly. When the three orders separated to elect their deputies, the nobility began to debate on what weight ought to be given the vote of the deputies of the provostships. Should their ballot count the same as that of an individual noble who had come in person, or should its value be equated with the number of nobles in the electoral jurisdiction who had signed the procuration? No agreement could be reached, and it was finally decided to hold a second assembly fifteen days later in which all members of the second estate were to appear in person. Surprisingly, the other two estates managed to choose their representatives without mishap. Perhaps there had been no rival candidates to protest against the method of voting adopted.[25]

In 1588 the estates of the bailiwick were convoked in the same manner, but nothing is known of what happened at the assembly. The unusual circumstances surrounding the estates of the League in 1593 led the towns of Vitry and Saint-Dizier to give their procurations to the deputy of Reims, and no bailiwick assembly was ever held. For the elections of 1614, it can only be

said that a preparatory assembly was held by the nobility of the provostship
of Vertus in the presence of the bailiff and the proctor of the Count of Vertus
and that the second estate of the bailiwick continued the practice adopted in
1576 of preparing a separate cahier.[26]

The elections in 1649 are of interest. The three orders assembled separately, the chamber of the clergy being composed in part of individuals and in
part of representatives of inferior jurisdictions. On the first ballot voting
was by head and the dean of the chapter of Vitry was elected. Immediately, a
protest was made by two persons who had voted for the Bishop of Châlons,
one claiming to have the procurations from twenty ecclesiastics of the subordinate bailiwick of Fismes and the other from eighty in Vertus. They, of
course, demanded a hundred votes in all, or preferably, that balloting be by
provostship for all in the assembly. The opposition argued with success that
only those present could vote, that it was not lawful to elect someone who did
not reside in the bailiwick, and that the bulk of the diocese of the bishop lay
outside of Vitry.

Two years later the nobility proved less bellicose. When they assembled,
some proctors appeared and announced that they held procurations from 346
nobles to vote for the Marquis of La Vieville and the Seigneur of Espence.
The nobility who were present appointed a committee of two to examine the
procurations, but the task was found to be so difficult that they decided to accept them all and then proceeded to elect unanimously Viéville and Espence.
In the order convoking the bailiwick in both 1649 and 1651, the bailiff had
specified that procurations were acceptable. In one instance his directive
had been respected, in the other it had not. The results were different because in one case there had been rival candidates and in the other there had
been no debate as to who should be chosen.[27]

The most difficult problem raised by the elections in Vitry was the number of votes that should be given to the deputies of subordinate jurisdictions
and to other holders of procurations. The bailiff does not seem to have specifically ordered any secondary assemblies. Whether they resulted from the
desire to avoid going to the bailiwick assembly, or on the inspiration of inferior magistrates, we do not know. Again it ought to be noted that the introduction of preparatory assemblies took place at about the same time as the
inclusion of the villages and the separation of the orders.

Chaumont-en-Bassigny

Nothing is known of the electoral procedure in the bailiwick of Château-
Thierry which broke off from Vitry during the sixteenth century, but we are
a little more fortunate in the case of Chaumont-en-Bassigny, a jurisdiction
situated to the south of Vitry along the borders of the Empire. It is difficult
to reconstruct the composition and activities of the bailiwick estates prior to
the Fronde. The usual select group of clergy, important seigneurs, officials,
lawyers, and representatives of the leading towns participated in the redaction
and reformation of the custom in 1494 and 1509. In 1588 the three orders
prepared a single cahier, but in 1614 the nobility submitted theirs individually.
There is also ample evidence of rivalry between the bailiwick officials and
the municipality.[28] However, it is the assembly of March 1, 1649, that provides the most interest. Sixty-four ecclesiastics, over half of whom were
curés, 154 nobles, and the deputies of thirty-four towns and other communities stood for their respective orders. After the usual preliminaries, the
three estates separated. The clergy and the third estate managed to name
their representatives with no more than the usual quarrels over precedence.
The nobles were not so fortunate, even though they wisely sought to speed the

proceedings by waiving this ticklish question "without prejudice to houses, qualities, dignities and rank." The initial vote gave the Sieur of Vaudremont ninety and M. de Verpelles sixty-three of the votes of those present. But the matter was not to be so easily resolved, one supporter of Verpelles announced that he had eighteen procurations and Verpelles himself claimed the vote of the subordinate bailiwick of Rosnay. Vaudremont, of course had a rival list of absentees who supported his candidacy, but this was not needed. The bailiwick officials ruled that procurations would not be counted in accordance with the letters of the king of July 20, 1614. Vaudremont had even felt secure enough to cast his vote for the third party, but Verpelles could not afford to be so generous and had voted for himself. [29]

Summary

The same extension of the suffrage to include the curés, lesser seigneurs, and villages took place in Champagne that has been noted in Picardy and the Île-de-France. In every bailiwick for which there is information, it can be shown that these elements were sooner or later allowed to participate in the elections. Indeed, the assembly in Meaux in 1496 was one of the earliest instances of a systematic effort to consult all the adult male inhabitants of a bailiwick. The reduction of the suffrage in 1509 when the custom was codified must be attributed to the decision that only the most important members of the three estates be summoned, but judging by the developments in Provins and other neighboring jurisdictions, suffrage was expanded again later in the century. The convocation of the villages made electoral assemblies in the subordinate jurisdictions advisable, but in Meaux and Sens there was a decline in their use and only in Troyes did a thoroughly developed system continue to exist. In Vitry and Chaumont the nobility and clergy sometimes named deputies in preparatory assemblies, and sometimes they came in person. This led to difficulty in deciding what weight should be given to the proctors and what to those who personally appeared.

Another feature of the procedure of this province was the frequency in which the three orders deliberated in a single chamber until the Wars of Religion. Provins is the only bailiwick in which the available documents indicate that deliberations were not together in 1560. By 1614 there is no instance in which we can prove that the three estates acted as a unit. Circumstantial evidence suggests that this change was brought about by the antagonism between the clergy and the secular orders in 1561 and by the inclusion of the villages. The nobility and clergy had no desire to be swamped by the superior voting power of the peasants. Then, too, the desire of the royal officials to separate the three estates in order to have a freer hand in their dealings with the third estate and the practice of the three orders deliberating separately in the Estates General in 1560 and thereafter may have had their effect.

5

THE ELECTIONS IN NORMANDY

The Provincial Estates

The plains of Picardy and the Île-de-France that extended eastward into Champagne also flowed westward into Normandy. Historical developments, however, counteracted the geographical unity of the region as a whole and made Normandy one of the best organized sections of France. Its medieval dukes and later rulers not only created provincial estates, but also a certain similarity in the institutions of the various subordinate jurisdictions, although the local historian who was unacquainted with the greater divergences in the other parts of France might dispute this statement.

Unfortunately, the archives of the estates of Normandy were lost during the seventeenth century and the departmental and communal archives that survived World War II contain little on the bailiwick elections to the Estates General except for the depositories at Rouen. Even before the war, Prentout had to search far and wide for the relatively scant evidence on which he based his excellent history of the provincial estates. But with his findings and the procès-verbaux of the elections in the viscounties and bailiwicks in October, and again in November, 1529, it is possible to establish the procedure used for choosing the representatives to the provincial estates.[1] These same viscounty and bailiwick estates were utilized in selecting the Norman delegates to the Estates General.

During the Middle Ages the provincial estates of Normandy, like those in most other parts of France, were composed of individually summoned ecclesiastics and nobles and the deputies of chapters and towns.[2] After the reconquest of the province from the English, the mode of convocation was changed, and by the dawn of the sixteenth century only the seven archbishops and bishops and six dukes and counts maintained the right of receiving writs of summons, a privilege they rarely exercised by actually attending the estates. In its place was substituted a system of electing deputies from the three estates in bailiwick and viscounty assemblies.[3]

The composition and activities of these local estates may be best studied for the year 1529. On September 11 the king issued orders for the provincial estates of Normandy to assemble and ratify the Treaties of Cambrai and Madrid. The grand seneschal-governor of Normandy instructed the deputies to meet at Rouen on October 15, and elections were held throughout the province in late September and early October. At Rouen a dispute arose which necessitated new elections in late October and early November.

The documents on these two series of elections reveal that in the bailiwick of Caen assemblies of the three estates were first held in the viscounties of Bayeux, Falaise, and Vire. In each of these assemblies those present, voting together, chose one deputy who was instructed to attend the bailiwick estates at Caen where he was to participate in the election of one deputy for the clergy and one for the nobility to represent the bailiwick in the provincial estates. Afterwards, he was to proceed to Rouen where he was to stand for his viscounty. No separate meeting was held for the viscounty of Caen. Rather the three estates of the area met with the deputies of the other three viscounties and chose the deputy for the viscounty as well as one for the clergy and one for the nobility of the bailiwick. The representation from Caen in the provincial estates therefore consisted of one deputy for each of the first two estates of the bailiwick and one for each of the four viscounties. The deputies of the viscounties were members of the third estate, but all three estates had participated in their choice. On the other hand, the deputies of the viscounties had taken part in the election of the clergyman and nobleman who attended the provincial estates. The intermixing of the three orders was complete. [4]

The same procedure was followed by the bailiwicks of Cotentin, [5] Évreux, [6] and Rouen [7] except that in the last, the viscounty of Rouen named three deputies in October and four in November rather than the usual one. There was no assembly for the bailiwick of Caux. The three estates of the five viscounties met separately and chose one deputy each from the third estate to go directly to the provincial estates. The right of selecting the delegate of the clergy and of the nobility was rotated between four of the viscounties. In 1529 the viscounty of Neufchâtel nominated the former and the viscounty of Arques the latter. The viscounty of Gournay, as a fief of the Duke of Longueville, was never given a turn and only her third estate was convoked. [8]

The bailiwick of Alençon provided another variation. The clergy and nobility of the bailiwick met with the members of the third estate of the viscounty of Alençon and chose one deputy from each estate to go to the provincial assembly. The other four viscounties meeting apart selected one deputy apiece to do likewise. The unique thing about these viscounty assemblies was that with one exception (Perche) only members of the third estate attended. [9] A more serious violation of the practice of the three orders voting together may be found in the bailiwick of Gisors. Here the nobility and clergy met on the same day but selected their deputies apart. The third estate of the five viscounties held separate assemblies, and each chose their own representative without outside interference. [10] Nevertheless, the Norman electoral procedure points to an amazing diffusion of the three traditional orders of French society. In only one of the seven bailiwicks did the three orders vote alone, and in only nine of the thirty-one viscounties did the third estate have complete control over the selection of the deputy.

The practice of the three orders voting together was paralleled by an unusually extensive suffrage. The curés were generally summoned in 1529 either to the viscounty or the bailiwick assemblies, though here and there they either did not attend or were excluded. This was particularly true in the viscounties where there was a large cathedral chapter as at Rouen, at Évreux where no curés appeared, or at Coutances or Avranches where less than six took part. Attendance was also quite poor in the bailiwick of Alençon. On the other hand, a very large number of curés and vicars appeared in the viscounties of Falaise, Caux, Pont-Audermer, and Pont-de-l'Arche, and the bailiwick of Gisors where there were no cathedral chapters. The cause for this phenomenon is not hard to find. The deans and canons of the chapters dominated the proceedings even to the point where the chapters of Évreux and Lisieux took turns naming the deputies of the bailiwick of Évreux. Later in the same century the chapters of Avranches and Coutances began to do likewise for the bailiwick of Cotentin. Small wonder the curés of Évreux asked in 1614 why they were convoked if they were denied the right to elect. Finally in 1626 it was decided that the two chapters and the cures would take turns naming the deputy of the bailiwick, each exercising this privilege every third year. [11]

Almost certainly all nobles with fiefs were convoked to the viscounty or bailiwick assemblies in 1529, and in some localities simple écuyers took part. On the whole, however, attendance on the part of the second estate was quite poor, and the number present almost never exceeded twelve. Only three took part in the estates of the bailiwick of Alençon and one, at Évreux. No noble of the sword appeared in the assemblies of the viscounties of Rouen and Pont-de-l'Arche.[12]

It is difficult to determine who participated for the third estate. Usually the clerks of the viscounty assemblies in 1529 were content to name from twenty to forty persons who were present from the third estate of the town and viscounty or simply the viscounty. The terminology used in the procès-verbaux suggests that any peasant who chose to lay down his hoe and trudge to town to vote could do so, but one may be pardoned for questioning how many actually did. In a few cases, as with the viscounties of Domfront, Gournay, Neufchâtel, Orbec, and Pont-Audemer, some persons were specifically listed as coming from parishes outside of the principal town, but we are not informed whether they had been elected by their neighbors, specially selected by an official to attend, or had just decided to come. At Falaise a determined effort was made to get one or two of the principal persons of each parish in the viscounty to attend, and at Pont-de-l'Arche each parish named a deputy. On the other hand, the inhabitants of the rural parishes did not participate in the viscounties of Verneuil, Gisors, Vernon, Pontoise, and Rouen.[13]

The next century marked a few changes in procedure. The curés of Évreux began to turn out in larger numbers and in 1614 threatened the position of the two chapters in the bailiwick. The nobles continued to regard the various representative institutions with indifference during the sixteenth century, but there is evidence of increased interest thereafter. The town of Rouen won the right of sending two deputies directly to the provincial estates in 1571, and Caen was given the privilege of sending one in 1586. Judging by what happened elsewhere, one strongly suspects that the vague summons so often sent to the inhabitants of the viscounties in 1529 was replaced in most localities by a direct order to the parishes to elect deputies. Furthermore, the marked differences between the handful of communities that participated in the elections in the viscounty of Orbec in 1529 and the two towns and 101 parishes that sent deputies in 1576 may have been duplicated in many other places. It is true that a reaction against the expansion of the electorate may have set in after the overthrow of the League. In the viscounty of Pont-de-l'Arche where the parishes had named deputies in 1529 and again in 1588, the treasurers of the parish churches were simply told to attend in 1600, no formal elections being held in the rural areas.[14]

We have established the composition and procedures followed in the viscounty and bailiwick estates during the sixteenth century as well as the limited number of documents permits. It is now necessary to see whether the usual composition of the estates was kept when deputies were named to the national rather than to the provincial assembly.

Rouen

The municipality, viscounty, and bailiwick of Rouen are the only jurisdictions for which there is much information. The municipality, of course, elected the deputies when the towns were convoked as in 1506.[15] When the Estates General was summoned by bailiwick, the deputies were chosen in much the same manner as if the Norman provincial estates had been convoked. The only difference was that the less populous viscounties usually agreed on a single deputy for the third estate rather than naming one each. Thus the delegates to the Estates General in 1560 consisted of one deputy for the clergy, one for the nobility, two for the viscounty of Rouen, and one for the third estate of the other viscounties of the bailiwick.[16]

A variety of difficulties arose in the elections of 1576. The three estates of the viscounty of Rouen assembled on October 5 and soon fell to quarreling. The chapter of Notre Dame protested against the claim of the twenty-four officials of the town to have one vote each. The town made complaints to the king against the nobility and against the lieutenant general, who had employed the clerk of the bailiwick rather than the clerk of the municipality for the assembly. Underlying all but the last quarrel was the fact that the three estates usually voted together and therefore the number of persons admitted for each order was important. The deputy of the chapter could hardly have been expected to have been pleased by an influx of townsmen.

On October 11 and 12 the bailiwick estates were held, and this time the two canons who represented the chapter were so displeased with the unimportant location of the seats which they had been assigned that they claimed that the proceedings were void. Nevertheless, one deputy from each estate was chosen to represent the bailiwick. About twenty-four officials of Rouen named a delegation of two to go directly to the Estates General, because in 1571 the town had won the right to deputize the provincial estates and without hesitation assumed the same privilege in regard to the national assembly. The protests raised in the two assemblies were sent to the king to be resolved. On October 31 he confirmed the right of the échevins to name two deputies to the Estates General and for the échevins, former councilors, and other town officials to attend the estates of the viscounty along with all nobles holding fiefs. This decree presumably defined the procedure that had been followed in elections to previous Estates Generals. Indeed, as early as October 8, the king had felt it necessary to write the provincial governor to make sure that the elections would be held in the accustomed manner.

That same day the two deputies of the town of Rouen reminded the échevins that no cahiers had been prepared, but since they had not then heard the king's ruling on the composition of the local assembly, it was decided to forgo the usual discussions with the other orders and to prepare a separate cahier for the town. November saw a new difficulty arise. The king ordered that one of the deputies of the town, who was a member of the local Parlement, be replaced to avoid any suspicions that might arise at seeing such an important official charged with submitting the complaints of the people, but the town exerted its independence and refused to comply with this directive.[17]

The elections in 1588 were carried out with much less difficulty. On July 9 the king took the precaution of ordering the municipal leaders of Rouen to assemble with the three estates of the bailiwick to elect one deputy from each order and two deputies from the town to attend the Estates General. A few weeks later these instructions were carried out in an assembly attended by the vicar-general, the deputies of the cathedral chapter, and other ecclesiastics including many curés, with about twelve nobles, over fifty municipal officials and bourgeois of Rouen, and the deputies of the viscounties. Since voting was by head, the town of Rouen not only dominated the third estate but the other estates as well. In addition, two deputies were specifically chosen by the town. These special considerations satisfied the town but not its deputies. One of them asked to be excused from attending the Estates General because his counterpart had been named first when he himself, as a former councilor, should have been given precedence over the incumbent of the office. The affair, like so many others, was finally settled at Blois.

Those who desired were invited to submit memoirs to the clerk of the municipality of Rouen or to the deputies of the viscounties to be turned over to the delegates to the Estates General. The special representatives of Rouen prepared a cahier based on the material given to them, and it was read before the municipal council. The clerical leaders of Rouen were not happy at the choice of the Bishop of Lisieux, a man from another diocese, as deputy of their order, and they assembled the clergy of their diocese to ask their archbishop to serve as their representative. Several persons were designated to receive the complaints of the ecclesiastics.[18]

Twice in 1590 the estates of the town and bailiwick met to name deputies to the Estates General[19] and this process was repeated for the estates of the League in October, 1592. A few ecclesiastics, nobles, and the officials of the municipality of Rouen joined with a deputy of the third estate of the viscounty of Rouen and one from each order of the viscounty of Pont-de-l'Arche to name the usual five delegates to the Estates General. No one appeared for the two other viscounties, but the delegates were declared chosen by the "larger and wiser part" of the bailiwick. When the deputy of the nobility later thought that it would be unlikely that he could attend, the municipal council did not hesitate to choose an alternate. Few incidents indicate more strongly the close relationship which existed between the orders.[20]

The electoral assembly of the bailiwick on July 29, 1614, was so well attended that everyone could not get in the hall reserved for the meeting. Several hundred curés and an equal number of nobles were there with the more important ecclesiastics, the usual large number of municipal officials, and the deputies of the third estate for the four viscounties. The customary number of delegates was elected and in October a single cahier for the bailiwick was prepared by the municipal officials and deputies of the clergy, nobility, and the third estate from each of the four viscounties.[21]

In 1651 the governor of Normandy presided over the estates of the bailiwick in great splendor. Present were the leading ecclesiastics, deputies of the chapters, 209 curés and vicars, 174 nobles, municipal officers and some bourgeois of Rouen, and the deputies of the viscounties. Six rather than the traditional five deputies were elected, as it was decided to send an assistant delegate for the clergy. The inhabitants of the bailiwick were invited to submit to the clerk of Rouen or the deputies of the various viscounties any memoirs they desired to be considered by those who prepared the cahier.[22]

There was an underlying presumption throughout the electoral history of Rouen that the same procedure ought to be used in electing deputies to the Estates General as was employed in the elections to the provincial estates. The council of Rouen drew this parallel on several occasions. The three orders deliberated and voted together. This practice put the town of Rouen in a powerful position because more of her citizens attended than came from the viscounties or other estates; this continued until there was an influx of nobles in the seventeenth century and an increased interest of the lower clergy which came a little earlier.

Alençon and the Other Bailiwicks

Little information exists concerning the elections to the Estates General in the other Norman bailiwicks. In Alençon in 1560 and in Cotentin in 1614 the three orders prepared a single cahier as might have been expected, but in 1651 the practice of the nobility and third estate voting together led to trouble in the former bailiwick. The nobles turned out in large numbers in the viscounties to elect deputies to the bailiwick assembly, but when their representatives arrived at Alençon, the lieutenant general insisted that the members of the third estate be allowed to vote by head with them. Thus the ballot of the artisan of Alençon was given equal weight to that of the deputy of the nobility of a viscounty, with the obvious result that the candidate of the lieutenant general was chosen, while the two men proposed by the nobility of all the subordinate jurisdictions were defeated. The nobles protested and on September 21, 1651, the royal council sustained their demands ordering that members of the third estate not be allowed to vote with the nobility in the future in conformity with the procedure practiced in 1588 and 1614. It is probable, judging by this decree, that the three orders had ceased to vote together by 1576. One fact becomes plain. The three estates had difficulty voting by head because the system opened the possibility of some official swamping the assembly with his henchmen and thereby capturing control of all three estates. [23]

Only traces can be found concerning the elections elsewhere. The viscounty of Valognes chose a deputy for the nobility to attend the estates of Cotentin in 1561, but no representatives arrived from two of the three viscounties, and the meeting had to be postponed. In 1588, fourteen clergymen, nineteen nobles, and sixteen members of the third estate of the same viscounty together elected seven deputies to attend the bailiwick estates. [24] There were also the usual disputes growing out of the electoral procedure, and these in turn led to rival representatives going to the Estates General. Two quarreling ecclesiastics competed for the honor of standing for the clergy of Évreux in 1576, and there were similar disputes between would-be deputies of the nobility of both Alençon and Caen in 1588 and of the clergy of Caux in 1614. [25]

Of more interest was the effort of the town of Caen to get a seat in the Estates General as Rouen had done. The attempt was first made in 1588, apparently on the basis that Caen's privilege of direct representation in the provincial estates which had just been recognized a few years before should be carried over to the national assembly. The effort was successful in spite of the hostility of Rouen at seeing a second town in the government matching its enviable position. In 1614 Caen was once more able to win direct representation. [26]

Wherever preparatory assemblies were held in France, there was a tendency to try to bypass the bailiwick and depute directly to the national assembly. This was especially true in Normandy where the viscounties had the right to send representatives to the provincial estates without the approval of the bailiwicks. It was but natural that they should seek the same privilege in regard to the Estates General. In 1588, for example, deputies appeared at Blois from one viscounty under the bailiwick of Rouen, one under Cotentin, two under Gisors, and two under Alençon. The diocese of Avranches added still another would-be representative to the list. [27] This adds further evidence that the same procedure was followed in electing deputies to the national as to the provincial estates. A possible exception was the practice occasionally followed in some viscounties of the nobility naming deputies to the bailiwick estates rather than attending in person. This occurred in the viscounty of Valognes in Cotentin in 1561 and in 1588, in the viscounty of Pont-de-l'Arche in Rouen in 1592, and in several viscounties in Alençon in 1651. However, there is insufficient evidence to prove that this procedure was never followed in electing representatives to the provincial estates.

Summary

In general, the history of Norman electoral procedure followed that of the national assembly. During the Middle Ages direct summons were sent to the bishops, abbots, and nobles to attend, and to the chapters and towns to elect deputies. Occasionally, the nobles of an area combined to send a representative or a town acted with the remainder of the viscounty. This practice was legalized by the formal adoption of elections by viscounties and bailiwicks throughout Normandy at about the same time that bailiwick elections replaced direct summons in the national assembly. In both the Estates General and the Norman provincial estates many aspects of the old procedure were maintained along with the new. In Normandy the cathedral chapter or principal town often continued to act in the name of the clergy or the third estate of a viscounty or a bailiwick. Only gradually after a long struggle did the curés and peasants win an effective voice. Sometimes the chapters were strong enough to ward off complete defeat, and in Évreux the curés never did progress beyond the right of naming the deputy every third year. Likewise, the towns of Rouen and Caen were so powerful that they were given separate seats in the estates, leaving to the other inhabitants of their respective viscounties the control of the delegate they had so long desired.[28] The same situation was apparent at the viscounty level. A long quarrel ensued between the town of Lisieux and the remainder of the viscounty of Orbec in which it was located. It was in evidence as early as 1529 and was finally resolved in the usual way by the town and parishes of the viscounty taking turns naming the deputy.[29]

These struggles within the clergy and the third estate were the dominant ones in the province. Royal officials caused less trouble than elsewhere, perhaps because the king had issued ordonnances denying them the privilege of being chosen as deputies to the provincial estates. There were, of course, infractions of this rule, but still few royal officials sat in the Norman provincial estates or in the Estates General.[30] They had little reason to cause trouble, and the difficulties in Rouen in 1576 and Alençon during the Fronde are among the few complaints that have been found against their handling of the elections. The relations between the three estates were friendly, although their practice of voting together led to a few quarrels over who was to be admitted to the bailiwick assemblies.

6

THE ELECTIONS IN ORLÉANS

The Government

Orléans was the largest and most poorly defined of the governments into which the Estates General was divided; it was composed of the pre-Revolutionary provinces of Orléanais, Touraine, Anjou, Maine, Berry, Poitou, Angoulême, and La Rochelle and Aunis. Sometimes this vast region was divided into several governments or appanages during the sixteenth century and on several occasions important sections were without any governor. It is not surprising, then, to find that in 1561 when elections were held for the Estates General of Pontoise, not one, but three governmental assemblies were convoked. One was composed of the eastern bailiwicks of Berry, Chartres, Étampes, Orléans, and Montargis; another of the western bailiwicks of Anjou, Maine, Touraine, Amboise, Blois, Perche, Loudun, and Laval; and still another of the southern jurisdictions of Poitou, Angoumois, La Rochelle and Aunis, and Saintonge, the last named jurisdiction being generally classified with Guyenne.[1]

There was little chance for any institutions to develop at the governmental level in a region so often subdivided. No meeting of the estates of the entire area ever took place, though there were some large assemblies of parts of the government as in 1561. These meetings were rare except for those in the southern jurisdictions where deputies from Poitou, Angoulême, and La Rochelle, joined with those of Périgord, Saintonge, Haut- and Bas-Limousin, and Haute- and Basse-Marche.[2] Little is known of these assemblies, beyond that they were rarely convoked after the sixteenth century.

Chartres

The study of the electoral history of the government may be best begun in the bailiwick of Chartres because of its close proximity to the Île-de-France. Here in 1468 over a hundred persons, including several canons of the cathedral chapter, attended the town meeting to elect deputies to the assembly of the estates at Tours.[3] The codification of the custom in 1508 necessitated a bailiwick assembly in which the lesser clergy, seigneurs with middle and low justice, and the inhabitants of the smaller towns and villages were excluded. A marked change may be noted, however, when the bailiwick met in 1529 to ratify the Treaties of Cambrai and Madrid. With a few exceptions, every town and castellany sent three deputies, one for each estate. The repeated use of the phrase "town and castellany" rather than "castellany" alone suggests that the smaller communities were not consulted, but certainly many of the lesser clergy and nobility were given a voice.[4]

The year 1576 marked another change in the method of convoking the bailiwick. The clergy and nobility were instructed to report to Chartres in person on October 8, and the parishes were ordered to elect deputies for the occasion.

By and large the inhabitants accepted the new procedure, but there were the inevitable exceptions. Election by castellany was fairly common, and occasionally members of the nobility and clergy attended as they had done in 1529. The choice of a priest to represent the third estate was not unknown. Once or twice the inhabitants of several localities combined to prepare a single cahier. Generally we are told that "the larger and wiser part" of the inhabitants of a parish attended, but sometimes there were indications that a few local leaders actually controlled the proceedings. Nowhere was this more clear than in the neighboring parishes of Saint-Loup, Luplanté, and Ermenonville-la-Petite where the inhabitants met separately the same morning and voted the adoption of identical cahiers. Some enterprising soul must have been busy the night before, preparing copies to distribute to his friends in each locality to be used the following day. On the other hand, a strong degree of independence is certainly indicated in some other parishes by the large number of people the inhabitants considered suitable for nomination to represent them at Chartres.[5]

The archives have little to offer concerning the elections in the bailiwicks in 1588, but some information is available concerning the town of Chartres in 1614. A general assembly of the parishes was held to elect deputies to attend the bailiwick estates. Apparently subordinate localities outside the walls of the town were summoned, for the parish of Thiville, which was under the temporal jurisdiction of the cathedral chapter, was instructed to have a deputy attend the preparatory assembly.[6]

The use of the parish as the basic electoral unit was continued during the Fronde, but the striking feature about the bailiwick assemblies at that time was the conflict that broke out in 1651, largely as a result of the aggressive attitude of several royal officials. Actual violence grew out of the refusal of the nobility to permit the lieutenant particular and the lieutenant criminal to take seats in their chamber in spite of precedents that had been established in 1614 and 1649. The two officials resolved to stand on what they conceived to be their rights, but nominal peace reigned as long as the officers of the king met in one place and the nobility in another. Unfortunately, the two groups were asked to join with the clergy and the third estate in a joint meeting. The nobility on entering discovered the lieutenant particular and lieutenant criminal seated in the places reserved for them. Several nobles dragged the two offenders from their seats. The ushers, guards, and members of the third estate drew their daggers and swords to revenge the insult done the lieutenant criminal who, as échevin of Chartres, had friends among the townsmen. A battle ensued in which one of the attackers was killed and several others wounded. The nobility emerged victorious and found themselves in complete possession of the assembly hall, which they proceeded to barricade. And none too soon, for when the townsmen saw the corpse and their wounded comrades, they sounded the alarm and massed two thousand strong around the assembly-building which housed the besieged nobility. The Marquis of Maintenon, who was the bailiff, courageously attempted to calm the mob, but at length, he decided to make his way with the lieutenant general from the besieged building to the hôtel de ville. As he passed through the angry crowd, he was threatened and shoved, but not attacked, so great was the affection and respect in which he was held. At the hôtel de ville he found the mayor and a few officials attempting to raise a company of militia to restore order, but without success, for the only officer present lacked enthusiasm for the project.

Meanwhile, the townsmen attacked the assembly-building. Some sought to enter the windows with the aid of ladders, others rushed the doors, still others made preparations to fire the beleaguered mansion. Slowly the nobles were shoved back beneath a hail of bullets which killed three and wounded others. Driven from chamber to chamber they at length asked for quarter, but they would have certainly been massacred had not the bailiff and lieutenant general returned at that moment and thrown themselves between the combatants with so much courage and authority that a reprieve was granted. Some of the prisoners were taken to the hôtel de ville; others were beaten by their guards and thrown into dungeons. That evening when a moderate degree of quiet had been restored, nearly all of the nobles were set free by the municipal authorities. The following day the nobility met in the country and elected a committee headed by Maintenon to complain to the king. For a month terror reigned in the town, and no one dared to go outside the walls for fear of violence. Companies of bourgeois mounted guard as in time of war. At length the nobility assured the municipality that there would be no reprisals and that they would stand content on the actions taken by the king who had already ordered an investigation. Well they might, for the king's council found the town at fault and ordered it to pay 80,000 livres to the nobility of the bailiwick. No doubt the testimony of the bailiff was decisive, for he reported that the attack had long been planned by the royal officials and that the gates of the town had been closed before the fight began. That very morning the officials were reported to have said that they knew how to make way with the nobility. Once more the royal officials were the aggressors, this time against the nobility, and once more the crown intervened to maintain the established order.[7]

Chartres had an interesting conflict with the barony of Châteauneuf-en-Thymerais. In 1560 and 1576 deputies from the smaller jurisdiction were seated without dispute in the Estates General because it was held as an appanage, but at the death of the Duke of Alençon in 1584, the barony was turned over to the Duke of Nevers and thereby lost the privileged status of being held by a member of the royal family. The deputies sent by the barony to the Estates General in 1588 and 1614 were challenged with almost uniform success by Chartres on the grounds that seigneurial, and not royal judges, had convoked the local estates and that the royal judicial cases of the area were turned over to the bailiwick officials of Chartres for judgement. During the reign of Louis XIII, Châteauneuf was recognized as being independent and elected deputies to the stillborn Estates Generals of 1649 and 1651, but in 1789 Chartres once more questioned her right to do so. Nothing is known of the electoral procedure followed in Châteauneuf except that both the curés and deputies of the parishes participated in the codification of the custom in 1552.[8]

Perche

The elections in the bailiwick of Perche were noteworthy because of the quarrel between the towns of Bellême and Mortagne over the question of which was the capital of the jurisdiction and, therefore, the place where the estates should meet. The rivalry was in evidence in 1558 when the custom was codified and became so intense in 1588 that deputations of the third estate were named in both towns to attend the Estates General. The quarrel was continued with equal vigor in 1614 and was renewed during the elections of the Fronde and in 1789. Little can be ascertained concerning the electoral procedure except that in 1529 the three estates deliberated together and neither the parish clergy nor the inhabitants of the villages participated. When the custom was codified in 1558, these two neglected elements were included. In 1576 at least one parish sent a deputy to the bailiwick assembly, and in 1651 they were all instructed to do so.[9]

Maine

Just south of Perche lay the larger seneschalsy of Maine. Here in 1508,

twenty-seven leading clergymen, forty-nine of the principal seigneurs, and
sixty-seven officials, lawyers, and other members of the third estate assembled to codify the custom.[10]   The electoral assembly of 1576 was attended
by much the same elements for the first two estates. Sixteen ecclesiastics
and sixty-five nobles stood for their respective orders. Only the complexion
of the third estate was changed to a noticeable degree. In the place of the
host of lawyers were substituted the deputies of twelve of the sixteen parishes
of Le Mans and of ten of the twenty-seven other communities that had been
convoked. The municipal officials of Le Mans were also present, but the les-
sor clergy, minor nobility, and the inhabitants of the villages were still excluded. The preponderance of Le Mans in the third estate was complete, for
her échevins and the deputies of her parishes outnumbered the proctors of
the other localities two to one. After the usual preliminaries the three orders separated to name their deputies and to select small committees to
prepare their cahier.[11]

In 1588 it was the clergy's turn to move towards a more democratic procedure. On the initiative of the bishop, the curés met in preparatory assemblies of the deaneries and elected deputies to the estates of the seneschalsy.
The canons of the cathedral chapter were so angered by this innovation that
they dispatched two of their number to Blois to challenge the right of the official delegation to their seats.[12]

The electoral assembly of 1614 was larger than the preceding ones, although there were no important innovations. The curés of the deaneries continued to send deputies with the connivance of the bishop and over the protests
of a large part of the upper clergy. A few more nobles attended, and this time
only one parish in Le Mans failed to send a deputy. Less than half of the
smaller towns responded, but this did not prevent those present from protesting against the predominant position of Le Mans, whose échevins and parish
deputies outnumbered the representatives of the third estates of the rest of
the jurisdiction. There was talk of the smaller localities naming a separate
deputation, so anxious were they to present their grievances before the crown
on the matter of the division of the taille within the seneschalsy, but in the
end a splitting of the third estate was avoided.[13]

In 1651 the lieutenant general changed the method of convoking the estates.
Preparatory assemblies were ordered in each subordinate bailiwick to elect
one deputy of the third estate to attend the seneschalsy meeting along with the
deputies of the parishes of the town and suburbs of Le Mans. Nothing is
known of these preparatory elections, and it is impossible to say whether the
rural parishes participated. The one important issue that arose in the seneschalsy estates grew out of the desire of the officials of the presidial seat
to attend en masse. The nobility and third estate strongly opposed this pretension, and the clergy gave some support. The lieutenant general sought to
resolve the difficulty by postponing the assembly for four weeks on the grounds
that some of the nobles had sent proctors rather than come in person. The
ruse was successful despite opposition, but we are provided with one more
example of how the nobility and third estate closed ranks to try to check the
aspirations of the royal officer class.[14]

One town, or more technically, county, sought to escape the predominant
position of Le Mans by gaining recognition as an independent jurisdiction. In
1560, 1576, and 1588, Laval refused to attend the elections in the seneschalsy,
but rather named deputations directly to the Estates General. On each occasion the delegation from the third estate of Maine successfully opposed their
pretensions. Persistence was to have its reward, however, for in 1593 Laval
was seated without question. Evidently the leaders of the League were anxious to swell the assembly whatever the cost.[15]   The nobility of the county did
not try to send deputies, but when they were taxed to pay the delegation of the

nobility of Maine to the Estates General of 1576, they followed the lead of the Count of Laval himself in appealing to the king's council. Here they were excused from contributing because of the privileges of the county. [16]

Étampes and Montargis

Little survives concerning the composition of the other bailiwick estates north of the Loire. At Étampes both the curés and the deputies of the parishes participated in the codification of the custom in 1556. The marriage between the town and the plat pays could not have been a happy one, however, for in 1576 they each sent their own deputy to Blois. The two factions did manage to agree on a common cahier in 1588.[17] The peasants were not consulted in the neighboring bailiwick of Montargis in 1484, but in 1496 when the Treaty of Étaples was ratified, a few curés attended and twenty-four towns were summoned. An elaborate system of preparatory elections was introduced in 1529 when it was a matter of ratifying the Treaties of Cambrai and Madrid. The three estates of each castellany assembled and named one person from every order to attend the bailiwick meeting. The method of convoking the jurisdiction was changed again two years later when the custom was codified; the clergy, including the curés, the seigneurs, and the deputies of the towns and villages were told to go directly to the bailiwick seat.[18]

Orléans

South of Étampes and east of Montargis straddling the broad bed of the Loire River lay the important bailiwick of Orléans. Here in 1496 the bishop, abbots, priors, chapters, seigneurs, and deputies of eleven towns of that part of the bailiwick exempt from the duchy of Orléans, met to ratify the Treaty of Étaples. The assembly to codify the custom in 1509 was larger because the duchy had reverted to the crown and was included in the bailiwick. The curés and villages were still excluded; the seigneurs with middle and low justice were not directed to attend in person, but rather joined together in the various castellanies and named deputies. This tendency to use preparatory assemblies was even more marked in 1529 when the assembly to ratify the Treaties of Cambrai and Madrid was composed almost entirely of the representatives of the three estates of the castellanies. In 1583, however, when the custom was reformed, a return was made to the practice of summoning individually important ecclesiastics, nobles, and officials, but having the lesser members of the three estates name deputies in assemblies of the castellanies.[19]

Only a limited number of documents survive concerning the election of deputies to the Estates General during the sixteenth century, but existing evidence indicates that the composition of the bailiwick assembly was not radically altered on these occasions. In 1614, during the period in which the elections to the Estates General were taking place, someone prepared a treatise explaining the procedure that had been followed in the bailiwick in 1576 and 1588. Preparatory elections, he said, had been held in the town of Orléans and in the castellanies to elect deputies to the bailiwick assembly. In the town the clergy and nobility had chosen one delegate each, and the inhabitants of every parish had selected two. In the castellanies, both royal and nonroyal, the three estates had assembled and named deputies. At the bailiwick estates, the usual preliminary joint meeting had been held and the three orders had then separated to name their deputies and prepare their cahiers. The purpose of the treatise was to counteract some noblemen's demands that the members of their order be convoked individually. These noblemen contended with justice that the present system gave no more voice to the thirty, forty, or fifty seigneurs in a large castellany than to the two or three who inhabited a small one. Their proposal, the treatise tells us, was bad because of the expense of everyone attending and the confusion that would result from such a large meeting. With evident satisfaction the author reported that the traditional system had been adopted by the bailiff and that some of the preparatory assemblies had already been held.[20]

Perhaps the actions of the clergy in 1614 gave the author less satisfaction, for the first estate of the diocese of Orléans met and named two of their number to go to the Estates General and three to attend the bailiwick assembly which was to meet sometime later. Those who went to the bailiwick assembly were instructed to ask the deputies of their order from the castellanies outside the diocese to accept their nomination. This was done with no apparent difficulty.[21]

Surviving documents on the elections of 1588 give support to the description by the unknown author. On August 2, the day following the joint meeting of the three orders, the third estate of the bailiwick assembled. Present were the municipal officials and the deputies, generally two, of twenty-two of the twenty-seven parishes of the town of Orléans and one deputy each from fifteen of the seventeen castellanies of the bailiwick. Thus the voting power of the town of Orléans was far greater than that of the remainder of the bailiwick, and this position of eminence was quickly demonstrated when five inhabitants of the municipality were named to the six-man committee to prepare the cahier. Later, on September 15, the cahier was approved, and two deputies were elected to take it to Blois.[22]

Neither the inhabitants of the castellanies nor the officers of justice who controlled them were satisfied with this procedure. In 1576 they had sent a separate deputation to the Estates General, but it had been refused seats. In 1588 the smaller localities in the bailiwick again sent a deputy to Blois, and this time he won the right to remain with the other representatives of the jurisdiction. By 1614 one finds the representatives of the third estate of Orléans at the Estates General being styled as deputies of the town or as deputies of the castellanies. The split between town and country, or perhaps to be more accurate, the split between the municipal oligarchy and the crown officials who controlled the voting of the rural areas, had become complete.[23]

A different procedure, of course, was followed in 1596 when the town of Orléans alone was asked to name deputies to go to the assembly at Rouen,[24] but a return to bailiwick elections was made in 1614 and during the Fronde. In February, 1649, the lieutenant general ordered the castellanies to hold preparatory assemblies for the members of the first two estates and the deputies from every parish. One deputy from each order was to be named to the bailiwick assembly. However, the principal clergymen of the diocese assembled and decided to repeat the procedure followed in 1614. They convoked all benefice holders, including curés, of that part of the diocese which lay in the bailiwick to an assembly at the episcopal hotel to elect the deputies of their order. The bailiwick officials expressed strong opposition to this move and pointed out that the king had ordered the elections to be held by bailiwick, not by diocese, and that some of the bailiwick clergy did not fall under the jurisdiction of the Bishop of Orléans, but rather that they were in another diocese. Their protests were to no avail, and at the appointed time the clergy assembled in the episcopal hotel and named a deputation to the Estates General. They did take the precaution of selecting a few persons to attend the bailiwick estates to ask the clergy present from outside the diocese to approve their choice. Unfortunately, the outcome of this dispute is not known. A quarrel occurred in the bailiwick meeting within the third estate, but not among the clergy.[25] The clergy proceeded in the same manner in the elections in 1651, but once more the results are unknown. The nobility does not appear to have resisted the preliminary assemblies in the castellanies at this time, and there is at least one clear instance of such a meeting.[26]

Gien

The small bailiwick of Gien was up the Loire River from Orléans. Here in 1614 the three orders voted separately. The municipal and royal officials of Gien met with a relatively large number of the local bourgeoisie and the deputies of the other towns and parishes of the bailiwick to name the representatives of the third estate. The predominance of the town of Gien over the rest of the jurisdiction was clear.[27]

Berry

The duchy of Berry was farther south in the valleys of the Loire and the Cher. Here the leading ecclesiastics, seigneurs, and the deputies of about twenty towns or comparable localities sufficed to ratify the Treaty of Étaples in 1496 and to codify the custom in 1539.[28] Attendance at the meetings to elect deputies to the Estates General later in the century was smaller still; this was caused by either the design of the officials or the indifference of the inhabitants. Only the delegates of the chapters of Bourges, three noblemen, and the deputies of seven towns attended the electoral assembly of 1561.[29] Less than twelve municipalities were involved in the preparation of the cahiers for the Estates Generals of 1576 and 1588, but in 1614 the number increased to thirty-one. Ten nobles were all that could be enticed to elect deputies to the estates of the League, but a much larger number participated in the elections of 1614.[30] This tendency towards increased attendance at the electoral assemblies was especially marked in 1649 when several archpriests and the deputies of the curés of a few subordinate jurisdictions sought admittance into the chamber of the first estate. Over a hundred seigneurs and the deputies of twenty-four towns and baronies were present. The designation of individuals as deputies of baronies indicates that there were preparatory assemblies that might have been attended by the inhabitants of the villages.[31] Within the towns the suffrage was limited, if one may generalize from the example of Bourges where thirty-two notables sufficed to elect the deputies to the bailiwick assembly in 1614.[32]

The elections in Berry were marked by several quarrels. In 1560 the clergy, officers of justice, and other members of the third estate had a dispute about some unknown matter, and the town of Issoudun was so provoked that it unsuccessfully sought individual representation at Orléans. In the electoral assembly of March, 1561, Issoudun renewed the attack charging that the deputy of Berry at the Estates General had taken advantage of his position and had made proposals that involved the suppression of judicial seats in the smaller towns. Nevertheless, this same deputy, who was again the candidate of Bourges, received the vote of four towns as opposed to the three that supported the position of Issoudun. Once more the patricians of a great town had had to beat off the challenge of the royal officials who controlled the smaller localities. In the future, the rivalry was partially solved by electing at least one deputy for the third estate from Bourges and one from Issoudun.[33]

The elections of the second estate in 1614 saw a lively contest develop between the Count of Nansay, a leader of the discontented nobility, and the supporters of the queen mother. The friends of Nansay arrived at the assembly with procurations from the Prince of Condé, the Duke of Sully, and a large number of other nobles. The loyal bailiff foresaw the results of the election unless he acted quickly. He refused to count the procurations, using as a justification a letter of the king which was on the subject and dated July 21, 1614. Even the vote of a noble elected by an inferior jurisdiction was given no additional weight. Nansay nevertheless received more votes than his rival, but the bailiff declared them both elected, in spite of protests that the letters of convocation had specified that only one deputy of the nobility be named and that a second delegate would add a heavy financial burden. Nansay and his faction continued to attempt to block the nomination of the queen mother's candidate the following day, but without success. Both gentlemen served in the Estates General.[34]

Blois

The town and bailiwick of Blois was to the west of Berry. Here in 1468, seventy-nine leading citizens of the town elected two laymen to go to the estates at Tours.[35] The composition of the bailiwick estates in the early period is indicated by the list of those who attended the meeting to codify the custom in 1523. Included were the abbots, priors, seigneurs, officials, and deputies of the chapters, monasteries, and eighteen towns and other communities. A somewhat similar group served to ratify the Treaties of Cambrai and Madrid six years later.[36]

There is not sufficient information to describe a bailiwick election to the Estates General before 1576. On August 14 of that year the lieutenant general sent orders to the subordinate officials and the échevins of the towns and bourgs telling them to have cahiers prepared and deputies named to attend a bailiwick meeting on October 1. The nobility and clergy were also informed. The échevins of Blois ordered the inhabitants of the town to assemble on August 28, but only twenty persons, including a nobleman and a monk, presented themselves at the appointed time. The assembly was postponed until the following day, when the threat of a 10 livre fine brought a much larger attendance. A committee was named to prepare the cahier, but no deputies were elected. Those who desired to make suggestions were told to put them in a box in the town hall to which only the échevins had a key. A month later when the box was opened, thirty memoirs were found inside.

On October 1 the three estates of the bailiwick met in the great hall of the Palace of Justice. Nine ecclesiastics, all but two of whom came from the town, stood for their order. No curés were present. Twenty-two nobles were at the morning assembly, but their number nearly doubled by afternoon when the three orders separated. The nobility held their meeting in the château, perhaps in the same room where the Estates General was to assemble a few weeks later. During their meeting a dispute arose when a noble stated that the bailiff of the subordinate jurisdiction at Châteaudun had held a preparatory assembly in which he had been named the deputy of his order. His vote should, therefore, count for more than that of the individual nobles who attended in person. This not unreasonable claim was rejected, and the balloting began. When it came to the turn of the deputy of Châteaudun, he refused to vote in his own right alone and protested to no avail that the election was null.

The town of Blois had not named deputies to the bailiwick assembly; any of her principal citizens who desired could attend. As a result two-thirds of the third estate came from the municipality. Only eight towns sent deputies, but about twelve are named as not answering the convocation. Only in Châteaudun was there a preparatory assembly in which the rural parishes had been convoked. After the usual quarrel over precedence, one deputy and an alternate to replace him if he were sick were elected. The same committee that prepared the cahier of the town was named to write the cahier of the bailiwick. The third estate was ordered to assemble again on October 22 to approve the cahier, but only Blois and Romorantin bothered to honor the summons.[37]

The municipal archives contain little on the elections in 1588, but the historian is more fortunate in regard to the elections of 1614. On July 7 of that year a general assembly of the town was held that was attended by many clergymen and nobles as well as those of the third estate. A box was set up to receive suggestions for the cahier, and over the protest of a few, it was decided that all nobles living in Blois who did not have the pursuit of arms as a profession should participate with the third estate of the town. On August 25 the three estates of the bailiwick met and named their deputies separately. Again the town completely dominated the proceedings with ninety-four of her citizens present and claiming the right to vote. The nineteen other towns represented were permitted only one vote apiece regardless of the number of deputies they had sent, but their plea that Blois itself be allowed only one vote fell on deaf ears. The same procedure seems to have been followed during the elections of the Fronde. Thus the procedure in Blois saw few changes after the introduction of bailiwick elections. The lower clergy and the rural areas were excluded, and the town completely dominated the third estate. The three orders voted and prepared their cahiers separately in the bailiwick assembly, but deliberated together in that of the town.[38]

Vendôme

In the neighboring duchy of Vendôme the cahier of the third estate in 1614 was prepared by the deputies of the town and suburbs of Vendôme. The exclusion of the other inhabitants of the duchy caused no difficulty, but at the Estates General the deputation was challenged on the grounds that Vendôme was not a royal town.[39]

Touraine and Amboise

Tours is along the Loire River to the west of Blois. Here in 1468 the clergy, bourgeois, men, and inhabitants were ordered to assemble and elect deputies to the Estates General. In theory at least, everyone was invited to attend, but only sixty bourgeois met with the proctors of the archbishop and three ecclesiastical corporations of Tours to name one clergyman and two laymen to go to the estates.

In 1484 the three estates of the bailiwick of Touraine were convoked rather than the municipality, but in spite of this the magistrates and a few clergymen of Tours chose three delegates to the Estates General in much the same manner as in 1468. The failure to act by bailiwick led to new elections being ordered. This time representatives of the towns of Chinon, Loches, Amboise, and Tours met with four clergymen and two nobles to choose together the delegates to the Estates General. The bulk of the urban population had no say and, of course, the rural population was excluded. The assembly to ratify the Treaty of Étaples saw an increase of three in the number of nobles and of one in the number of towns that were present. The clergy did a little better, but the priors and curés were still absent.[40]

The assemblies to codify and reform the custom were better attended. In 1507 the upper clergy, seigneurs with high justice, officials, lawyers, and deputies from the chapters and eight towns participated. In 1559 when the custom again claimed the attention of the bailiwick, the curés, lesser seigneurs, and the deputies of hundreds of villages were also included.[41]

Unfortunately it is not known to what degree this extension in the suffrage was reflected in the elections to the Estates General during the sixteenth century, and it can only be said that in 1588 the rural parishes were convoked. The existence of individual cahiers for the nobility and clergy in 1560 and for the third estate in 1588 proves that the orders normally prepared their remonstrances separately. [42]

In contrast, there is abundant information on the elections in 1614. The curés and lesser seigneurs were included in the summons and the urban and rural parishes were told to send two deputies each. By and large the rural areas obeyed, but there were some variations in the towns. At Châtillon-sur-Indre the deputies were elected in a general assembly of the municipality rather than by its two parishes. At Chinon each parish named two deputies, but instead of going to Tours, they met together, prepared a cahier for the town, and chose two of their number to bear it to Tours. In all, deputies from about one hundred parishes were present at the bailiwick estates, a goodly showing. The attendance of only twenty-four nobles pointed to their lack of interest; a far greater number had been present in 1559.

The bailiwick assembly opened on July 14 with the mayor and échevins of Tours asking to be seated in front of the deputies of the parishes. One of the parish deputies arose and, speaking in the name of the deputies, denied the municipal officials precedence and even challenged their right to be present because only deputies of parishes had been convoked for the third estate. Furthermore, the échevins had generally participated in the parish elections in Tours. To permit them to enter would be to create a fourth estate. A deputy from Chinon backed this position, and the interpretation of the parishes was accepted.

After the usual preliminaries, the orders separated. The third estate was told to elect one deputy from each of the eight parishes of Tours, one from each of the seven royal seats, and six from the plat pays to prepare the cahier of the third estate of the bailiwick and to elect one or two deputies to the Estates General. The order caused further quarreling, this time between the deputies of the town and those of the plat pays, over the relative number of seats allotted to each. Meanwhile, the municipal officials appealed to the king and on July 25 the royal council ruled that the mayor and two échevins had precedence in the assemblies of the bailiwick and would sit with the twenty-one deputies of the parishes and a clerk in the meetings to prepare the cahier and elect the representatives to the Estates General. The parishes protested against this decision and on August 10 the council found it necessary to issue a second decree. Finally, on August 21, the cahier was completed and signed by twenty-five persons including the clerk. Once more the crown had intervened to protect the privileges of the municipal officials. In doing so, the procedure used in 1588 was quoted as the guide. [43]

Meanwhile, the Archbishop of Tours had insisted that the clergy meet before him on the first afternoon of the bailiwick assembly to elect deputies, but the proctors of the chapter of Saint-Martin of Tours refused, claiming that they were exempt from his jurisdiction. This was not the first time that the chapter had taken an independent position. In 1576 and 1588 it had sent deputies to the Estates General where they had been seated with the clergy of Touraine. In 1614 the chapter followed the same course with equal success, though it was decided that in the future individual representation would not be granted. [44]

In 1651 the bailiwick officials repeated their instructions of 1614, but their orders were not always obeyed. The principal inhabitants of Chinon chose a representative to go to Tours rather than leave the task to the parishes of the town as directed. It is not known what disputes occurred at the bailiwick estates. [45]

One characteristic of the elections in Touraine was the struggle of the bailiwick of Amboise to get a separate seat in the Estates General. In 1484 the town sent deputies to the assembly of Tours and in 1560 the three estates of the bailiwick of Amboise did likewise, though their deputies were also admitted into the Estates General. In 1561, Amboise dispatched a delegation directly to the assembly of the government just as other independent bailiwicks. Amboise did not deputize anyone to the Estates General in 1576, but in 1588 the bailiff assembled the clergy and third estate of the town and suburbs to prepare a cahier and elect two representatives to the national assembly. About three weeks later the plat pays and parishes of the bailiwick of Amboise also prepared a cahier and turned it over to the two deputies chosen by the municipal assembly to be taken to the Estates General. The deputies of Amboise were not seated at the national assembly because of the opposition of the deputies of Touraine who argued that Amboise was under their jurisdiction. A second assembly of the town of Amboise was held in which a former bailiff was charged to go to Blois and support their pretensions. He was successful and on October 4 the third estate ordered that the deputies of Amboise be given deliberative voice. Thus the clergy and third estate of the town and suburbs of Amboise named deputies directly to the Estates General.[46]

The quarrel was renewed in 1614 and in an order of the council dated October 23, the right of Amboise to have a seat in the Estates General was again recognized. Inevitably the convocation of the Estates General in 1649 and in 1651 saw the same question raised. The lieutenant general of Touraine ordered Amboise to send deputies to the bailiwick assembly at Tours. The nobility seemed to have had no objection, but the third estate resisted as vigorously as they had done nearly three quarters of a century before. One of the most amazing things about the government of France is that a bailiwick should have successfully defended its right to have seats in the Estates General in 1588, 1614, and 1649 only to have it questioned again in 1651. Each time the royal council had made decrees in its favor. Nothing was ever settled under the old regime.[47]

Anjou

Anjou with its capital city of Angers lay farther down the Loire River. Here in 1506 the municipal council named deputies to the estates of Tours.[48] The shift to bailiwick assemblies at first had no great effect. Only the inhabitants of the town stood for the third estate when the custom was codified in 1508, and in 1560 the rural areas were ignored, leaving to the échevins a preponderant voice in the election of the deputies of the third estate. The rivalry between the Catholic and Protestant nobility in 1560 was so bitter that the partisans of both religions came well armed. After the three orders separated to name their deputies, the Huguenots demanded that some of their number be chosen, and they were strong enough to get two of their candidates elected. The Catholics were present in greater numbers that afternoon and asked for new elections, their spokesman claiming to have procurations from about five hundred gentlemen. The Huguenots tied handkerchiefs to their hats and around their necks in order to be recognized by their compatriots. They moved angrily toward the speaker, and he was fortunate to escape with his life, but several persons were wounded in the confusion. Order was restored when the Duke of Montpensier, who was the governor of the area, arrived with four or five hundred men. The Huguenots, knowing Montpensier to be a devout Catholic, thought it best to retire, and the governor ordered a new assembly which broke the earlier elections and chose persons loyal to the Roman church.[49]

The election of 1560 was not the only violent one in Anjou. In 1588, four hundred nobles assembled and chose an ardent adherent of the League. The minority, headed by the royalist governor, withdrew with the intention of electing another deputy. The pro-League officials of the presidial seat refused to support this venture, and with such insolence that a tumult broke out. Barricades were raised and the governor could maintain peace only by abandoning his design of contesting the election of the League candidate.[50]

In 1614 it was the turn of the third estate to provide excitement. The protagonists, as might have been expected, were the bourgeoisie of Angers and the royal officials of the seneschalsy. The latter had recently won a victory in the municipal elections and were set to capture the deputation to the Estates General as well. To ensure victory they summoned twenty towns to the seneschalsy estates, more than had been invited in the earlier period. Aided by the increased suffrage, the royal officials quickly got two of their number chosen as deputies and managed to halt the efforts of Angers to replace one of them by its own candidate. The bourgeoisie did win partial revenge when eight deputies were chosen by the parishes of Angers to prepare a cahier. Four were merchants, two advocates, one a bourgeois, and only one a councilor at the presidial seat, though he was later joined by another. Thus, the cahier represented the viewpoint of the bourgeois oligarchy, but the deputies stood for the royal officials. The other towns took no part in the preparation of the cahier, and the complaints of the villages were scarcely considered. Perhaps the peasantry were indifferent; for in the subordinate seneschalsy of Saumur where they were convoked, only a third attended the assembly. Here a committee was named to prepare the local cahier and a deputy elected to take it to Angers where it received little consideration.[51]

The elections of 1651 provide no exception to the tumultuous history of the assemblies in Anjou. As was so often the case national issues were confused with local ones. This was particularly true in the town of Angers where the officers of the presidial seat had long controlled the municipal government. In May, however, the popular party in the town got their candidate elected mayor, but the bulk of the council remained unchanged. A sharp clash between the mayor, supported by the overwhelming majority of the people of the town, and the council and royal officials was inevitable. The three orders assembled on June 28 in the royal palace at Angers, where, after hearing the letters of the king read, they separated to name their deputies. The pro-Mazarin bishop had seen to it that only the ecclesiastical communities of the towns had been convoked, the rural clergy being excluded for fear that they were too tainted with the ideas of the Fronde. Even so, one of the three "official candidates" might have been defeated had not the bishop insisted that everyone vote before him by voice rather than secret ballot. This was enough to insure a peaceful election with the desired results.

The nobility was less easily controlled. The Duke of Rohan, who doubled as governor of the province and who was a sympathizer with the Fronde, managed to get his two candidates elected with the aid of the procurations of many absentees. Unfortunately he had not chosen them well, for one was a Huguenot. The majority of those present leaned towards the royal cause and protested against the election of a Protestant. They won moral support from the clergy and chose two representatives of their own. The electoral dispute was carried to the king's council where a decision was rendered against the candidates of the Duke of Rohan.

Even more bitter was the election in the third estate. The royalist lieutenant general sought to defeat the pro-Fronde mayor and bourgeoisie of Angers by altering the electoral procedure. The procedure followed in 1614 called for the third estate to be composed of the seventeen magistrates of Angers, about one third of whom were for the mayor, two deputies from each of the sixteen parishes who were all of the popular party, and one deputy from each of twenty towns in the province. The great weight given to the parishes of Angers insured a royalist defeat unless the procedure was changed. The lieutenant general was equal to the task and convoked from eighty to one hundred parishes of the province to whom he gave not one but two votes each. By one means or another he managed to get the bulk of the new voters on his side. The mayor of Angers protested strongly against this innovation which greatly weakened the position of the town and demanded that the traditional usage be followed. The rural parish deputies, on the other hand, argued that they made up the greater part of the province and should therefore have a heavy voice. At length the Duke of Rohan had to intervene. He was not then ready to break with the lieutenant general and though sympathetic, he advised the mayor to accede in return for being elected deputy. It was by no means a victory for the town, however, for the assembly named the lieutenant general as a second representative and chose a royalist committee to prepare the cahier. Thus the lieutenant general and officials at the presidial seat won by calling the rural parishes to their aid in the seneschalsy assembly for the first time.[52]

Like so many other places, Anjou faced the problem of subordinate jurisdictions trying to assert their independence. In 1614 the seneschalsy of La Flèche sent a deputation to Paris. At the insistence of Anjou, the royal council denied it a seat, but, at the same time, ordered that in the future the jurisdiction be treated as a separate entity. In 1651 the officials of La Flèche confidently ordered an assembly to elect deputies to the Estates General. The clergy and third estate of each parish were told to send deputies, and the nobility were to appear in person. Saumur likewise sought independence on this occasion.[53]

Loudun

The seneschalsy of Loudun was located south of Anjou and west of Touraine, but it had long been connected with the two larger jurisdictions in what was sometimes considered a subordinate capacity. A deputy for the nobility was present at the Estates General of 1560, and the tiny seneschalsy was represented in the assembly of the western part of the government the following year. In 1576 two deputies were elected for the nobility and two for the third estate, but only the latter can be traced to Blois where they were given seats under the bailiwick of Touraine. By 1588 the right of Loudun to a separate seat was established, and her representatives for the secular orders were enrolled on the registers. A quarrel appeared between two factions within the third estate. Each elected its own deputy, and both were seated. In 1596 the three estates submitted a common cahier to the assembly at Rouen, and in 1614 they sent representatives to the Estates General. On this last occasion the clergy and nobility elected their deputies without difficulty, but it was necessary for the third estate to assemble several times because of the rivalry between the Catholics and the Protestants. In their first meeting the syndics of the parishes had procurations in favor of the Catholic candidate, but they were regarded as void because they had not been given in general assemblies of the inhabitants. A second meeting was ordered for the following week and this time a Protestant was chosen, but the royal council ordered a new election on the grounds that the procedure of 1588 had not been followed. The third estate assembled a third time, and after some bickering, the Catholics and Protestants separated and each named a deputy. Again the council declared the elections null, but because the Estates General was about to open, it ordered that both deputies be given seats. The presence of the

representatives of the parishes in the assembly marked an increase in suffrage, for only the inhabitants of the town of Loudun participated for the third
estate when the custom was codified in 1518.[54]

Poitou, La Rochelle and Aunis, and Angoulême

Poitou, La Rochelle and Aunis, and Angoulême were claimed by the governments of Orléans and Guyenne. In 1560 the deputies from Guyenne made
no effort to acquire the three jurisdictions, but in 1576 they lay claim to all
three and were successful in getting the clergy of Poitou and Angoumois to
deliberate with them. In 1588 a long debate on the subject took place, this
time between a deputy of the third estate of Bordeaux and one from Poitou.
It ended with the king's council awarding Poitou to Guyenne. On November
15, 1614, the council reversed itself and returned Poitou to Orléans. Since
the three jurisdictions met with Orléans a majority of times, including the
meeting in 1614 for which there are more details of how each government
voted, the discussion of their electoral procedure is included here.[55]

In 1514 the customs of the three jurisdictions were codified. Present in
each case were only the bishops, abbots, deputies of the chapters, important
seigneurs, royal officials, and lawyers of the leading towns. In 1559 the suffrage in Poitou was extended in a meeting to reform the custom to include the
priors, several curés, lesser seigneurs, deputies of a dozen towns, and some
parishes.[56]

A somewhat different system was used in Poitou to choose deputies to the
Estates General. In 1560 the three orders met together in the presence of the
seneschal to receive instructions before separating to elect deputies and prepare cahiers. Present for the clergy were the vicars-general or proctors of
the Bishops of Poitiers, Maillezais, and Luçon, the abbots, priors, and the
deputies from the chapters and large churches of Poitiers, a few monasteries,
and certain subordinate jurisdictions. Each diocese had held a preparatory
assembly to elect a delegation to the estates of the seneschalsy as had several
other localities, such as the barony of Saint-Maixent and the castellany of
Montreuil-Bonnin. Nothing is known of these preliminary elections in 1560
beyond that their existence gave a preponderance of power to the clergy of
Poitiers who attended in large enough numbers to outvote the other two dioceses who relied on representatives. Details on the activities of the other
two estates are also lacking.[57]

The elections in 1576 reveal the activities of the town of Poitiers. Each
of the twenty-six parishes was directed to elect two deputies to the estates of
the seneschalsy. In addition, the échevins chose five noblemen to sit with the
second estate and four bourgeois to participate with the third estate. One of
these noblemen, Pierre Rat, Sieur of Sabuert and president of the presidial
seat, was elected in the estates of the seneschalsy to attend the national assembly for the third estate. Thus the office-holding nobility sought admission
into the second chamber of the local assembly, but one of their number was
content to serve as deputy for the third estate. The clergy dominated by the
canons of Poitiers chose their deputies in a separate assembly.[58]

The practice of holding preparatory elections caused some difficulty. The
diocese of Luçon sent a deputy directly to the national assembly where he was
received "to present his cahier without prejudice to the deputies of Poitou."[59]
The subordinate seneschalsy of Montmorillon sent delegates to Blois for the
three estates, but the king in council ruled against their pretensions and ordered them to give their cahier to the delegation from Poitou. Representatives from the third estate of Châtellerault were more fortunate and were
given separate seats, even though in 1560 this duchy had sent its delegation
to the electoral assembly of the seneschalsy of Poitou.[60]

In 1588 the parishes of Poitiers once more elected two deputies apiece to attend the estates of the seneschalsy and to help the municipal council prepare the cahier. A box was set up to receive the suggestions and four échevins were chosen to participate in the assembly of the second estate as they had done in 1576. Only a few of the rural nobility attended the electoral meeting on August 25 where they opposed the admission of the échevins into their chamber. The reason for this action is not difficult to find. Most of the rural nobility was for the League, while the town nobility was for the king. As so often happened each group elected a deputy. The struggle was continued in the Estates General where in the end both deputies were seated. The king's council and the second estate at Blois sought to regulate the number of échevins admitted into the second estate of the province. The mayor of Poitiers even claimed to have precedence in the chamber of the nobility as first baron of Poitou. The crown hoped that the mayor and four or five échevins would be seated in accordance with the traditional practice and that their heirs would be recognized as nobles, but the nobility decreed that only the mayor and one échevin would be accepted.[61]

The subordinate jurisdictions continued to cause trouble in 1588. Representatives, for the most part from only the third estate, of Niort, Fontenay, and Châtellerault sought admittance to the national assemble, but as in 1576 only the deputy of the last named place was able to win separate status.[62] In 1614 Fontenay renewed the conflict with vigor by sending deputies from both the first and the third estates, but the representatives of Poitou managed to win from the royal council a decree against their rivals. On the other hand, Poitou accepted without opposition the seating of the delegation from Châtellerault. This belated recognition of its independence did not prevent Châtellerault from having its own electoral difficulties. The Huguenots demanded that one Catholic and one Protestant be chosen for the third estate. The bailiff delayed the elections until he received a ruling from the royal council to the effect that the members of the two religions should meet together and elect one or two representatives by a plurality of votes.[63]

The elections of 1614 provide further information on the procedure followed by the estates of Poitou. In a directive sent to Richelieu, then Bishop of Luçon, the royal governor directed that the future Cardinal assemble the first estate of his diocese to meet with the other two orders to prepare cahiers and to elect one deputy from each estate to attend the assembly of the seneschalsy at Poitiers. Whether the lower clergy and the inhabitants of the rural parishes actually participated is not known, but even if they did, they did not get a vote equal to that of the town. The clergy of Poitiers attended in large enough numbers to outvote easily the deputies from the subordinate jurisdictions. This situation is amply demonstrated by the fact that between 1560 and 1614 Richelieu was the only clergyman elected by the estates of the seneschalsy who was not from Poitiers, and his success was due to the support he received from the bishop of that city. Likewise, the participation of the deputies of its numerous parishes gave Poitiers a dominant position within the third estate. The poor attendance of the rural nobility and the acceptance of part of the municipal nobility in the second estate gave the town some influence there as well.[64]

In 1649 the subordinate jurisdictions were again directed to hold assemblies to elect deputies from the three estates to attend the estates of the seneschalsy. The procedure followed in the subordinate jurisdictions varied widely. At Montmorillon a handful of officials named the delegation of the third estate, but in the barony of Saint-Maixent the three estates, including the inhabitants of the rural parishes, were told to meet and elect deputies to attend the meeting at Poitiers. The bulk of the clergy, as usual, assembled by diocese to choose representatives. In the estates of the seneschalsy the three orders deliberated and voted apart.[65]

The same general procedure was followed in 1651. The nobility, about three hundred strong, attended the seneschalsy assembly. The roll of this order was headed by the mayor of Poitiers as first baron of Poitou and included were fourteen peers and échevins, all owners of seigneuries. Small wonder one noble candidate referred to the town as "the center and true support of the nobility" when he solicited its support before the elections. The deputies from the town and the numerous parishes of Poitiers continued to dominate the third estate. Some subordinate jurisdictions sent deputies, but there is no indication how they were chosen.[66]

Thus while the directives of the royal officials who convoked the estates indicate the desire that a wide suffrage be achieved by the use of elections in the subordinate jurisdictions, these meetings did not always take place except for the clergy, and in the diocesan estates of Poitiers and perhaps elsewhere the curés were generally excluded. The nobility held no preparatory elections, but came directly to the assemblies at Poitiers. The third estate elected those who attended the seneschalsy estates, but the rural parishes were sometimes, if not generally, ignored.

Less is known of the elections in La Rochelle, for the municipal archives were lost soon after Cardinal Richelieu captured the town in 1628. It can only be said that the three estates sent deputies to the Estates General in 1560 and to a meeting of the southern part of the government of Orléans in 1561, but being a Protestant stronghold no proctors attended the Estates General in 1576, 1588, or 1593. In 1614 only the secular orders sent representatives. The municipal officials were specifically authorized by the king's council in that year to choose one deputy for the third estate. Another was elected by the bourgeoisie of the town. Soon thereafter the seneschal of La Rochelle and Aunis decided to assemble the estates of his jurisdiction in the following manner. The Protestant and Catholic clergy were to elect the deputy of the first estate, the échevins of the town and the nobility were to act for the second estate, and the remainder of the municipal leaders of La Rochelle were to name deputies for the third estate in conjunction with the proctors of the other places in the seneschalsy. However, the clergy does not seem to have ever assembled, and the town did not wish to name any more representatives. The nobles met and elected the seneschal, and the parishes of Aunis chose the procureur of the king at the presidial seat. This last official had a unique method of campaigning. He charged the sergeants who delivered messages to the parishes concerning the elections to say that he wished to be designated as deputy and would pay his own expenses if chosen. His technique was successful. Thus each of the three deputies who sat for the third estate under the banner of La Rochelle had been chosen by a different group. It is not surprising that differences arose among them in the Estates General where the deputy of the municipal officials was attacked by his two compatriots. The king's council in the end gave them each an equal voice.[67]

To the south and east of Poitou was situated the seneschalsy of Angoulême. Little is known of the electoral procedure followed here. The town was among those invited to send representatives to the estates of Tours in 1506, and the seneschalsy regularly elected deputies to the Estates General. It is only for 1649 that we can describe the provincial assembly. The meeting of the three estates began with the usual quarrels over precedence. The lieutenant general claimed the seat immediately to the right of the seneschal, but the clergy, who had traditionally held this place, would have none of it. They were supported by the nobility in their determination to oust the presumptuous official. At length they succeeded, and the seneschal and the advocate of the king were able to make their harangues. The roll was then called, and it was revealed that only five clergymen were present. Most of the nobles were absent, and it is not known what representation there was for the third estate beyond that the municipal council named several deputies to attend for the town and castellany of Angoulême. By the time the roll call had ended, it was evening and the three orders dispersed. The following day they assembled separately to elect their deputies and name several persons to prepare the cahiers. Three weeks later, the nobility met again to approve their cahier.[68]

Summary

The elections in the government of Orléans reflect the same trends which have been found elsewhere. There was a marked increase in the suffrage among the clergy and third estate, although here and there the curés and the villages were still excluded during the Fronde. Attendance for the nobility also increased, and the limitation of that order to those who had high justice in the assemblies to codify the customs around 1500 was not apparent in later meetings. The increased suffrage resulted primarily from the initiative of officials who issued the writs of summons or who influenced their contents. These officials included the members of the Parlement who presided over the assemblies to codify the customs, the bailiffs and lieutenant generals, and in at least one case the local bishop who convoked his diocese. The motivations of these officials doubtless varied, but it is certain that in Anjou, at least, it was the desire to defeat the bourgeois oligarchy of Angers that led the lieutenant general to summon the parishes.

The struggle between the royal officials and the bourgeois oligarchy can be seen in many other places. By the time of the Fronde the former had generally emerged victorious and had begun to tackle the other orders as well. In Maine, Anjou, Angoulême, and especially Chartres, there were quarrels that grew out of their presumptions. Other disputes appeared, but they were not between the three estates, but rather between Protestant and Catholic, royalist and Leaguer, and royalist and Frondeur. Religious and political affiliations were more important marks of division than social classes.

On the other hand, in 1560 and thereafter the three estates almost invariably deliberated and voted apart. We can only speculate whether the separation of the orders resulted from the increased suffrage, the ambition of the officer class, or some more obscure cause.

7

THE ELECTIONS IN BURGUNDY

The Provincial Estates

Burgundy lay to the east of Orléans and the south of Champagne. Her glorious days had ended with the death of Charles the Bold less than a decade before the convocation of the Estates General of 1484, but her dukes had left enough of an imprint on her institutions to differentiate them from those of the surrounding jurisdictions. The province had as its nucleus the duchy of Burgundy. To it was added the so-called pays adjacents of Charolais, Auxerre, Bar-sur-Seine, and Mâcon. These four localities began to be represented in the assemblies of the duchy during the fifteenth century, thereby forming the provincial estates of Burgundy. The provincial estates usually met every third year. Between sessions the interests of the province were looked after by the élus, a group of five, one of whom was drawn from the clergy, one from the nobility, and two from the third estate. The fifth was appointed by the crown.

Like most provincial estates that of Burgundy was exclusive in its composition. For the clergy, the Bishops of Autun and Chalon, the abbots, deans of priories, and delegates of the chapters were summoned. All nobles with fiefs were convoked, but usually only from thirty to fifty appeared. Twenty-five towns were represented, generally by their mayors or échevins. In addition, the local estates of Charolais, Mâconnais, and Bar-sur-Seine sent deputies. Auxerre did not, but rather a few important towns took turns being represented. In all about three hundred persons had the privilege of attending, but rarely more than a third that number appeared during the latter part of the sixteenth century.[1]

Although the bailiwicks of Burgundy usually elected the representatives from the province to the Estates General, in several instances the provincial estates named deputies. In February, 1440, they sent a delegation to the national assembly at Bourges in the company of an embassy from their duke. This precedent was not sufficient to prevent the crown from ordering the bailiwicks to elect deputies to the Estates General of January, 1484. When the provincial estates met the preceding December to hear the report of a delegation they had sent to court on other matters, they decided to ignore the royal directives and to depute by province in order to be in a stronger position to preserve their privileges. The pays adjacents of Charolais, Bar-sur-Seine, Mâcon, Auxerre, and the bishopric of Autun elected separate delegations.[2]

In 1560 the crown once more directed the Burgundian bailiwicks to send representatives to the Estates General. Again there was a movement to substitute election by the provincial assembly, but this time the close tie between the Cardinal of Lorraine, who was the principal figure at court, and his younger brother, who was governor of Burgundy, was sufficient to prevent this action. Bailiwick elections were to be preferred, Lorraine wrote, because they gave the people more ease in making their remonstrances and also saved the cost of a special meeting of the provincial estates.[3]

The crown itself changed the method of convocation when it ordered a national assembly to meet in 1561 and told the provincial estates to name delegates. The estates opened on March 20, and each order deliberated separately, making its own decision about what to offer the king and whom to elect. The only untoward incident was a complaint by the nobles that only twenty members of their order had been convoked. More than three hundred gentlemen, they said, should have been called; it was difficult for those present to speak for the remainder.[4]

The élus were in session in July, 1576, when they received copies of letters ordering the bailiwicks to elect deputies to the Estates General. They immediately asked that these letters be revoked and the provincial estates assembled to name the Burgundian delegation in order to obtain "a union of the body of the three estates of the province." The crown complied to the extent of permitting the provincial estates to assemble to consider the question, but by the time the meeting opened, the bailiwicks had already chosen their deputies to go to Blois. Nevertheless, a proposal was made to ignore the bailiwick elections and have the cahiers prepared in these local meetings brought to the estates to be used in the preparation of a provincial cahier for each order. The three orders separated to consider these suggestions. At length it was decided to recognize the actions of the bailiwicks, but to name in addition one deputy from each order to represent "the body of the three estates." The third estate dissented, and when the other orders persisted in electing a clergyman and a noble, they clearly stated that they would pay no part of the costs of what they considered an unnecessary luxury.[5]

The élus again got advance word of the convocation of the Estates General in 1588 and immediately sent a deputation to Paris to ask that the provincial estates be assembled to take action on the elections and the cahiers. The request was granted and on August 20, after the bailiwick meetings, the provincial estates opened at Dijon. The deputies chosen in the bailiwicks to go to Blois were recognized as the representatives of the duchy as well, and the cahiers of the duchy were simply added to those of each bailiwick. This time no special deputies were elected. There were some complaints about the choice of royal officials to be delegates, and this practice was forbidden in the future. Once more the struggle between the municipal and royal bureaucracies had come to the fore.[6] In 1614 the major responsibility concerning the elections and the cahiers again rested with the bailiwicks. Thus the Burgundian estates named all or most of the deputies in 1483 and 1561, some of the deputies in 1576, but was content to approve the actions of the inferior jurisdictions on other occasions. A degree of provincial unity was kept, but not as much as in Brittany, Dauphiné, or Provence. The bailiwick estates are therefore of considerable importance.

Dijon

The three estates of Dijon prepared their cahiers and elected their deputies apart in 1560. No information has been found to indicate the composition of the electoral assembly beyond that the cahier of the third estate was submitted in the name of "the towns and plat pays."[7] The significance of the term plat pays should not be overemphasized, for the true nature of the suffrage was revealed in 1576 when deputies from the towns of Dijon, Auxonne, Nuits, Saint-Jean-de-Losne, Talant, and Beaune sufficed to prepare the cahier for the third estate and elect deputies to go to Blois. The other localities in the bailiwick were ignored, and Dijon gave notice of her determination to play a dominant role at an early date when her échevins decided that if their candidate was not elected in the bailiwick estates, he would go to Blois anyway in the name of the town. The precaution turned out to be unnecessary, and the lesser towns followed the lead of the capital. The municipal elections to the bailiwick assembly were no more democratic. The échevins of Dijon sufficed to choose the deputy, but the other inhabitants were invited to submit suggestions for the cahier, which was prepared by one man and approved by the échevins.[8]

The same procedure was followed in 1588, but this time the lesser towns did not accept both of Dijon's candidates. Étienne Bernard, a favorite of the Duke of Mayenne and incidentally an inhabitant of Dijon, was substituted for one of them. Here the hands of Mayenne or his associates were plainly visible.[9] In 1593, twenty-four municipal officials of Dijon named Bernard to go to the Estates General again. There is no evidence that other towns were consulted, but earlier a bailiwick assembly had elected Bernard to the meeting ordered for Reims.[10] In 1614 the échevins again decided to name a deputy to go directly to the Estates General, but when the other towns at the bailiwick assembly refused to consent to this action, they abandoned their design. Later the king asked that the clerk of the provincial estates also be named for the bailiwick, and the échevins consented without protest. Little is known of the activities of the other orders except that they voted apart. In 1614 the estates deliberated in different parts of the same chamber.[11]

La Montagne

A detailed procès-verbal survives for the elections in 1588 in La Montagne, a bailiwick centered around Châtillon-sur-Seine to the northwest of Dijon. The curés and proctors of the rural communities were convoked, but no less than fifty-three of the former failed to appear. The first two orders, voting separately, chose their deputies without mishap, in spite of some rivalry among the twelve nobles who had responded to the summons. Twenty-five were absent. The events in the third estate are of more interest. The deputies of the small towns and rural areas selected the lieutenant general of the bailiwick notwithstanding the opposition of the mayor and échevins of Châtillon. The municipal hierarchy was not content to accept this defeat and appealed to the Parlement of Dijon and the provincial estates on the grounds that a royal official would not press the petitions they intended to make against the government of the king. Indeed, they pointed out, the lieutenant general was the son of the advocate of the king, the brother-in-law of the lieutenant particular, the uncle of the procureur of the king, and was related by marriage to the clerk of the bailiwick as well. Small wonder the mayor and échevins saw little chance of making known at Blois their complaints against the local administration. The rumor was current that the lieutenant general had conspired with a man deputed by several rural communities to get elected. One wonders if the ambition of the royal officials does not explain the presence of the rural communities, as it had in Amiens in 1576, for the suffrage was the most generous in Burgundy. When the Burgundian estates and the Parlement failed to break the election of the lieutenant general, the magistrates of Châtillon dispatched an échevin to Blois where he was given a seat.[12] In 1614 the same electoral procedure was followed. Again the majority of the curés were absent, but there was no difficulty when the lieutenant general and another royal official were elected for the third estate.[13]

Auxois

Six towns sent deputies to the bailiwick assembly of Auxois in 1576, but several more had been convoked. The three orders named their deputies and prepared their cahiers separately. As late as 1651 the curés were not present in the electoral assembly, and only eight towns participated.[14]

Autun

Little survives on the electoral procedure used in the bailiwick of Autun, but a few interesting facts are known. In 1576 Georges Venot was elected deputy of the third estate and given the mission of asking for the suppression of the clerical jurisdictions. This put him in an embarrassing position, for he was the bailiff of the church. If he succeeded at Blois, he would lose his employment. He petitioned the town to spare him the journey that was likely to cost him so dearly, but the municipal council was at that moment engaged in a suit with the chapter on the subject of temporal justice and was little disposed to change its cahier or to deny itself of the services of one of the ablest and most prominent citizens of the community. Their knowledge of the character of the man and the power of the mandate system were regarded as security enough for his loyalty. Venot went to Blois and must have acquitted himself in an honorable fashion for in 1588 his son, who was scarcely twenty-one, was elected to return to the Loire as the deputy of the bailiwick, and in 1614 he was deputed to Paris. A second son represented the town in the estates of the League.

The three orders voted separately in Autun. It is not known who was convoked except that during the League the lesser towns and villages of the bailiwick did not participate. Fifty leading citizens of Autun elected the deputy for the third estate. The clergy deputed by diocese; in 1576 the Bishop of Autun sent an order to the archpriest of Beaune directing all benefice holders to assemble to name deputies. Beaune may have been in the diocese of Autun, but it was also in the bailiwick of Dijon. Once more the confusion of boundaries in the old regime presents itself.[15]

Chalon-sur-Saône

In the bailiwick of Chalon-sur-Saône as elsewhere in Burgundy, the three estates elected their deputies separately in 1576. Only nine important towns participated for the third estate and a committee of three sufficed to prepare the cahier. After the deputies had departed for Blois, the rumor spread that the municipal magistrates who had controlled the elections and the preparation of the cahier had leaned too far toward the side of peace and toleration. The strongly Catholic inhabitants of Chalon forced their town officials to call a municipal assembly, and the eighty-five persons who attended revised the cahier and dispatched two deputies to take it to Blois. All this was done without consulting the other towns of the bailiwick. The revised cahier was not received warmly by the deputies of the bailiwick who were already at the Estates General, but with the aid of the delegate of the nobility and other Burgundian representatives, a third and compromise version was produced at Blois, sent to Chalon, and approved in an assembly of the towns on December 10. At the same time the deputation of Chalon to the Estates General was accepted giving the little bailiwick four deputies for the third estate.

Once more, in 1588, the leaders of Chalon leaned toward the side of peace, and once more the election of tolerant deputies by the third estate was challenged. Here the similarity ceases, for this time the matter was taken to the Duke of Mayenne, who was governor of Burgundy, and to the estates of the province where the original deputation was finally accepted. The end of the Wars of Religion made possible undisputed elections in 1614.[16]

Mâcon

The four bailiwicks of Mâcon, Auxerre, Bar-sur-Seine, and Charolais had local estates in the sixteenth century, but the county of Mâcon was the only one of these so-called pays adjacents of the duchy of Burgundy that was able to keep its local estates until the Revolution. The estates probably had its origin in the fourteenth century. After the county was ceded to the Dukes of Burgundy in 1435, the institution continued to develop in spite of its integration with the Burgundian estates. By 1441 it had achieved the composition which was to characterize it throughout its history. For the clergy, the bishop, the two chapters of Mâcon, and the abbots of Cluny, Tournus, and Saint-Rigaud alone were summoned. Often the bishop and abbots were represented by proctors. All gentlemen holding fiefs in the county were convoked, but rarely did more than six or twelve attend. The third estate was made up of deputies from the towns of Mâcon, Tournus, Cluny, and Saint-Gengoux-le-Royal. During the religious troubles, Romenay, Marcigny, and Bois-Sainte-Marie were occasionally convoked.[17] The first two of these three towns were included in the electoral assembly of 1560 along with the six clergymen, about the same number of nobles, and the deputies of the regularly convoked municipalities. Most of the deliberations were in common in that year, but the basic decisions on the contents of the cahiers and the naming of the deputies were made by the individual orders. Nevertheless, the group as a whole had a reviewing power, for the representatives elected to go to Orléans were described as standing for "the community of the estates," and the cahiers of the nobility and the third estate were signed by the Bishop of Mâcon as president of the assembly.[18]

Thereafter the three orders acted apart, and the Bishop of Mâcon ceased to sign the cahiers of the secular estates. The rivalries during the time of the League increased the interest of the nobility in the estates, and in 1588 over twenty-five attended a session in which trouble between the Guises and royalist faction was narrowly averted. The other orders remained at their usual size with six attending for the clergy and four municipalities sending deputies. The absence of one town in 1614 made a noticeable difference.

The estates of Mâconnais was certainly far from democratic. Most of the clergy were excluded, and within the privileged towns general assemblies of the inhabitants were rare. Municipal cahiers were prepared in 1588 and perhaps at other times. A group of "poor rustics and peasants" did dare to submit a series of articles to the deputy of the third estate in 1560, but there is no evidence that the practice was continued.[19]

Auxerre

In the bailiwick of Auxerre the three estates deliberated separately in 1576, 1593, 1614, 1651, and presumably on other occasions. Like Autun, the clergy was convoked by diocese, and its deputies and cahiers were referred to as coming from that ecclesiastical jurisdiction rather than the bailiwick. The most unusual occurrence in the elections took place in 1593. The Abbot of Orbais, who was the secretary of the clergy in the League assembly at Paris, informed the canon of Auxerre that the Estates General was in session, but that no deputy from the area had been chosen. He asked that this oversight be corrected. In an assembly composed only of the ecclesiastics of the town of Auxerre, the Abbot of Orbais himself was elected as their deputy. The clergy excused themselves for not consulting the members of their order outside of the town and also for not sending a representative from their own number to Paris on the grounds of extreme poverty occasioned by the activities of the anti-League forces. Little is known of the composition of the bailiwick estates beyond that the curés and deputies of the villages participated in the reformation of the custom in 1561, that the curés attended the local estates in 1592 and the electoral assembly in 1614, and that the parishes were convoked during the Fronde to help choose deputies.[20]

Bar-sur-Seine and Charolais

The electoral processes in the two remaining bailiwicks remain in even greater oblivion. One can only state that Bar-sur-Seine regularly sent complete delegations from the three orders to the Estates General and that the clergy prepared a separate cahier in 1614.[21] The local estates of Charolais were functioning as early as the fourteenth century. The estates consisted of eleven ecclesiastics, almost all the nobles possessing fiefs, and the deputies of five towns, but in 1611 about half the clergy and three fourths of the nobility were absent. Unfortunately, no documents survive concerning the elections to the Estates General, but habitually the three orders deliberated apart.[22]

Bresse, Bugey, and Gex

Three bailiwicks that had previously had little historical connection with the duchy of Burgundy sent deputies to the national assembly in 1614 where they sat with the representatives of the Burgundian government. They were Bresse, Bugey, and Gex; they had belonged to the Dukes of Savoy until 1601, except for a brief intermission during the reigns of Francis I and Henry II. Each had its local estates whose privileges were recognized at the time of the French annexation, and their assemblies were convoked periodically until the Revolution. The three jurisdictions also sent deputies to a regional assembly and eventually to the still larger Burgundian estates.

The estates of Bresse assembled in Bourg in 1614 where each order chose its deputies separately. The seventy-five odd nobles who were present represented the largest number to attend the local estates until 1789. About half that number from Bourg and neighboring communities acted for the third estate. Much the same procedure was followed during the elections of February, 1649.[23]

The three orders deliberated separately in the estates of Bugey where thirty-two nobles signed the register of the second estate in 1651. Twenty-two towns regularly sent deputies to the estates.[24]

The bailiwick of Gex was the smallest of the three jurisdictions consisting of only twenty-eight parishes in the eighteenth century. Here the three orders also deliberated separately. About ten nobles usually attended the estates after 1750, but there are no figures before that date. The rural communities sent deputies. The bailiwick was geographically and economically so closely associated with Geneva which was ten miles away that it remained in the Swiss customs union until 1926. The Bishop of Geneva wrote letters recommending the deputy of the clergy in 1614. In the same year, a nobleman of Swiss extraction served as deputy, and some Genevese were charged to pay part of his expenses. In 1789 more Genevese nobles sought to vote in the electoral assembly on the grounds that they held land in the bailiwick.[25]

Summary

Suffrage in Burgundy did not widen as rapidly as in the other governments that have thus far been studied. Few changes can be noted during the course of the sixteenth century, and if we except the lands taken from Savoy, only in La Montagne, Auxerre, and possibly Autun were the curés or villages ever consulted. Also, there were fewer disputes between the royal officials and the bourgeois oligarchy in Burgundy than in many other places. The explanation for the differences lies in part in the existence of strong provincial estates to check the ambitions of the royal bureaucracy and protect local privileges. The estates codified the custom of Burgundy, removing any need for the members of the Parlements and the local royal officials to summon large bailiwick assemblies for this purpose. Auxerre was an exception; as a pays adjacent it prepared its custom separately in 1571 in a meeting in which the curés and villages participated, and these oft-neglected groups took part in an election to the Estates General thereafter. The most serious quarrel between royal officials and a municipal oligarchy took place in La Montagne, and there the curés and villages were given the right to vote. Another reason for the divergent procedure used in La Montagne and Auxerre was their proximity to Champagne, where curé and peasant voted as a matter of course. Ideas and practices had little respect for the vague provincial boundaries of Renaissance France.

Available records indicate that in the bailiwick estates, the three orders voted apart, but at the provincial level they acted together on several occasions.

8

THE ELECTIONS IN LYONNAIS

The Government

The government of Lyonnais, as it was constituted for the purposes of the Estates General, consisted of a widely diversified area. It included part of the rich Rhône valley with its great banking, commercial, and industrial city of Lyon, the plateau and mountains of Auvergne, the surrounding heavily forested, hilly areas in La Marche, Bourbonnais, and Forez, and the lowlands to the north in Nivernais. There were no regularly convoked estates of the government or common economic-social interests to unite the area. Auvergne was ever the stronghold of feudalism, but the seneschalsy of Lyon was largely controlled by the merchant aristocracy of the capital city, although at the close of the Middle Ages the Church could not be ignored. The old seigneurial nobility was neither numerous nor especially influential.

Lyon

The elections in the town and seneschalsy of Lyon are of exceptional interest because the richness of the communal archives makes it possible to study the electoral procedure for the third estate from the second decade of the fifteenth century. Prior to 1483, letters of convocation were addressed either to "the councilors, bourgeois, men, and inhabitants" of Lyon as in 1421 or to "the clergymen, bourgeois, and inhabitants" as in 1435,[1] but the variation in the royal directives had little influence on the procedure followed. The consulat alone elected the deputies to the estates in May, 1421, January, 1423, October, 1427, September, 1428, and to other meetings.[2] In March, 1428, the consuls and the representatives of the cathedral chapter voted together for the deputies of the clergy and third estate, but in 1435 when the letter of convocation was addressed to both the clergy and lay population of the town, the consuls acted alone.[3] The estates of 1468 saw the procedure of 1435 repeated. In that year Louis XI addressed the letter of convocation to "the clergymen, bourgeois, men, and inhabitants of our town and city of Lyon" and directed that one clergyman and three laymen be named to a meeting of the Estates General. The royal order was read before an assembly of the consulat and other notable persons, including the maîtres des métiers, but no action was taken at that time. Later, with only the consuls present, a lawyer was named to represent the clergy; a nobleman, the bourgeoisie; and a third person, the merchants of the town.[4]

The failure of the consuls to consult the clergy, even in the matter of naming a deputy to represent that order, was caused by a quarrel with the archbishop and chapter over their possession of rights of justice in the town. The twelve consuls, all drawn from the leading bourgeois, had been successful in wresting control of the government from the lesser inhabitants, but they were having difficulty defeating the claims of the clergy. The choice of a

member of the urban nobility to represent the bourgeoisie reflects the high
social status of the principal families. Indeed, after 1495 the office of consul
carried with it ennoblement. The relegation of the maîtres des métiers to a
minor role comes as no surprise considering the power of the ruling oligarchy, and from the beginning of the sixteenth century the maîtres were
selected by the consuls, not by the members of their respective guilds.

In 1483 the method of choosing the representatives to the national assembly was officially changed, and the three estates of the seneschalsy named a
delegation that included one member from the third estate. The consuls were
not happy at this turn of events and a few days later chose a deputy to the
Estates General. Six notables of the town were invited to meet with them to
elect still another. One of the notables selected protested against this action
on the grounds that such a large delegation was a useless extravagance. When
he was outvoted, he demanded the convocation of a greater number of people
to decide. The consulat had no intention of granting this request, but did indicate that one of the nominees was going to Tours on private affairs and
would therefore be content with a small present. Both deputies named by the
town attended the estates and made their report to the consulat on May 31,
the day after their return. Thus the change from convocation by town in 1468
to convocation by seneschalsy in 1483 did not destroy the power of the municipality, or rather of the consulat, to name deputies.[5]

The crown returned to the system of election by towns in 1506. On April
27 the consulat named a delegation to ask the king to marry his daughter to
the Duke of Angoulême. About six weeks later the delegates made their report. Only then were the notables and maîtres des métiers assembled to
learn what had happened at the estates and to ratify the proposed marriage.[6]

When the three estates of the seneschalsy were convoked in 1560, the
consulat held an assembly of several hundred notables, including the clergy,
legal officials, terriers — a group of rich, retired bourgeois who lived on
landed estates — and the maîtres des métiers. After some debate on the procedure to be followed, the consulat was asked to represent the town in the
estates of the seneschalsy and to prepare a cahier.

The seneschalsy meeting began on October 31 in the presence of the
vicar-general, the deans and canons of several churches of the town, and
other ecclesiastics. The parish clergy was absent. The names of only six
nobles appear on the roll, but others also attended. The consuls of Lyon and
the deputies of the towns and villages of the plat pays comprised the third
estate. The plat pays had participated in an assembly with Lyon in 1425, and
by 1556, if not earlier, had been formed into a distinct community consisting
of five jurisdictions. In each jurisdiction the syndics of the parishes met and
named deputies to their local assemblies or to the estates of the seneschalsy.
In 1560, deputies from these localities made their appearance in the electoral
assembly for the Estates General where they threatened the consulat's control of the third estate.

After the usual preliminaries, the three orders separated to prepare cahiers and select deputies. On November 2 they reassembled; the cahiers of
the clergy, nobility, and town of Lyon were read and the names of their deputies announced; at least nominal approval was given by the assembly as a
whole. The representatives of the plat pays had not deliberated with the town
of Lyon, but rather had prepared a separate cahier and named their own delegates to the Estates General. When called upon to have their remonstrances
read, their spokesman refused. The assembly protested, saying that the cahier would have to be approved by the entire assembly before it would be received by the Estates General or crown, but this was of no avail. The plat
pays persisted and her representatives were given seats at Orleans with the
others from Lyon.[7]

A few months later the Estates General was again convoked. This time the seneschalsy of Lyon was instructed to send deputies to an assembly of the government in March at Moulins where representatives were to be named to the national assembly. The procedure followed by the town of Lyon was similar to that used in 1560. The consulat assembled the terriers and maîtres des métiers, the latter representing forty-six guilds, to invite them to make suggestions to be included in the cahier. About seventy-five persons availed themselves of this privilege, and a large delegation was named to attend the estates of the seneschalsy. There, the plat pays again decided to elect a separate delegation.[8]

The feud between the town and the country was renewed in the seneschalsy assembly in 1576. The deputies of the plat pays refused to prepare a cahier and elect deputies with the representatives of Lyon, and insisted on a separate assembly. The archbishop protested that to concede to this demand would create a fourth estate, but the plat pays were nevertheless granted permission to meet eight days later to name two deputies to go to Blois. The archbishop and principal clergy of Lyon sufficed to nominate the deputy of the first estate, and we are vaguely informed that the larger and wiser part of the gentlemen of Lyonnais stood for their order. The action of the plat pays left to the consulat the joyful necessity of electing two of their own number to go to Blois in the company of the procureur of the town to give advice. Meanwhile, the cahier was prepared by a single individual and ratified by the consulat.[9]

By 1588 the seneschalsy officials were willing to concede that it was impossible to get the town and plat pays to vote together. On October 9 the lieutenant of the seneschalsy directed the consulat to assemble all the orders and estates of the town, including the terriers and maîtres des métiers, to elect deputies and prepare a cahier for the Estates General. The consuls resisted this effort to democratize the electoral procedure and pointed out that they had already chosen two competent deputies, as in truth they had. Four days later the consulat again took up the question of the elections because of criticism that the number of electors had been too small, but once more they reiterated their determination that the two consuls they alone had selected would go to Blois. They did consent to receive the memoirs of the inhabitants of the town. The plat pays also named two deputies.[10]

Again in October, 1592, the consulat alone named the deputies of the town to the estates, and the plat pays sent their own delegate. The submission of Lyon to Henry IV in 1594 brought changes in the municipal government designed to increase royal control. In the place of the twelve consuls, four échevins were named, and a provost of the merchants was installed who owed his nomination largely to the king. Two years later when a return was officially made to the convocation of the towns to a national assembly, the échevins called a general assembly of all the estates of the municipality. About a hundred persons drawn from the clergy, bourgeoisie, and officers of finance and justice attended. The inclusion of this last group reflected the determination of the king to control the town. A cahier was prepared and a deputy named to take it to Rouen.[11]

On August 4, 1614, the three estates of the seneschalsy assembled and heard a letter read convoking the Estates General. When this preliminary was completed, the first two estates separated and elected their deputies. Neither the town of Lyon nor seemingly the plat pays took action at this time. Several days later the terriers and the maîtres des métiers from fifty-six guilds were assembled by the échevins and asked to suggest articles for the cahier and to give the consulat authority to name the deputies to the Estates General, a request that was granted without opposition. Having taken these precautions, the provost of the merchants and the échevins met and elected

the former to go to the Estates General. Immediately thereafter, a second
assembly was held. This time it was made up of the ecclesiastical corporations, officers of justice and finance, advocates, procureurs, and other notable citizens. The provost of the merchants announced that the consulat had
already elected a deputy. Those present were then invited to name a few of
their number to assist in the preparation of the cahier, and a box was placed
in the hôtel de ville to receive suggestions that individual citizens wished to
make. Thus every group and each individual was permitted to make suggestions for the cahier, but, of course, the échevins kept careful control over
what was actually included in that document. Meanwhile, the échevins named
two assistant deputies to go to Paris to help the provost of the merchants and
to replace him if he became sick.[12]

The municipal elections in Lyon in 1651 were held in the same manner as
in 1614. The échevins were empowered by the terriers and maîtres des métiers to name the deputies of the town to the Estates General. This they did.[13]

Most striking about the electoral history of Lyon is how little the procedure changed during the course of nearly two hundred years, and this regardless of the directions given in the letters of convocation. Whether the town
or the seneschalsy was convoked, the end result was that the consulat alone
named the bulk of the deputies for the third estate. At the most the terriers
and maîtres des métiers were called upon to authorize their acts and make
suggestions to be included in the cahier. The submission to Henry IV led to
the enlargement of this group to include the ecclesiastical corporations, royal
officials, and other notables, but the larger assemblies served in an advisory
capacity only. The échevins remained in control, and only in 1588 was a
serious effort made to increase the suffrage.

The consulat, composed of patricians in every sense of the word, could
co-operate with the other orders without any feeling of inferiority. True, the
seigneurial rights enjoyed by the Church in the Middle Ages led to friction
between the ecclesiastics and bourgeoisie during the fifteenth century, and
this rivalry perhaps explains the separation of the orders in 1468 and 1484,
but it was scarcely a major factor thereafter. The nobility of the sword were
not numerous in Lyonnais and caused the town few difficulties. The only internal conflict which appears in the procès-verbaux was within the third estate — to some extent between the consulat and the rest of the town, but more
so between the capital city and the plat pays. The lesser towns and villages,
controlled as they generally were by royal notaries and minor crown officials,
were jealous of Lyon and the powerful merchant oligarchy who governed there.
In every assembly of the seneschalsy, they asserted their independence. Here,
as in so many other places, was the conflict between city and country, between
the merchant princes and the municipal officials of the former and the crown
officials and the petty bourgeoisie of the latter.

Bourbonnais, Beaujolais, Forez, and La Marche

Beaujolais lay to the north of Lyon; Forez, Bourbonnais, and La Marche
lay to the west. These four jurisdictions belonged to the Bourbons at the close
of the Middle Ages, and with the possible exception of Beaujolais, they had
estates which were frequently assembled during the late Medieval period. In
1483 they met on order of their duke to name deputies to the Estates General
of Tours.

The electoral procedure followed in this area is poorly known. It can only
be said that the estates of Bourbonnais consisted of the upper clergy, seigneurs, and deputies of about thirty towns and communities, judging by the
list of those who attended the meetings to reform the custom in 1521 and to

ratify the Treaties of Cambrai and Madrid in 1529. As late as 1614 the rural curés were not included. In that year two rival delegations of the clergy were sent to the Estates General where their elections were annulled by the king's council, the first because only twenty-five ecclesiastics had participated in its election and the second because of other electoral irregularities. A dispute between the deputies of the third estate was also brought before the council, but little can be gleaned from the record on how the elections were held.[14]

The third estate of Beaujolais was dominated by the town of Villefranche-sur-Saône. In 1614 the royal and municipal officials and a few important bourgeois met in the town hall and elected the lieutenant general to go to the Estates General. Then the échevins informed the deputies of the castellanies of their decision. Without reluctance the smaller communities adhered to the choice of the principal town of the jurisdiction. Perhaps they were receiving more attention than was customary. In 1576 the municipal leaders consulted only three other towns before reaching a final decision. Twelve years later they were less considerate and named a deputy to the Estates General without referring to anyone outside the municipality. It is not surprising that in 1592 the consuls of Lyon thought it sufficient to write their counterparts in Villefranche asking that a deputy be sent to the national assembly to elect a Catholic king. Truly the rest of Beaujolais suffered from neglect. Except for 1484, the deputies of the clergy were the same as those of Lyon. The bailiwick was in that diocese and the representatives of the first estate were probably chosen at the episcopal seat for the entire area. Nothing is known of the activities of the nobility.[15]

The estates of Forez met frequently during the century following the outbreak of the Wars of Religion, but the custom developed for the nobility and the thirteen "good towns" to assemble at different times except when there was a matter of common concern to be considered. They each had a syndic to represent their interests when they were not in session. Thirty-three nobles participated in the elections to the Estates General in 1614, and the cahier was prepared by the nominee and four other persons. At one time or another, at least nineteen towns took part in the assemblies of the thirteen "good towns." Fifteen sent deputies to the assembly to choose representatives in 1614. The increase doubtless resulted from the growing demand for representation during the Wars of Religion. The clergy had no separate sessions, and after Forez' reunion with the crown may have met at Lyon with Beaujolais and the rest of the diocese. The three jurisdictions always sent the same delegation to the Estates General in the sixteenth century.[16]

La Marche sent five deputies to the Estates General of 1484, but in the sixteenth century the two seneschalsies into which the county was divided sent separate delegations to the national assembly. The presence of deputies from Basse-Marche in 1560 is attested by an edict establishing a royal seat at Dorat at their request, but only in 1588 and 1614 did anything like a full delegation attend the Estates General from the two jurisdictions. The electoral procedure remains unknown except that during the reign of Charles VII the three estates voted together. In 1521 when the custom was codified, the parishes sent deputies, but the curés were not specifically summoned. Over a century later, in 1651, more than two hundred ecclesiastics, including curés, four or five hundred nobles, and the deputies of the towns and parishes attended the estates of Basse-Marche.[17]

Haute-Auvergne and Basse-Auvergne

Forez, Bourbonnais, and La Marche form a half-moon around Auvergne, a mountainous province subdivided into two areas — Haute-Auvergne and

Basse-Auvergne — each with its own estates. Sometimes the estates of Haute-
and Basse-Auvergne assembled together during the fifteenth century, sometimes they deliberated separately. When the estates of Haute-Auvergne met,
the three orders deliberated together. In Basse-Auvergne thirteen privileged
towns were so tightly knit together that they acted apart from the clergy and
nobility until in the latter part of the sixteenth century, when the syndics of
the first two orders were given deliberative voice in their assemblies. Even
when the estates of the two Auvergnes met together, the municipalities of
Haute-Auvergne were excluded from the proceedings of their fellow townsmen
to the north. Such peculiarities need not concern us, however, for in 1484 and
thereafter Haute- and Basse-Auvergne sent individual delegations to the Estates General. For this reason it is advisable to treat their histories separately.[18]

The membership of the first estate of Basse-Auvergne was limited to the
more important ecclesiastics. When the custom was redacted in 1510 only
one bishop, seven abbots, four priors, and the deputies of the two chapters
participated, but half again as many were summoned in 1529 to ratify the
Treaties of Cambrai and Madrid. Only the upper nobility was called during
the early part of the sixteenth century, but the suffrage for the second estate
was expanded thereafter, and in 1651 no less than 209 nobles participated.[19]

Thirteen "good towns" stood for the third estate of Basse-Auvergne in
1484, but in 1560 the towns and communities of the plat pays managed to be
heard as well. The letter of convocation was sent to the royal governor, and
he directed the three estates to meet at Clermont on November 17. The échevins of Clermont, who were entitled to convoke the thirteen towns, ordered a
preparatory assembly of the municipalities on the tenth. Here it was determined to ask the other towns and communities of the plat pays to send deputies to Clermont on the sixteenth to submit articles they desired to have included in the cahier. On the seventeenth the three estates met as scheduled
in the presence of the governor to discuss their common problems, but each
order prepared its own cahier and named its own deputies. The only difficulty
grew out of the failure of the deputies of the plat pays to accept the minor role
assigned to them. In spite of the protests of the thirteen "good towns," they
prepared a cahier of their own and elected a deputy to take it to the Estates
General.[20]

The "good towns" had only themselves to blame for initiating the plat pays
into the assemblies of the estates. In 1480 and 1554 the inhabitants of the plat
pays had participated in meetings at the invitation of the privileged thirteen.
The reason for this generosity is not difficult to find. The crown wanted to
levy a tax on the "good towns," and they in turn hoped to persuade the plat
pays to share the burden. Some of the villages failed to appear in 1554, but
one locality sought a permanent position among the "good towns." This demand was anticipated by the privileged thirteen, for in that year and again in
the preparatory meeting for the Estates General of 1560, their spokesman
specifically stated that the consultation of the plat pays was not to be taken as
a precedent for the future. Be this as it may, in 1576 the plat pays had become sufficiently organized to have its own syndic and was more determined
than ever to receive due consideration.[21]

The "good towns" of Basse-Auvergne met again in March, 1561, to hear
the report of their deputies to Orléans. After a brief consultation with the
other orders, they elected deputies to attend the estates of the government at
Moulins on the twentieth of the month. This time the plat pays was not consulted, but fifteen years later it was to find a powerful ally in the officials at
Riom.[22]

Through an error in the royal chancellery, letters ordering the election
of deputies to the Estates General were sent in 1576 to the seneschalsy officials at Riom. These officials seized their opportunity and directed the three

estates, including the plat pays, to meet at their seat. The échevins of Clermont protested immediately, arguing that the thirteen towns had always spoken for the third estate of Auvergne, that they alone had the right to convoke the deputies of these localities, and that the meeting should be held at Clermont. Once more the entrenched interests of the patricians of the great towns were attacked by royal officials. The crown intervened on behalf of the échevins, but to no avail. The deputies of three or four hundred towns and bourgades gathered at Riom and elected a delegation to go to Blois, but the officials were not completely successful in their effort to supplant the provincial estates. The clergy followed the new directives of the king and met at Clermont under the direction of their bishop. Twelve of the thirteen towns responded to the call of the échevins of Clermont to choose representatives, only Riom preferred to follow the royal officials who controlled the town. Some of the nobles attended the seneschalsy estates, but they were so few in numbers that another meeting was held at a later date at Montferrand. At Blois the quarrel was renewed when the deputies elected at both Riom and Clermont claimed to represent the third estate. Again the king in council sided with the thirteen towns and ordered that future meetings be held at Clermont. The deputies chosen at Riom were nevertheless given seats.[23]

The privileged towns had triumphed, but their position remained insecure. The crown officials at Riom were unreconciled, and the plat pays continued to demand representation, a desire quite understandable since the "good towns" controlled taxation. In 1587 the governor sought to solve the problem by recommending that twelve additional towns be admitted to the deliberations, but it was not until the elections of 1588 that matters were brought to a head. The letters of convocation were once more sent to the seneschalsy at Riom, and the officials quickly assembled the estates. Again the king intervened, acknowledged his error, and directed that the estates meet at Clermont in accordance with the traditional practice. This time he was obeyed, but when the deputies assembled, a new dispute arose. A second seneschalsy had been created in Basse-Auvergne with its seat at Clermont, and there were thus two seneschals who claimed the right to preside over the estates. A bitter quarrel ensued with the échevins and royal officials at Clermont co-operating to check the claims of those of Riom. The upshot of the whole affair, of course, was the election of two sets of delegates in rival meetings sponsored by the two officials. Once more the king's council had to act. The rights of Clermont were safeguarded, but the number of towns representing the third estate was increased to nineteen. The six new localities were to be chosen for a term of six years, initially by the plat pays, but thereafter by the assembly of the third estate. The quarrel between the thirteen towns and plat pays was thus terminated, and in 1614 and 1649, nineteen towns chose the delegations to the Estates General. The rivalry between Clermont and Riom, on the other hand, persevered until the Revolution in spite of order after order issued by the king in council.

In summary, the "good towns" initiated the experiment of consulting the plat pays, but it was the quarrel between the royal officials at Riom and the municipal oligarchy at Clermont that led to the disputed elections in 1576. The quarrel was renewed in 1588 with the royal officials at Clermont also playing a part, and the king in council protected the "good towns" by admitting only a tiny fraction of plat pays. The bulk of the towns, bourgs, and villages of Auvergne never participated in a legal election to the Estates General. Even in the privileged municipalities, few took part in the choice of deputies to the electoral assemblies. The first estate did no better; only the upper clergy was convoked by the Bishop of Clermont when he assembled his diocese for a meeting of the estates.[24]

The three orders of Haute-Auvergne deliberated together during the fifteenth century, but little is known of their activities thereafter. When the custom was redacted in 1510, the clergy was represented by one bishop, two abbots, two priors, and one chapter. The nobility was more numerous, but only six towns spoke for the third estate. In 1560 several bailiwick officials and the proctors of five towns met to name representatives to the Estates General, the deputies of the other orders having been elected in an earlier assembly. Every town wanted one of its citizens chosen, for they all had remonstrances to make at Orléans which concerned themselves alone. The procureur of the king protested, saying that the crown had directed that only one deputy be elected from each estate and that it would be expensive to send more. Nevertheless, three deputies were then named, and at some other time three more were chosen to go to Orléans. The latter were either elected in the assembly in which the clergy and nobility chose their representatives or by the individual towns.[25]

Haute-Auvergne witnessed the same increase in suffrage in the first and second estates after the middle of the sixteenth century that has been noted elsewhere. In 1649, 26 ecclesiastics were convoked as opposed to the 6 who had participated in the estates of 1510, and 105 nobles were convoked as opposed to the 24 who voted in 1588. Nevertheless, in 1649 the lower clergy and the nobles without fiefs were still excluded.[26]

For a time it looked as though the same pattern would unfold in the third estate. The six towns that had participated in 1510 were increased to ten by 1569, but for some unexplained reason the suffrage was reduced thereafter. In 1576 and 1588 only the "towns and provostships" of Saint-Flour, Aurillac, Maurs, and Mauriac participated.[27] The use of the word "provostship" should not be taken to indicate that preparatory assemblies that included the smaller towns were held to elect deputies. In 1614 Saint-Flour refused to let several other towns in the provostship participate in the elections on the grounds that as the principal town and capital it represented the province. This attitude was taken despite the fact that several of the rejected towns had taken part in the bailiwick assembly in 1569, and one had done so as early as 1510. In 1649 the suffrage may have been further restricted. Instead of the principal towns in the four provostships being told to name deputies to the bailiwick assembly, the consuls of each were summoned. At Maurs, however, the older procedure was followed anyway, and an assembly of "the larger and wiser part" of the inhabitants was held to elect deputies to the estates. At Saint-Flour twenty persons sufficed to name the delegation, and it is doubtful if Aurillac or Mauriac were more generous.[28]

There was a bitter rivalry between the towns of Saint-Flour and Aurillac. In 1588 Aurillac sent to the Estates General a special deputy who was seated. In 1614 there was further trouble. Henri de Noailles, the bailiff of Haute-Auvergne, summoned the three estates to meet at Aurillac. Saint-Flour sent a delegation, not to participate, but to protest that as the capital and principal town in the province it should be the seat of the assembly. The sixty-year-old Noailles refused to change the place of the meeting. He was too sick to move and comforted himself with the thought that Aurillac also claimed to be the principal town in the province. The deputation from Saint-Flour departed angrily expressing the belief that they were in danger of arrest. When they arrived home they summoned an assembly which named deputies to the Estates General. Meanwhile, the assembly at Aurillac had also elected a delegation, but only that of Saint-Flour was given a seat at Paris. In 1649 both Saint-Flour and Aurillac again laid claim to be the principal town. Officials in both localities summoned the estates. The electors from the provostships of Maurs and Mauriac preferred Aurillac, but Saint-Flour named a deputation anyway.[29]

The three estates of Haute-Auvergne ceased to vote together by the middle of the sixteenth century. The division of the estates may have grown out of the frequent meetings of the towns when the other orders were not convoked. Once the towns had become accustomed to act alone, it is not surprising that they continued to do so even when the other estates were in session.

Nevers and Saint-Pierre-le-Moutier

The elections in the duchy and peerage of Nevers are especially interesting because there a noble, not of royal blood, exercised the right to assemble the estates to elect deputies to the Estates General. As this privilege was constantly challenged by the royal officials of the bailiwick at Saint-Pierre-le-Moutier, the elections in the two jurisdictions must be considered together. The bailiff of Saint-Pierre and his subordinates were ever ready to argue that only royal officials could convoke the estates, and well they might, for little remained if all the pretensions of the duke were allowed. Guy Coquille, the great spokesman for the ducal family, insisted that Nevers was a province and that as a province it possessed both a geographical and a moral unity in which all the inhabitants had the same spirit and customs. As such, even the clergy and the other royal enclaves in the midst of the ducal territory fell under the jurisdiction of the House of Nevers leaving little for the royal officials. On the other hand, the bureaucrats at Saint-Pierre sought to exercise political control over the seigneurial lands. [30]

As was so often the case, the pretensions of the various officials caused little trouble before the last quarter of the sixteenth century. In 1483 Nevers and another territory of the prince (Rethel), sent the same deputies to the Estates General, and the royal enclaves elected deputies at Saint-Pierre-le-Moutier. When the custom was codified in 1534 the ducal officials presided over the assembly which included the clergy and even the protesting deputies of Saint-Pierre itself. [31] The elections in 1560 saw the town council of Nevers prepare the municipal cahier, after receiving the suggestions of the populace. Those who attended the ducal estates named a deputy to take the articles "agreed on in the assembly of the three estates" to the duke, for they wished to propose nothing before the king without his consent. [32]

The rivalry between the bailiff and the ducal officials began in earnest in 1576 and fortunately Pierre de Blanchefort, who became the deputy of the nobility, left an account of what took place. The bailiff was determined to entice as many inhabitants of the duchy into the bailiwick estates as possible. He wrote Blanchefort begging him to attend the assembly at Saint-Pierre. As an inducement he hinted that many nobles would like to elect him as their deputy. Blanchefort tactfully replied that he would attend the assembly if his health permitted. This encouraged the bailiff, and he suggested that Blanchefort inform the other nobles in his neighborhood of the meeting since he himself was not acquainted with "all the nobility of the province." The bailiff was seeking to expand his supposed conquest.

Meanwhile, Blanchefort had received a letter from the officers of the peerage ordering him to attend the meeting of the estates of the duchy and enclaves at Nevers. The tactful Blanchefort decided to obey both summons and with several companions set off for Nevers. There the nobility, deliberating alone, prepared a cahier and elected Blanchefort as their deputy by a plurality of votes. Blanchefort vainly protested that his health would not permit him to attend, but he was "finally vanquished." The next day he set out for Saint-Pierre, after indicating to the worried officials at Nevers that he did not intend to participate in the assembly, but only to thank the bailiff for his kind letters. When he arrived, the officers of the king immediately sought to win his support, arguing that the letters of convocation had been addressed only to the royal bailiwicks. This Blanchefort knew to be incorrect, for he had been shown the royal letters to the duke. He remained firm. The royal officials were irritated to learn that the duke had received letters of convocation, but felt it wiser to turn their spleen against the clergy who, they claimed, were directly under royal protection and therefore obligated to attend the assembly at Saint-Pierre. Once more they were disappointed, for the right of the peer to convoke the ecclesiastics had also been recognized.[33]

In 1588 the battle was renewed by the bailiwick officials, and this time they managed to get the clergy to assemble at Saint-Pierre in spite of the disapproval of the crown. Nevers had no deputies from the clergy to send to the Estates General, but for the first time during the century Saint-Pierre had a full contingent.[34]

Neither the duchy nor the bailiwick was represented at the estates of the League, but in 1614 the rivalry was revived with increased bitterness. The royal officials protested against the crown's decision to send a letter of convocation to the duke and tried to get the clergy and the towns of the duchy, even Nevers, to attend the bailiwick assembly. The duchess, who was then in residence, caught the messenger to her capital and had him thrown in prison. The ducal officials began to carry the attack, and agents were sent to the clergy to persuade them not to desert as they had done in 1588. Their efforts were largely successful, and the ecclesiastics assembled alone under the leadership of the bishop and chose the two candidates of the duke, one of whom registered as the deputy of the bailiwick and one as the deputy of the duchy. Most of the nobility, towns, and clergy of the duchy later attended an assembly held at the château in great splendor, following closely the ceremony used in the Estates General with the duke playing the role of king. After the initial speeches, the three estates separated, and the secular orders elected their deputies. The bailiff could muster only three nobles at his assembly at Saint-Pierre, and they named two deputies who, incidentally, were friends of the duke. Only two or three ducal towns sent representatives; and the officials of the presidial seat, completely in control, elected two of their most violent colleagues. In the Estates General the quarrel continued with the duke himself successfully pleading the cause of his duchy before the council.[35] The Duke of Nevers again assembled the estates of his duchy to elect deputies to the Estates General in 1649 and 1651.[36]

In neither the duchy nor the bailiwick were the villages convoked, and the town council of Nevers assumed the bulk of the responsibility of naming deputies to the ducal assembly and preparing the cahier. In 1614, and perhaps earlier, the curés were consulted.

Summary

The electoral procedure in Lyonnais was far from democratic. The curés and deputies of the villages were generally excluded from the electoral assemblies, and only a small minority of the population participated in the great urban centers. Nevertheless, the number of towns convoked in Basse-Auvergne and Forez increased during the period, and the plat pays of Lyon sent deputies directly to the Estates General. These developments were brought about in part by the rivalry between the local royal and municipal officials and in part through the insistence of the excluded localities themselves.

The three orders usually deliberated together in the various provincial estates during the fifteenth century, but thereafter they acted separately. This change may have been brought about by the practice of convoking only the "good towns" on those occasions when the matters under consideration did not effect the other orders. This prepared the towns to act separately in electoral assemblies for the Estates General. The only quarrels, other than the perennial one between the crown and municipal officials, were between the town and the clergy of Lyon, the rival municipalities of Saint-Flour and Aurillac, and the royal officials of Saint-Pierre-le-Moutier and the Duke of Nevers.

9

THE ELECTIONS IN LANGUEDOC

The Provincial Estates

Languedoc was a long, rather narrow province extending from the valley of the Garonne and the Pyrénées north and east to the mountains of Auvergne and the Rhône River. It possessed active provincial estates, estates of the seneschalsies, and estates of the individual dioceses. Few parts of France were so well supplied with representative institutions, and by the eighteenth century their composition, functions, and duties had become fairly well defined. Students of this period state with justified assurance that the provincial estates consisted of 23 archbishops and bishops, 23 barons, and 68 deputies from towns or dioceses who possessed in all forty-six votes, exactly the number of the first two orders combined. Beyond this facade of order lay all the confusion and all the infinite variation so characteristic of France before the Revolution.

The first representative institutions to appear in the province were the estates of the various seneschalsies. Later, during the fourteenth century, it became common to assemble the estates of several of these jurisdictions in one place, but with each of them deliberating alone much of the time. These meetings gradually led to the formation of the provincial estates and to a corresponding decline in the use of the seneschalsy estates. During the sixteenth century the seneschalsies seldom assembled except to elect deputies to the Estates General. Often while the provincial estates were in session, however, the deputies of the three oldest seneschalsies got together and discussed problems relative to their particular area.

Since the provincial estates of Languedoc were in reality the estates of the seneschalsies meeting together, their composition and that of the smaller institutions was much the same in the post-Medieval period, although earlier many who went to the estates of the seneschalsies did not go to the larger assembly. Attendance at the provincial estates was especially poor on the part of the first two orders, and the number convoked was slowly reduced until the reign of Charles VII when the makeup of the clergy became fairly consistent. Twenty-two archbishops and bishops were recognized as comprising the first estate. The composition of the second estate varied for a longer period, and it may not have been until the dawn of the seventeenth century that its number also became fixed at twenty-two. From twenty-five to thirty-five towns sent deputies during the reign of Charles VII, but here, too, there were changes. Assemblies of the dioceses were formed, and they also began to elect delegations to the provincial estates. During the sixteenth century the custom was established of granting one vote to the chief town and one to the deputy of the third estate chosen in the diocesan assembly; this gave the third estate the same voting power as the other two orders combined. Of course there were many exceptions to this rule. The capitals of the dioceses of Comminges and Montauban were outside of Languedoc, and the third estate of these areas was represented only by a syndic. For some reason Vivarais was treated in a similar manner. Two consuls from Le Puy were the sole deputies of the third estate of Velay. On the other hand, several dioceses contained two towns that could depute proctors with voting rights. The municipalities generally sent more than one deputy, but regardless of the number, each town had only one vote. Custom, ruled by chance rather than reason, ever decided except for the clergy, who should be admitted and who should not; but the idea of a balance in the voting power of the orders had become so strong by 1694 that when a bishopric was established at Alais, thereby adding another prelate to the provincial estates, additional votes were given to the nobility and third estate. This balance was of importance because the three orders usually, though not always, voted by head.[1]

Although the seneschalsies formed the basic electoral unit in Languedoc for the Estates General, the provincial estates were also interested in what took place. In October, 1560, the three orders elected together one deputy to participate in the estates of Orléans, and named a committee to prepare a cahier.[2] The following March the provincial estates met to name deputies to the Estates General of Pontoise. On the motion of the third estate, it was decided that the three orders would initially deliberate apart. The reason for this action may be easily surmised. The king had asked for advice on how to pay the mortgage on the royal domain, and the secular estates had determined to offer him part of the temporal goods of the church for this purpose. The concurrence of the clergy could hardly be expected, and the orders separated. The secular estates then got together and prepared a joint letter to the king containing their generous offer, leaving the clergy to protest alone. On the matter of deputies, the clergy and lay orders managed to reach agreement, and representatives were sent to Pontoise in the name of the three estates of the province.[3] Not until January, 1652, were the provincial estates again in session during the period when elections to the national assembly were being held. In that year the three orders named a delegation of six to attend the national assembly along with representatives of the seneschalsies.[4] During the intervening century the provincial estates had done little in regard to the national assembly.

Toulouse

The estates of the seneschalsies played a more important role in the elections to the Estates General, but so few documents survive concerning their activities that it is difficult to reconstruct their history. As might be expected the town of Toulouse clearly dominated the activities of the third estate of the seneschalsy of that name. Like many other towns, the municipality claimed direct representation in the Estates General. In 1560, 1576, 1588, 1593, and 1614, a deputy was elected by the municipal council and supplied with a special cahier. Furthermore, all the other deputies of the third estate from the seneschalsy in 1560, 1576, 1588, and 1614 were natives of Toulouse and played prominent roles in its history.[5]

Less is known of the assemblies of the three estates of the seneschalsy, but surviving documents suggest strongly that attendance was limited to those of the seneschalsy who had seats in the provincial estates. The electoral assembly of 1576 consisted of the Archbishop of Toulouse and five bishops, or rather of their vicars-general who stood for them, several nobles, and the deputies of six or eight towns or dioceses. This highly select group named together the deputies for the three estates and instructed them to work together at the national assembly.[6]

A dispute arose at the Estates General in 1588 between three deputies who claimed seats in the chamber of the third estate. It was charged that the seneschal had not convoked the nobility to the electoral assembly and that only sixteen of the thirty-six persons entitled to participate for the three orders had done so. The third estate at Blois examined the powers of the rival deputies and finally ruled that all of them would be seated, but gave precedence to the one elected by the sixteen voters. It is interesting that even the challengers admitted that only thirty-six persons could vote in the large seneschalsy of Toulouse; actually less than half that number did so. It is also worthy of note that the seneschal, who was accused of not summoning his fellow nobles, sat for the second estate. [7]

The failure to keep adequate records of the procedure followed in the elections to the Estates General was clearly revealed in 1649. In that year both the seneschal, who was a partisan of the Duke of Orléans, and the Archbishop of Toulouse, who headed the rival Mazarin faction, appealed to an official of a neighboring jurisdiction who had been a deputy in 1614 to learn how the elections ought to be held. Of particular interest was the matter of who should be summoned and whether the three orders ought to vote together or apart. Upon these questions depended the outcome of the bitterly contested elections.

Before the seneschalsy estates met, the seneschal must have found documents indicating who had been summoned in the past, for instead of following the erroneous advice of the deputy of 1614, he convoked his jurisdiction in the traditionally exclusive manner. Only one bishop and the vicars-general of the archbishop and five other bishops attended for the first estate. The proctors of three nobles, the syndic of the second estate of Albi, and the deputies of three towns and six dioceses completed the assembly. The one innovation was that the estates met at Gaillac, rather than at Toulouse. The reason for this change becomes apparent when one remembers that there were rival factions headed by the seneschal and the archbishop. The seneschal chose Gaillac because it was in the archdiocese of Bourges. There the archbishop could not participate "with the preeminences of his archepiscopal dignity," a situation which left a true man of his age no alternative but to absent himself and send his vicar-general instead. The Orleanists had successfully excluded their most dangerous rival, and they proceeded to threaten and cajole those who attended to support their candidates by methods which included the substitution of a voice for the usual written ballot. They were largely successful, for the three estates voting together named an Orleanist bishop and the seneschal among others as deputies. There were the usual complaints. The town of Toulouse made a strong protest against choosing a royal official as one of the representatives of the third estate; even the south was not free from the rivalry between the two leading elements of that order. The loudest protests came from the vicar-general of the archbishop. He charged that several persons who had the right to vote had not been summoned. The estates, he argued, ought to consist of the bishops and barons of the seneschalsy who were deputies born, and one delegate for the clergy, one for the nobility, and two for the third estate of each diocese.[8] His statement was correct in regard to the bishops and barons who had hereditary seats in the provincial estates, but his claim that the diocesan estates should send deputies is open to question. It is necessary to investigate the composition of these assemblies and determine what action they took in regard to the Estates General.

The civil dioceses, upon which the local estates were based, were jurisdictions which largely replaced the old jugeries and vigueries during the financial reforms of the fifteenth century. It would be too much to hope that their boundaries would conform with those of the ecclesiastical dioceses, and they did not. It would be equally erroneous to expect a broad suffrage, for theirs was among the most restricted in France. The civil diocese of Toulouse contained about two hundred communities at the close of the sixteenth century, but only ten master towns were permitted to send deputies to the diocesan estates. In 1625 the number was increased to eleven. The nobility had at first been admitted but, through indifference to an institution that served mainly to collect taxes, they withdrew only to seek to re-enter during the seventeenth century. The three barons of the diocese who held seats in the provincial estates had especially strong claims. The Archbishop of Toulouse, or his vicar-general, was the only representative of the clergy who had the right to attend. No deputies were sent to the provincial or seneschalsy estates for the nobility and clergy, and the third estate delegated only its syndic and the first consul of the ville de tour, for the towns took turns furnishing the second deputy. There were no elections in the modern sense. Indeed, the representatives of the towns in the diocesan assemblies were consuls or persons chosen by the municipal magistrates alone. It is of interest that the town of Toulouse played no part in the diocesan activities, but was separately administered. The procès-verbaux of the diocesan assemblies to elect deputies to the seneschalsy in 1614 and 1649 indicate that the procedure described above was also followed when a delegation was named to the Estates General. In the elections of 1649, more of the confusion of boundaries of the old regime was revealed. Five of the eleven towns stated that they were also in the seneschalsy of Lauraguais and did not wish to pay toward the costs of sending two deputations to the national assembly.[9]

The diocesan assembly of Lavour was no more democratic. The bishop, the syndic of the chapter, and one noble made up the contingent from their respective orders. The third estate consisted of two consuls from each of five master towns and one from each of three. Twenty-four other communities took turns being represented, two of them sending their magistrates each year. This small group handled the administration of the diocese, but when it came to participating in the estates of the seneschalsy or of the province, the bishop or his vicar-general, the baron, the first consul of Lavour, the syndic of the diocese, and the deputy whose turn it was from one of the five principal towns made up the entire delegation.[10]

The diocesan assembly of Saint-Papoul at the close of the old regime still consisted of only eight deputies for the third estate, four of whom came regularly from three towns and the other four were taken in turn from a number of communities. A bishop and a privileged baron also resided in the jurisdiction. The bishop and six master towns normally controlled the diocesan estates of Rieux, but during the period of the Wars of Religion there were a few assemblies in which about fifty communities were represented and several members of the other two orders attended. Only small parts of the dioceses of Comminges and Montauban were in Languedoc, but their bishops and syndics of the third estate attended the provincial estates as well as those of the seneschalsy.[11] The dioceses, except for Albi, never named deputies for the clergy or nobility, and usually the principal towns took turns furnishing a consul to accompany the syndic to the estates.

Lauraguais

The seneschalsy of Lauraguais did not become independent until 1554. By that time the composition of the diocesan, seneschalsy, and provincial estates of Langeudoc had been largely determined. As a result, the important communities in Lauraguais continued to take part in the meetings of several diocesan estates, for the most part in the seneschalsy of Toulouse. The area did not have a regularly convoked assembly of its own nor did it participate in the provincial assembly on an equal basis with the three older seneschalsies. It did, however, send deputies to the Estates General. Our knowledge of the electoral procedure depends on a description of the assembly in 1614 given years later by the juge-mage of Castelnaudary, who had been a deputy. He firmly stated that all prelates, abbots, priors, archpriests, nobles, and first consuls of the towns with royal judges were convoked, and the cathedral chapters and the master towns of the diocese sent deputies. This relatively generous suffrage for Languedoc may be explained because the estates of Lauraguais were not regularly convoked; hence the trend towards an increased suffrage could be satisfied without complaints that traditional usage was being violated. The same reasoning suggests why the three estates voted for their deputies separately, but it would be a grave error to exaggerate the degree of democracy practiced here. The curés were excluded, many rural communities were ignored, and the first consuls were summoned, rather than the municipalities being asked to hold elections. Furthermore, the juge-mage did not hesitate to add that the nomination for the clergy belonged to the Bishop of Saint-Papoul, as the senior ecclesiastic, if he wanted it. [12]

Carcassonne

Carcassonne was the second of the original three great seneschalsies that made up Languedoc. The electoral meeting of her estates was held at the town hall in 1614 under the presidency of the Bishop of Carcassonne. Four other bishops attended and three sent their vicars-general. Seven nobles were there in person or by proxy. Ten towns and nine dioceses sent deputies. The three orders elected their delegates together and appointed a committee to prepare a common cahier. The same procedure was repeated when the seneschalsy named its deputies in 1649. [13] These assemblies were small, and when one considers that the bishops and nobles present served by right rather than by election, and that the deputies of the towns owed their nominations only to their respective municipal councils, it becomes obvious that the overwhelming majority of the three orders was excluded, except in so far as they could participate in the ten diocesan assemblies which had the right to choose one deputy each. But even these local estates added few to those consulted.

The estates of the diocese of Castres was made up of deputies from fifteen towns and the bishop or his vicar-general. Nobles were not normally admitted and the towns took turns sending the deputy to the provincial estates. The assembly of the diocese of Carcassonne consisted of the bishop or his vicar-general, the consuls of the town of Carcassonne, and two magistrates from each of eight other master towns. In addition, towns in four inferior districts took turns sending one deputy each. The estates of the diocese of Lodève was no more democratic. Two towns were always represented, but forty-eight others alternated, each sending one deputy every twelve years. The bishop but not the nobles was admitted. Twenty-four towns sent deputies to the diocesan estates of Narbonne and seven to those of Saint-Pons. Fifteen towns always had the right to attend the diocesan estates of Mirepoix, but this generosity cost little because ten of the towns had to withdraw from the meeting before the deliberations began. Five barons had the right to enter, but they rarely appeared and no deputies were elected from their order to attend the provincial estates. The third estate of the diocesan estates of Agde consisted of ten persons. Eight were chosen by four towns, each of whom sent two deputies. The ninth came from one of three towns who took turns naming him each year and the tenth came from one of eleven towns who also took turns naming him each year. Pézenas always furnished the deputy of the diocese to the higher assemblies. The Bishops of Alet and Limoux attended the estates of the seneschalsy and the province, and both towns sent their consuls, but the two dioceses had a single diocesan assembly to which was convoked only the magistrates of a handful of master towns. One noble resided in the two jurisdictions who had the right to participate in the provincial estates. [14]

Part of the diocese of Albi lay in the seneschalsy of Toulouse and part in Carcassonne. As a result, the estates were frequently told to send deputies to the assemblies of both seneschalsies. In 1576 the Parlement issued a decree forbidding this practice and directing the diocese to take part in one assembly only. In 1614, however, the estates of Albi determined to ignore the ruling and send deputies to both larger assemblies where they were admitted. Present at this meeting of the estates of Albi were the vicar-general, the deputies of two chapters, and the proctor of one of the other two ecclesiastics who had the right of being admitted. Two nobles sent proctors, but five others who had seats failed to do so. For the third estate, the consuls from eleven master towns were present along with a goodly number of consuls from the other 111 communities that were invited to participate. The estates of Albi were more democratic than most of the diocesan assemblies, but still the overwhelming majority of the first two orders was excluded, and the master towns exercised the preponderant influence in the third estate. More serious, the people of the communities had little direct say as to the activities of their consuls in these assemblies. The three estates voted together.[15]

Béziers, the tenth diocese in Carcassonne, also presented a problem. Two towns regularly sent deputies to her diocesan estates, and twenty-four others took turns sending someone every six years. Difficulties arose because Béziers claimed to be an independent seneschalsy with the right to send deputies directly to the Estates General. Under the leadership of the lieutenant general, a meeting of the seneschalsy was called in October, 1614, to elect deputies. The Bishops or Vicars-General of Saint-Pons, Béziers, and Agde were present along with the consuls of six towns and the deputies of several dioceses, although many of them had also been present at the estates of Carcassonne a little while before. No nobles attended. The lieutenant general explained that Carcassonne had refused to recognize the position of Béziers as an independent seneschalsy, but that the governor had given permission for them to meet. Those present then proceeded to choose together the lieutenant general, but he was not seated in the national assembly.[16]

Beaucaire and Nîmes

The third great seneschalsy in Languedoc was that of Beaucaire and Nîmes. Its electoral assembly in 1576 consisted of the proctors of the Bishops of Nîmes, Uzès, and Viviers; the deputies of the nobility of the dioceses of Nîmes and Viviers; the deputies of the towns of Nîmes and Uzès; and the deputies of the third estate of the dioceses of Nîmes, Uzès, and Viviers; in all, ten persons, to whom must be added a syndic general of Languedoc, who attended on order of the provincial governor. One might think that this little group could elect deputies without difficulty, but this was not the case. When the representatives from Vivarais discovered that the other two dioceses had two deputies from the third estate — one from the principal town and one from the diocese — to their one, they withdrew rather than accept this mark of inequality. It was necessary to hold a second assembly. Once more the seneschal of Beaucaire and Nîmes ordered Vivarais to send only one deputy for the third estate, but he was disobeyed and two were chosen.[17]

The electoral assembly in 1614 was better attended by the lay orders. About six nobles were present or sent proctors and the third estate of Gévaudan was represented in addition to the dioceses of Nîmes, Viviers, and Uzès. This time Vivarais was permitted to have two deputies for the third estate, but the diocese was still not content and insisted that one of her inhabitants be chosen to go to the national assembly.[18]

In 1649 it was necessary for the lieutenant general of Beaucaire and Nîmes to explain that tradition called for only those people to be convoked who had the right of entrance into the provincial estates. The province, he argued, was a pays d'état, not a pays d'élection, and therefore was not governed specifically by the instructions contained in the royal letters of convocation. When the estates met in March of that year, only the Bishops of Viviers and Mende were present for their order. Five nobles or their proctors were there along with deputies from the dioceses or estates of Nîmes, Uzès, Vivarais, and Gévaudan, and from the town of Nîmes. With few difficulties they chose together their deputies to the Estates General.[19]

When the jurisdictions that named deputies to the seneschalsy of Beaucaire and Nîmes are studied, the reader is struck by the greater participation of the nobility there than elsewhere in Languedoc and by the tendency of the subordinate jurisdictions to send deputies directly to the Estates General. The first phenomenon is explained by the fact that three of the diocesan estates, Vivarais, Velay, and Gévaudan, had their origin as local assemblies of the three estates and performed many functions other than tax collection. The nobility had therefore continued to exercise their right of attendance. The deputations to the Estates General may be accounted for by Vivarais, Velay, and Gévaudan being large areas that bore the title of bailiwicks, a fact that led the clerks of the royal chancellery to send them letters of convocation upon occasion. The vicissitudes of the religious struggles and the ambition of local royal officials also were factors.

The seneschal was able to control only the diocesan assemblies of Nîmes and Uzès. At the end of the old regime the estates of Nîmes was composed of the bishop or his vicar-general and the consuls or deputies of eight master towns. Eight other towns took turns being represented every other year. The electoral assemblies of the sixteenth and early seventeenth centuries appear to have included even fewer of the third estate, and both the bishop and his vicar-general were often absent. One unusual incident that occurred was in 1561 when the town of Nîmes, strongly influenced by the Protestants, prepared a cahier in a municipal assembly and elected a delegate to present it at the Estates General. The estates of Uzès was smaller. Only nine master towns had the privilege of attending, although two others were occasionally permitted to send nonvoting deputies.[20]

The estates of Vivarais presumably sent deputies to the meeting of the seneschalsy at Nîmes in 1560, though insufficient documents survive to admit proof. As a bailiwick, though a subordinate one, Vivarais was also asked to name deputies directly to the Estates General and the syndic of the estates was elected to attend. In 1561 Vivarais chose a large delegation to go to the provincial estates which met at Montpellier on March 20 to name deputies to the national assembly. In 1576 Vivarais sent deputies to the estates of the seneschalsy at Nîmes and, on order of the royal chancellery, to the Estates General as well. Since only the secular orders were adequately represented in the diocesan estates, the clergy named their deputy to Blois in a separate assembly. Vivarais probably received a double summons again in 1588, but the war prevented the estates from meeting to choose deputies to go to Blois, and the area had to be content with the consuls of the principal towns naming one delegate for the third estate. Thereafter, Vivarais was not asked to send representatives directly to the national assembly and accepted a role more comparable to the other dioceses, though in 1614 a request to the seneschalsy estates that someone from her territory be elected was satisfied.[21]

The most unusual feature in the composition of the estates of Vivarais was the absence of the clergy. On the rarest occasions was the bishop or his vicar-general admitted because of his ecclesiastical position, but the former attended regularly as one of the barons de tour. Sometimes the secular orders named a deputy for the first estate anyway. Sometimes they were content to leave this duty to a special assembly of the clergy, as when they were directed to send representatives to the Estates General in 1576. Ten barons known as the barons de tour took turns presiding over the assemblies and representing their order in the provincial estates. Several others were permitted to attend the estates of Vivarais, but most often the only noble who personally participated was the one whose turn it was to preside. The others usually sent their bailiffs with their proxies. The third estate consisted of the consuls of thirteen towns. These towns also took turns sending someone to the provincial estates. Thus the great majority of the three orders was excluded. During the Wars of Religion inhabitants of the plat pays sought, without permanent success, the privilege of electing a deputy to the estates. Some simple gentlemen fared no better during the Fronde. The orders deliberated together and voted by head using the secret ballot from the middle of the sixteenth century.[22]

The neighboring estates of Gévaudan consisted of eight ecclesiastics, eight barons who took turns representing their order in the provincial estates, and twelve more who had the right of attendance, and the consuls or deputies of eighteen towns. The three orders ordinarily deliberated and voted together. They were not always content to depute only to the estates of the seneschalsy. In 1588, and perhaps at other times, the bailiwick obeyed the summons of the king and sent a delegation directly to the national assembly. No noble was elected by the estates that year because so many of the order were absent and those present were deeply divided. A committee was named to prepare the cahier.

None of the deputies chosen by the estates of Gévaudan in 1588 ever went to Blois. A canon accompanied by a friend took the place of the Bishop of Mende who had been officially elected. Then, on the last of November, the Bishop asked a local advocate, Jacques Desasalmartin, in the presence of the syndic of the estates and several other persons, if he would go to Blois as representative of the third estate, since those elected had found that they were unable to attend. Decasalmartin agreed and was seated on arrival at the Estates General. Few instances indicate more clearly the casual way in which deputies were so often named or why the list of those elected corresponded so poorly to those who actually attended the national assembly.[23]

The estates of Velay, like the other representative institutions of the region, was exclusive. The composition of the orders varied, but at the close of the Medieval period ten ecclesiastics were convoked, with sixteen barons and the consuls of Le Puy. The economic-social demands of those excluded had some effect during the Wars of Religion when both royalist and Leaguers increased the suffrage to give the estates they held the appearance of full assemblies. Several more nobles won the right to be summoned, and a few towns were given the privilege of taking turns being represented. How often this aristocratic body named deputies to the Estates General is not certain. In 1484 and probably in 1560 the estates sent deputies to vote in the elections of the seneschalsy of Beaucaire and Nîmes, but in 1576 and 1588 Velay dispatched deputies directly to the Estates General. In 1614 the three estates elected together a nobleman to go to the Estates General, but one deputy of the third estate was named by the master towns alone and another by the consuls of Le Puy. In 1649 the three estates elected their deputies together and chose a committee composed of the three orders to prepare the cahier.[24]

There was a town, a diocese, and a bailiwick of Montpellier, all at one time subordinate to the seneschalsy of Beaucaire and Nîmes. In 1560 the town participated in the estates of the seneschalsy, but the bailiwick sent a deputation directly to the Estates General. Thereafter, Montpellier behaved as an independent jurisdiction, and even the town played no further role in the estates of the seneschalsy. One is unable to ascertain whether the composition of the assemblies of the bailiwick was comparable to that of the diocese, but the latter was controlled by seven towns. The first consuls of some other communities were permitted to attend part of the deliberations.[25]

Foix

The three estates of Foix must also be considered at this time, for their representatives deliberated with those of Languedoc in the Estates General of 1614, although the inhabitants of the area did not participate in the estates of the province. Little is known of the early history of the estates of Foix except that near the close of the fifteenth century the House of Foix-Navarre united them with the estates of Béarn, Bigorre, Gabardan, Marsan, and Né-bouzan to form an Estates General for their domains in that part of France. Only after the Bourban accession to the throne of France did Foix send deputies to the national assembly.

Few were permitted to participate in the estates of Foix. The Bishop of Pamiers and five abbots were summoned for the first estate. Only a limited number of nobles could attend, a mere thirty-seven being convoked in 1520, but the participation of the second estate increased somewhat during the Wars of Religion and immediately after the death of Henry IV. In 1520, twenty-eight communities were summoned, but after 1693, twenty towns and twenty-five bourgs and villages were invariably convoked. The three estates nearly always deliberated together; this procedure gave the nobility a preponderant voice. In 1614 the three orders elected their deputies together and named a committee of six to prepare the cahier. A similar procedure was employed for the elections in 1649 and 1651.[26]

Summary

The two most striking features of the elections in Languedoc were the almost universal practice of the three estates voting together and the extremely narrow suffrage permitted by all three orders. The bishops, a few privileged nobles, and the consuls of the more important towns were in complete control almost everywhere. The practice of this small group of nobles and consuls taking turns serving as deputies to the larger assemblies reduced to a farce the elections in many places. One must not suppose that everyone was content with this situation. There was a mild demand for an enlarged suffrage during the Wars of Religion, and during the Fronde the disenfranchised clergy and nobility made a determined effort to achieve political power.

Their drive reached its most serious proportions in the seneschalsy of Toulouse, although it was also an important factor as far away as Vivarais. The chapter of Saint-Étienne of Toulouse was the spearhead of the movement in the first estate, but sought votes only for the chapters and ignored the regular clergy and curés. The dissatisfied nobility claimed that twenty-two nobles had usurped the right to sit in the provincial estates. Supported by the Parlement of Toulouse, they demanded that all gentlemen be admitted to the diocesan assemblies and that one member of the second estate be chosen by each diocese to sit in the provincial estates. If this arrangement had been followed, it would have given twenty-two seats to the diocesan nobility, and twenty-two would have remained with the privileged nobles. Unfortunately for the chapter clergy and the disenfranchised nobles, they allied themselves with the rebellious local Parlement, and their movement was therefore discredited at the eventual triumph of Cardinal Mazarin. The oligarchy that controlled the provincial estates had been more discreet, and as a result was able to hold its pre-eminent position until the Revolution.[27]

The failure of the suffrage to expand as much in Languedoc as elsewhere undoubtedly stemmed from the existence of strong provincial estates that were able to impose their procedures on the electoral assemblies and prevent the seneschalsy officials from changing the suffrage at will. It was more than a coincidence that in Lauraguais, where there were no traditional estates, the suffrage was wider than in the three older seneschalsies. The provincial estates also kept royal officials under control in other ways. There were fewer quarrels between the municipal and royal officials; the case of the lieutenant general who sought independence for Béziers so that he could be elected to the Estates General was exceptional. Finally, the virtual absence of assemblies in the sixteenth century to codify the customs must be noted. A province that had long used written law had little need for these meetings that had proved a powerful force for the extension of the suffrage in the north.

The limited suffrage was paralleled by the practice of the three estates voting together. The fusion of the orders was almost complete; perhaps if the representation of the three estates in the north had remained as select, they too would have continued to act in common.

10

THE ELECTIONS IN GUYENNE

The Provincial Estates

The government of Guyenne had as its nucleus the wealthy, commercial region of Bordeaux and the Garonne Valley so long held by the English, the less endowed forested area of Lannes to the south, and Saintonge on the northern bank of the river. The Treaty of Brétigny in 1360 added Agenais and the mountainous region of Rouergue, Périgord, and Quercy to the English possessions; the conquerors quickly incorporated these provinces with the older territory. Finally, a part of the foothills of the Pyrénées fell to the government, although the Bourbon territories of Navarre and Béarn successfully resisted these expansive tendencies throughout the old regime.

It has often been assumed that the provincial estates of southwestern France died out after the English were expelled. Nothing could be further from the truth, for the municipal archives reveal that assemblies of the third estate were frequently held during the sixteenth century. Probably the establishment of élections in Guyenne between 1621 and 1623 marked the decline of the provincial and local estates of the area.

Actually, there may have been two provincial estates in southwestern France as well as numerous local ones. In addition to the estates of Guyenne, which included Bordeaux and the seneschalsy of Guyenne, Agenais, Périgord, Condomois, Bazadois, Rivière-Verdun, Quercy, Rouergue, Armagnac, Lannes, and Comminges, assemblies were held in 1549, 1569, and possibly on many other occasions that included Saintonge, Haut- and Bas-Limousin, and Périgord in the government of Guyenne, and Poitou, Angoulême, La Rochelle, and Haute- and Basse-Marche in the governments of Orléans and Lyonnais. In truth, so little is known of these provincial estates that it would be dangerous to generalize further than saying that the local estates had ample experience in sending deputies to deliberate in larger assemblies.[1]

Saintonge

The seneschalsy of Saintonge possessed one of the least known of these local estates. Its composition is indicated by the assemblies to ratify the Treaty of Étaples in 1496 and to codify the custom in 1521. These meetings were limited to the prelates, abbots, and deputies of the chapters and monasteries for the clergy; the counts, barons, castellans, and seigneurs with high justice for the nobility; and some royal officials, lawyers, and the mayor of the seat of the jurisdiction.[2] The only election to the Estates General for which there is information took place in 1588. In that year Saintes was the only town consulted. A local committee prepared the cahier for the seneschalsy, and it was read before an assembly of the inhabitants of the municipality. The mayor and échevins asked the lieutenant of the governor to name the deputy of the third estate, and his choice fell on the lieutenant particular.

Immediately, the municipal officials regretted their decision and, arguing that
the lieutenant particular was an enemy of the town, asked that the local royal
officials meet with them to select a deputy. The request was granted, and an
election was held in which a councilor of the presidial seat was chosen in lieu
of the lieutenant particular. The councilor, Geoffroy Turmet, Seigneur of
Breuil, accepted, but the lieutenant particular did not receive this rebuff gra-
ciously, and a few days later he threatened the mayor with a 500 écus fine if
he did not deposit the cahier and procès-verbal of the election with the clerk
of the seneschalsy. This the mayor refused to do. A new difficulty arose
when Breuil decided not to go to the estates because of the dangers of travel
and his ill-health. Another deputy was elected, but for some reason he never
reached Blois. At length the king notified Saintonge that no deputy for the
third estate had arrived and a third electoral assembly was held. Again
Breuil was elected and again he refused to go. Once more the échevins and
other notables met to choose a deputy and this time they were careful to name
someone who would brave the dangers of the road. Meanwhile, the nobility
elected their deputy and prepared their cahier separately. Nothing is known
of the activities of the clergy. [3]

Marennes was a subordinate jurisdiction in Saintonge until 1646 when it
became an independent seneschalsy. The role of those convoked in 1651 included about one hundred clergymen, two thirds of whom were curés, all the
seigneurs, and the syndics of the parishes. [4] It is not known whether the suffrage in Saintonge had become equally generous by this time.

Guyenne

The seneschalsy of Guyenne with its capital of Bordeaux was situated to
the south of Saintonge. There, as in Saintonge, only the members of the upper
clergy and nobility were summoned to codify the custom in 1521. The one
difference was the presence of representatives from over twelve towns. [5] The
elections to the Estates General of 1560 were no more democratic. The deputies from two chapters at Bordeaux and several of the archpriests of the
diocese assembled at the episcopal palace under the leadership of the vicar-
general. This small group authorized the deans and canons of the two chapters to prepare the cahier of the clergy. A month later the cahier was approved and two deputies were named to take it to the Estates General. The
assembly of the second estate was equally limited, with only ten nobles appearing. They elected an absentee "for themselves and for all the other
seigneurs,... of Guyenne."[6] Nothing is known of the activities of the third
estate.

In 1576 the chapter of Saint-André of Bordeaux elected a deputy and prepared a cahier for him to take to the ecclesiastical assembly of the archbish-
opric, and the jurats of Bordeaux instructed the villes filleules, or lesser
towns, in the seneschalsy to send deputies with cahiers to the electoral assembly of the third estate. [7] The events that took place at the meeting of the
seneschalsy escape the historian.

There are more details of the activities of the third estate in 1588. On
August 8 deputies from seven towns, baronies, or similar jurisdictions met
with the jurats of Bordeaux. It was decided that each town, including Bordeaux, would have one vote regardless of the number of representatives present. A delegate was elected, but the jurats withdrew from the meeting without
voting, no doubt in protest against being given no more voice than the lesser
localities. The delegates who remained decided to elect a second deputy, but
they postponed this action until the thirteenth because so few towns were represented. On the thirteenth, only five towns appeared, and it was decided to

delay the election of a second deputy for still another week in the hope of securing a larger attendance. The meeting on the thirteenth also saw the representatives of the towns and the jurats of Bordeaux fail for a second time to
agree on a common course. The third summons to the third estate of the
seneschalsy must have been accompanied by threats, for about twenty towns
sent deputies to the meeting on the twentieth. The jurats once more refused
to act with the delegates of the lesser towns and decided to elect one of their
own number to sit in the Estates General. Finding themselves deserted, the
deputies of the lesser towns chose a second delegate alone. Thus the third
estate of the seneschalsy of Guyenne sent representatives from two factions
to the Estates General where after a long dispute they were both seated on
order of the royal council. Since the lesser towns were controlled by the
royal officials, we have once more the officer class, with the support of the
smaller communities, quarreling with the bourgeois oligarchy of a great town. [8]

In 1614 the Archbishop of Bordeaux selected a committee of ten to prepare the cahier of the clergy under his supervision. Only seven ecclesiastics
met with him to choose the deputies to the Estates General, but three of them
were referred to as deputies of "the curés and other benefices" of the diocese, which indicates that the lesser clergy were indirectly represented. The
archbishop was elected, and this choice was later approved in a larger assembly which included the ten archpriests of the diocese and several other
persons. The suggestion of the archbishop that an assistant deputy also be
chosen was received with little enthusiasm because of the additional expense
entailed. Finally, it was agreed that he could name an assistant to replace
him if he were absent from the estates, but that at no one time should the
diocese be charged for more than one deputy.

In 1614 more of the clergy were consulted than in 1560, but even in the
later election the rural curés were excluded except for the small indirect
representation in the first electoral assembly. The archbishop with a few
advisors, and not the seneschal, had determined who should be convoked, and
it is interesting that the archbishop summoned only the desired persons from
the diocese of Bordeaux, rather than use the boundaries of the seneschalsy as
the limiting geographical factor. His actions met with considerable opposition from the clergy itself on the grounds that the procedure of 1588 was not
being followed, but it is impossible to ascertain what that procedure was. [9]

Nothing is known of the activities of the nobility in 1614, but the jurats of
Bordeaux claimed the right to assemble the third estate just as the archbishop
had the clergy. The villes filleules and subordinate seats of the seneschalsy
were instructed to send deputies to Bordeaux, and on the appointed day two
deputies were elected. The lieutenant general, who did not recognize the
privileges of the town, also presided over an assembly in which a deputation
was named for the third estate, and the elections directed by the jurats were
nullified. The dispute was settled by a decree of the royal council which permitted a deputy from each faction to be seated, but severely criticized the
lieutenant general for not following the traditional usages. Once more the
crown had protected its subjects from its own officials. [10] The quarreling
continued during the Fronde, and a second convocation of the estates of the
seneschalsy was necessary before the accustomed form was observed. [11]

Lannes

The estates of the seneschalsy of Lannes met frequently after the expul-
sion of the English. During the reign of Charles VII, the Bishops of Dax,
Bayonne, and Aire and several abbots and priors made up the first estate; the
principal barons and seigneurs, the second; and the deputies of the seven

towns, the third.[12] It is not known who attended the electoral assembly for
the Estates General of 1484, but the three estates met at Dax and submitted a
single cahier to the king. This cahier, and a reference to a municipal official
in Bayonne being elected by "the people of the three estates of the seneschalsy," indicates that voting was done by head and not by order,[13] a procedure that had been followed in the deliberations of the estates during the previous reign.[14]

By 1529 the representation in the clergy had been expanded to include the
proctors of the cathedral chapters and in the third estate, to include the deputies of some baronies and provostships.[15] In 1561 over twelve towns, baronies, and parishes in the provostship of Dax alone were represented. Very
few nobles attended either of these assemblies.[16]

The extension of the suffrage was paralleled by internal disputes that led
the clergy of the seneschalsy to subdivide into dioceses and use that ecclesiastical subdivision as a basis of electing deputies to the Estates General.
The dioceses of Aire and Dax sent deputations to the Estates General in 1560
and again in 1576 in the company of the diocese of Bayonne. Dax alone was
represented in 1588, but in 1614 her representative and that of Bayonne carried on a dispute in the Estates General itself.[17]

The towns and provostship of Dax, Saint-Sever, and Bayonne also fell to
quarreling. The first two sent separate delegations to the Estates General of
1560. Neither Saint-Sever nor Bayonne attended the electoral assembly held
at Dax in March, 1561, and Saint-Sever alone was represented in the Estates
General of 1576. In 1588 the third estate of the provostship of Saint-Sever
gave their cahier to a deputy of Bordeaux to take to Blois, but sent no representatives, nor did her two rivals take any action. Saint-Sever alone deputed
to the Estates General of 1614 for the third estate, but in that year the nobility, who had rarely attended the estates of Lannes and had sent no deputies to
the Estates General during the sixteenth century, dispatched a delegate representing the three seats.[18]

The rivalry in the third estate continued in 1649. Bayonne protested
against the decision of the seneschal to convoke the estates at Dax, and her
deputy left the assembly when precedence was given to Dax and Saint-Sever.
The fight was renewed in the electoral assembly of 1651.

These rivalries brought to an end the practice of common deliberations
on the part of the three estates. When the clergy determined to depute by
diocese, they automatically cut themselves off from the secular orders. When
the royal officials and municipal leaders of the three important towns could
not agree on who was to have precedence or where the estates were to be
held, they acted alone, or did nothing at all. The nobility was indifferent and
rarely participated. Hence, one is not surprised to find the third estate of
Dax naming its deputies without consulting the other orders in 1561, or the
third estate of Saint-Sever meeting alone in 1576, or preparing a separate
cahier in 1614.[19]

Haut-Limousin and Bas-Limousin

The province of Limousin, which lay in the northeast corner of Guyenne,
was divided into two sections. The one to the north was known as Haut-
Limousin and was centered aroung Limoges. The other, Bas-Limousin, included the rival towns of Tulle, Brive, and Uzerche. Each section had flour-
ishing estates during the fifteenth century. Occasionally they met together,
but for the most part they followed their own course, and always during the
sixteenth century named separate delegations to the Estates General. During
the reign of Charles VII the three orders of each section deliberated together.

The suffrage was quite limited: only the bishops, abbots, priors, and deputies of the chapters participated for the clergy; the nobles with fiefs, for the second estate; and seven towns in Bas-Limousin and five in Haut-Limousin, for the third estate.[20]

There is no significant information relative to the elections in Haut-Limousin in 1560, but early in 1561 the consuls of Limoges joined some of the syndics of the towns and parishes of the seneschalsy to elect a deputy for the third estate to attend the governmental assembly at Bordeaux. When the estates of Guyenne were ordered to assemble again on June 10, the consuls of Limoges alone named the representative of the third estate. In neither instance were the people of Limoges consulted. Little can be added concerning the elections thereafter except that by 1614 there had been some extension of the suffrage. The curés participated as did some representatives of the plat pays. This fact did not prevent the town of Limoges from successfully claiming the privilege of naming a deputy. The three orders voted in different chambers that year.[21]

We are better informed concerning the electoral procedure of Bas-Limousin where the chief characteristic was the rivalry between the lieutenant generals in Brive, Tulle, and Uzerche, the most important towns in the seneschalsy. In 1560 and 1561 the estates of Bas-Limousin met at Uzerche to elect representatives, but almost nothing is known of these assemblies other than that over 150 nobles were assessed to pay the costs of their deputies to the estates at Orléans and that at least six deputies represented the third estate at that same meeting.[22]

The assembly of the estates in 1576 escapes the historian, but the procès-verbal of the meeting in 1588 has survived. Tulle was chosen as the meeting place by the governor. All ecclesiastical communities were told to send deputies; and the remainder of the clergy, even the prioresses and curés, were to attend in person. However, only 97 were present or represented; and 184, mostly curés, were absent; 90 nobles with fiefs attended or sent proctors, and 75 were absent; 73 towns and parishes sent deputies, but 93 failed to do so. Those absent were fined. The three estates separated to name their deputies, and the first two accomplished their task without difficulty. The majority in the third estate decided to elect three officials from Tulle and Uzerche, but two notaries who held procurations from twenty-eight parishes of the plat pays protested, saying that they had been instructed by the king to elect only one person and to send three to Blois would place too great a burden on the province. Their complaint was to no avail, for the three officials were elected. To make matters worse, the lieutenant general at Brive, angered that Tulle had been chosen by the governor as the meeting place for the estates, had previously assembled his jurisdiction on his own authority. Two deputies, one being the lieutenant general, had been elected and they were given seats at Blois even though the governor and the estates at Tulle had declared this assembly to be null. Thus five delegates attended the Estates General for the third estate of Bas-Limousin — a far cry from the one delegate ordered by the king and requested by the plat pays.[23]

In 1614 the lieutenant general of Brive again ordered the estates to meet in his town. The magistrates of Tulle and Uzerche protested and obtained letters from the king on July 31 ordering the lieutenant generals of the three jurisdictions to meet at Uzerche to work out an agreement. When the lieutenant general of Brive did not appear at the appointed time, the other magistrates again protested, and on August 17 the king ordered the estates to meet at Tulle. The royal command arrived too late, for a week earlier the lieutenant general of Brive had been elected deputy by an assembly of the third estate of his jurisdiction. The estates which met at Tulle on the twenty-seventh chose the lieutenant generals of Tulle and Uzerche. If the lieutenant general of Uzerche was unable to attend, his son was to take his place. This proved to be the case, for between the elections at Tulle and the opening of the Estates General, the lieutenant general of Uzerche died. When the deputies arrived at Paris, the lieutenant generals of Tulle and Brive patched up their differences and acted in concert in an effort to deprive the son of their fellow official from Uzerche of his seat. The third estate ruled that all three could attend, but have only one vote between them. Such was the jealousy between the royal officials, but all seemed interested in the rivalry. Even the little town of Laguenne took the trouble to plead that the estates should be held at Tulle, the traditional capital, the seat of the bishop, and the most centrally located town.[24]

The three estates of both Haut- and Bas-Limousin ceased to act together during the first half of the sixteenth century. This change was paralleled by an increased suffrage in the third estate, especially in Bas-Limousin. Since the procès-verbal of the elections of 1588 stated that the third estate was much more numerous than formerly, it may have been the first time all the villages had been summoned. On the other hand, in 1614 only sixty nobles voted, a marked decrease from the ninety who found their way into the meeting of 1588.[25]

Périgord

The seneschalsy of Périgord was to the south of Limousin. The three estates were active, and the capital city of Périgueux frequently sent deputies to the assemblies of the towns of the kingdom. Lists of those convoked to the estates survive for 1529 and 1553. They indicate that the bishops, abbots, priors, and deputies or syndics of the chapters were called for the first estate; 125 nobles, for the second estate; and the consuls or syndics of about a dozen towns in 1529 and twenty-seven in 1553, for the third estate. The curés and villages were not consulted.[26]

Attendance was never as great as the size of the summons warranted. In the assembly of March, 1561, to elect deputies to go to the estates of the government at Bordeaux, only a fraction of those listed above appeared; three fourths of the towns failed to send deputies. Nevertheless, enough were present to make it advisable to avoid confusion by naming twelve persons from each order to prepare a cahier and elect together at least one deputy from each estate to attend the meeting at Bordeaux. The preceding year one deputy of the third estate had been elected in a different manner. A councilor had been sent to court by the municipal officials of Périgueux to try to prevent troops from being stationed in the town and, while there, had been told to represent the town in the Estates General at Orléans. He sat with the other deputies from his order who had been elected by the three estates of Périgord.[27]

Little is known of the electoral procedure followed in 1576, 1588, or 1593, but the existence of individual cahiers for the third estate in 1576 and 1588 suggests that the three orders decided to act separately.[28]

This period saw an ever increasing divergence of interests within the third estate. The three principal towns of the province, Périgueux, Bergerac, and Sarlat, were controlled by a mixture of wealthy bourgeoisie and royal officials who found it to their advantage to co-operate against the inhabitants of the less fortunate localities rather than to indulge in their usual quarrel. The three towns and those who controlled them possessed many privileges; the mayor of Périgueux even claimed precedence over the simple seigneurs of the province. The inhabitants of the lesser towns who had seats in the estates and the peasants of the plat pays, who were for the most part excluded, placed much of the blame on the more privileged group of their order for the heavy taxation and the sufferings occasioned by the civil wars. Feeling their interests neglected, they made many demands in the estates of the province including that of having a separate syndic for the plat pays to look after their interests. The crown, as usual, favored the privileged towns, but the movement did not stop short of open rebellion and was terminated only by the grant of some concessions to the smaller towns that were already included in the estates. Once these towns were satisfied, they dropped their allies from the fields, so that the developments of the 1590's in Périgord brought more of a strengthening of the position of the secondary localities than an increase in rural suffrage.[29]

The estates of Périgord met in 1614 to elect deputies to the Estates General, and the list of those who attended reveals that few changes had taken place in the composition of the orders since 1553. About thirty persons attended for the clergy, the curés still being excluded. One hundred and fourteen nobles and thirty-one towns were present or represented, a consul or syndic nearly always standing for his municipality. The only significant innovation was the introduction of some gentlemen without justice into the second estate on the order of the seneschal and the lieutenant general. The three orders elected their deputies and prepared their cahiers separately.[30]

The two meetings of the estates of Périgord to elect deputies to the Estates General during the Fronde were attended by the same elements as in 1614. The three estates continued to elect their deputies and prepare their cahiers separately.[31]

Quercy

Farther south the estates of the seneschalsy of Quercy were composed of the Bishop of Cahors, nine other clergymen, twenty-five nobles, and the deputies of twenty-two towns in the assemblies of 1486 and 1512. By the close of the sixteenth century the number of those summoned increased to twelve for the clergy, twenty-nine for the nobility, and twenty-seven for the towns and similar jurisdictions. It is surprising to find that no ecclesiastical communities were convoked. More expected was the absence of nobles without fiefs, curés, and proctors of the villages. The three estates generally deliberated together, but in 1576 the nobility elected their own deputy and named a committee of four to prepare a cahier. In 1614 each order elected its own deputy and after doing so, joined together to choose the syndic of the province as a fourth representative.[32]

Bazadois, Condomois, and Albret

There are only scattered documents concerning the elections in the seneschalsies of Bazadois, Condomois, and Albret. The first two possessed thriving estates, and the smaller towns of the three jurisdictions were convoked in 1614 and during the Fronde. The jurades of Condom acted for the commune in 1614.[33]

Agenais

The historian is more fortunate in regard to the neighboring seneschalsy of Agenais. In 1468 the town of Agen was instructed to send one clergyman and two laymen to the estates at Tours, but in 1483 the three estates of Agenais were called upon to name deputies. Only the upper clergy participated for that order, and the consuls of a handful of towns made up the delegation from the third estate.[34] In 1529 about six ecclesiastics, several nobles, and the consuls or deputies of about forty towns ratified the Treaties of Cambrai and Madrid.[35] The procès-verbal of the third estate in 1576 indicates further changes. The consuls or deputies from about sixty towns representing "the larger and wiser part of the consulats" composed the third estate. The proposal by some consuls that two deputies, one Protestant and one Catholic, be chosen for their order was rejected, following the intervention of the seneschal who pointed out that the king had ordered the election of one delegate for the third estate only. No reference was made in the procès-verbal to the other two orders.[36]

In 1614 the town of Agen clearly dominated the proceedings of the third estate. Its jurade, composed of consuls and former consuls, elected two deputies to the Estates General. This selection was confirmed the following day by the consuls of the lesser towns, who showed their independence only to the extent of adding a third name to the list. A committee was selected to prepare the cahier of the third estate of the seneschalsy, but the jurade of Agen also gave an individual cahier to the two deputies it had named.[37] The procedure in 1649 was similar. This time the jurade of Agen was content to present a single candidate who was accepted by the other towns. The only noteworthy event was the complaint of the third estate that the clergy had not properly chosen its delegate, the Bishop of Agen, because only those abbots, priors, archpriests, and curés of the diocese had been summoned who were favorable to his candidacy. Whether the protest of the third estate was justified or not, it does indicate the presence of the lesser clergy. At no time before 1789 were the villages consulted. The estates of Agenais met again in 1651, and each order named its deputies separately.[38]

Armagnac

The Armagnac clergy did not often attend the estates during the fifteenth century, but the Archbishop of Auch, the Bishop of Lectoure, the abbots, and the deputies of the chapters probably had a right to participate, and some of them did in the elections of 1484. Nobles with fiefs composed the second estate, and towns and communities with no seigneur other than the king or count were summoned for the third estate.[39] The estates continued to meet until the early part of the seventeenth century, but very few documents survive, not one of which pertains to the elections to the Estates General. Material on the assemblies of 1631 and 1632 does reveal something concerning the procedure followed during the seventeenth century. Preparatory assemblies which were attended by the local syndic of the nobility and other members of the second estate and the consuls of the towns were held in the seven subordinate jurisdictions. Villages with seigneurs were not convoked to the preparatory assemblies, and the bulk of the nobility did not attend. In the assemblies of the seven subordinate jurisdictions, the secular orders, voting together, elected deputies to the estates of the seneschalsy. The clergy did not participate in the meetings, and acted separately in 1651 during the elections to the Estates General. In that year the clergy held preparatory assemblies in the archpriestships and in at least one of them, the curés were invited to attend.[40]

In 1639 Armagnac was subdivided, a second seneschalsy being established at Lectoure. There the three estates assembled together to elect deputies in 1649, but each order voted apart.[41]

Comminges

The county of Comminges was situated to the southeast of Armagnac. The long, narrow territory extended from the Pyrénées to within a few miles of Toulouse. Assemblies of the estates occurred in exceptional instances during the Middle Ages under the counts, but it was only after the annexation of the county to the crown in the middle of the fifteenth century that meetings became regular. Sometimes the estates met four or five times in a single year during the Wars of Religion, but the establishment of the élus in 1621 made the estates unnecessary as a tax collecting institution. They were convoked rarely thereafter, and the last known meeting was held in 1668.

The composition of the estates of Comminges between 1520 and 1522 is known. Two bishops, four abbots or priors, and one abbess represented the first estate. It is not known whether all nobles with fiefs were allowed to attend during this period, but it seems certain that the number summoned after the middle of the sixteenth century was quite restricted. The consuls from twenty-five towns composed the third estate. For some unexplained reason the number of persons who attended the electoral assemblies during the Wars of Religion was much smaller. The meeting of September 19, 1576, was marked by the presence of only the vicars-general of two bishops, the syndics of the nobility, the consuls of twelve towns, and two or three other persons. A second meeting of the estates in October of the same year saw about eight nobles also in attendance. The three orders deliberated and elected their deputies together in 1561, 1576, 1588, and 1614. No documents survive on the elections of the Fronde. Only in 1560 did an order submit an individual cahier at the Estates General. This unilateral action may be explained by the fact that only the third estate was represented at the meeting of the Estates General in that year.

The most noteworthy characteristic of the elections in Comminges was the quarrel with Toulouse. A few communities of the county lay in that seneschalsy, and the Bishop of Comminges and the syndic of the diocese were members of the estates of Toulouse and of Languedoc. Nevertheless, the bulk of the county was in Guyenne and regularly deputed to her provincial estates. It is not surprising that difficulties arose on this matter in 1576 and perhaps earlier. The seneschal of Toulouse saw in Comminges just another diocese in his jurisdiction, and he ordered the estates of the county to name deputies to attend the estates of his seneschalsy on September 25 to elect deputies to the Estates General. The county named Jean Bertin, who had already been chosen to attend the Estates General, to go to Toulouse with instructions to protest that Comminges was a part of the estates of Guyenne and not of Toulouse. At Toulouse, Bertin agreed to participate in the meeting to prepare the cahier and elect deputies, but again protested with representatives from Rivière-Verdun and several other places normally considered in Guyenne. A few weeks later the estates of Comminges assembled and disavowed the actions taken at Toulouse as "completely breaking our privileges, liberties, and ancient customs." Bertin suggested that to save the expenses of his trip to Blois, the deputy of the third estate of Toulouse be asked to act for Comminges as well. The plan was greeted by strong disapproval, so anxious were those present to keep completely free from the ambitious designs of the neighbor to the north. The independent position of Comminges was recognized by the Estates General, and on January 26, 1577, Henry III decreed that Comminges was attached to Guyenne, not to Languedoc. The county was not to contribute toward the payment of the deputies of Toulouse to the Estates General and in the future was not to be convoked to the estates of Languedoc or of Toulouse.

Nevertheless, in 1588 the seneschal again ordered the estates of Comminges to send deputies to the electoral assembly of the seneschalsy of Toulouse. Once more Comminges protested and sent its deputies directly to
Blois. In 1591 when the Estates General was ordered to meet at Orléans, the
seneschal of Toulouse tried once more to include Comminges in his jurisdiction, but with no more success. The county belligerently retained its independence and condescended to send deputies only to the frequent meetings of
the provincial estates of Guyenne.[42]

Rivière-Verdun

The jugurie of Rivière-Verdun was situated to the west of the Garonne
River a few miles north of Toulouse. Unfortunately, almost nothing survives
relative to the history of the estates. It can only be said that in February,
1649, the representatives, usually the first consuls, of twelve towns met to
elect the deputy for the third estate. These consuls in turn seem to have been
chosen by their respective municipal councils alone. No mention was made of
the other orders. Indeed, they may not have assembled. No noble and only one
delegate of the clergy ever sat in the Estates General from the area. Apparently the estates of Rivière-Verdun were not assembled after 1659.[43]

Bigorre

The county of Bigorre was a possession of the Bourbons and sent deputies
to the Estates General only after the accession of Henry IV. Like the other
jurisdictions of the region, Bigorre had its own estates. It had been included
in a regional Estates General with Béarn, Marsan, Gabardan, Foix, and Né-
bouzan near the close of the fifteenth century as a part of the state-building
activities of the House of Foix-Navarre, but being outside of royal control,
Bigorre had no connection with the provincial estates of Guyenne.[44]   Nine
clergymen, all bishops, abbots, priors, or commanders, acted for the first
estate. Nine barons were convoked in 1614 and during the Fronde, but gentlemen of lesser distinction occasionally claimed the right of entering the estates. Fourteen towns or equivalent jurisdictions sent deputies. Those excluded were numerous, but even the few who could attend the estates did not
always avail themselves of the privilege. The three orders sometimes deliberated apart, but the deputy of the clergy in 1614 specifically drew his powers
from acts given in three estates of the county as well as in an assembly of the
diocese of Tarbes at a later date. Unfortunately, no procès-verbaux have
been found of the meetings which named deputies to the Estates General.[45]

Rouergue

The last jurisdiction to be considered in the government of Guyenne is the
seneschalsy of Rouergue. During much of the Middle Ages the seneschalsy
was attached to Languedoc, but as a by-product of the Hundred Years War it
was joined to Guyenne. During the fifteenth century the estates of Rouergue
sometimes named deputies to the Estates General and on other occasions the
towns of Millau and Rodez acted for the third estate.[46]   About 1623 a member
of the estates prepared an account of the deliberative procedure. This account revealed that the estates took turns meeting in the rival towns of Rodez
and Villefranche under the presidency of the Bishop of Rodez. Once assembled the three orders deliberated and voted together. This rule favored the

third estate because it had more representatives than the other two orders combined since only nobles with high justice were summoned.[47] The three estates did not alter their regular procedure when they elected ten deputies to participate in the Estates General of 1614, and those chosen were empowered in the name of the three estates of the seneschalsy.[48]

The estates proceeded in a different manner in the elections of 1649. The seneschal touched off a heated debate when he read a list of names purported to be those whose election the king desired. The Bishop of Vabres remarked pointedly that since his majesty had already chosen the deputies, there was no need for them to assemble. The seneschal, embarassed, admitted that it was really the governor who made the request. The three estates separated, and with characteristic independence the nobility elected three persons whose names had not been included on the official slate. The roll of the estates for 1651 indicates that about twenty-five clergymen, including several abbesses, were convoked. Excluded were all of the lower clergy. More than twice that number of nobles, and the consuls of about seventy towns were also summoned. The rural communities and the bulk of the population of the municipalities were excluded even at this late date.[49]

Summary

The suffrage expanded and the three orders separated into different chambers in Guyenne as they did elsewhere. Neither phenomenon progressed as far as in the north, but both went much further than in Languedoc. Circumstantial evidence suggests that the existence of provincial and local estates in Guyenne made for these relative differences. The assemblies checked the aspirations of the royal bureaucracy and preserved the traditional procedures to the best of their ability, and thereby prevented as complete a change as in the north, but they were not as strong as those of Languedoc and could not come as close in stopping all innovations. Furthermore, the absence of assemblies to codify the customs in the late sixteenth century removed an influence that often made for an extension of the suffrage, while the tendency of the clergy and the nobility to absent themselves from the local and provincial estates undoubtedly accustomed the third estate to working alone. Quarrels between the royal officials and the great towns and rivalries between different towns within the same jurisdiction were frequent, but perhaps less so than in the north.

11

THE ELECTIONS IN BRITTANY, DAUPHINÉ, PROVENCE, AND OTHER JURISDICTIONS

Brittany

The government of Brittany was one of the seven that had provincial estates that were periodically convoked during the Renaissance. These provincial estates were so strong that they always served as the electoral assembly for the Estates General, but there are insufficient documents to determine how the deputies were actually chosen until 1576. In that year the nobility named six members of their order as candidates; the clergy also presented a list of six candidates; and the third estate, eight. It was decided that the clergy and third estate would choose four from the list of the candidates presented by the nobility. In turn, the secular estates were to select three or four deputies from the list presented by the clergy, while the first two orders were to select six deputies from the candidates named by the third estate. Thus no estate was to have any voice in the final selection of its deputies, but each was assured that no one who was regarded as likely to betray its interests would be elected from its ranks. On the following day the nobles decided that they wanted all their candidates to go to Blois. They won their point on the condition that all the candidates of the other orders be considered as deputies also and that only four deputies from each of the first two estates would be paid by the province. Thus in 1576, the deputies of Brittany were officially named and empowered by the assembly as a whole, but each order elected its own representatives. To assure that the deputies did not act in the name of their order rather than in the interest of their province, it was stipulated that "no two estates could propose, conclude, ask, or voice anything in the said Estates General unless all three were present."[1]

In 1588 Brittany once more chose deputies to attend the Estates General during the regular session of her estates. This time the three estates named their deputies together.[2]

Still another variation in electoral procedure was employed by the estates in 1614. Six members of each order were named deputies: the deputies of the clergy were elected by the nobility and the third estate, those of the nobility by the clergy and the third estate, and those of the third estate by the other two orders. Thus no estate had any voice in naming its representatives. Provincial solidarity was preferred to social union with other parts of France.[3] In 1651 when deputies were again chosen to go to the Estates General, the strength of provincialism was equally apparent, and those selected were empowered by the estates as a whole and not by their respective orders.[4]

Every cahier the estates of Brittany took to the Estates General was submitted in the name of the province as a whole. No single order ever made a cahier of its own. Unfortunately, there is little direct information on how these documents were drawn up before 1614. In that year a committee of four persons from each order was named to perform this task. Individual suggestions were to be submitted to the clerk of the estates and given to the committee for consideration. However, the committee failed to complete its work at the appointed time, and the assembly authorized its deputies to the Estates General to draw up a cahier. In 1651 a committee was named to prepare the cahier and a box was set up to receive suggestions.[5]

The three estates of Brittany were far from democratic. Nine bishops, the abbots and priors, and the deputies of the chapters stood for the first estate. The curés and the lower clergy were not represented. Even those of the clergy who had the right to attend did not always avail themselves of the privilege. In 1576 only five bishops, one abbot, and the deputies from nine chapters were present; in 1588 only fifteen clergymen attended, but in 1614 the number increased to twenty-two.

Nobles with fiefs had the right to attend the estates of Brittany during the sixteenth century, and at the commencement of the seventeenth century simple gentlemen also gained admission. Generally, few nobles cared to exercise this privilege during this period, but the turnout was usually larger when deputies were elected to the Estates General. In 1576, 115 nobles participated, and in 1588, ninety. Perhaps some officials had made a special effort to secure a large attendance, or perhaps the nobles themselves were more interested because of the elections to the Estates General. In 1614, however, neither the presence of the royal family nor the convocation of the Estates General was sufficient to bring as many nobles to the assembly as in the preceding or following year. Only eighty-three attended. On the whole, the participation of the nobility slowly increased during the late sixteenth and early seventeenth centuries and then grew rapidly from 1651 to 1728 when attendance reached 978. This increase reflects the growing interests of the nobility in the provincial estates.

The number of towns that sent deputies also increased. In 1576, seventeen were represented; in August, 1588, twenty-one; and in 1614, thirty-one. The rural population and the smaller towns were excluded, and in the larger towns the bourgeois oligarchy named the deputies. Truly the estates of Brittany were controlled by the aristocracy.[6]

One must not suppose that all the inferior jurisdictions were content to see the dominant role played by the provincial estates in the election of deputies to the national assembly. In 1560 the dioceses of Cornouailles and Tréguier elected their own deputies. In 1576, Nantes, Morlaix, and another town sent deputies directly to the Estates General. In 1588 only two towns tried to act independently, and in 1614 the number was further reduced to one.[7]

Dauphiné

Like Brittany, Dauphiné possessed a provincial assembly that named deputies to the Estates General. Unfortunately, a large part of the archives of the estates have been lost, and only the elections in 1614 can be described in detail. The estates assembled at Grenoble on August 7 of that year, and after dealing with several other matters took up the question of the preparation of the cahier. It was decided that the estates should meet separately the following morning to discuss the articles they would like to have included. On the eleventh the articles prepared by the individual orders were read before the assembly, and a committee was named to prepare a provincial cahier for the three estates. Although this committee was large, the major part of the work was done by the Bishop of Grenoble. On several issues agreement was difficult, and in these cases the third estate was granted the privilege of submitting an individual petition. Two days later the deputies to the Estates General were named by the three orders voting together. Like those of Brittany, the deputies of Dauphiné stood for the province as a whole and not for their respective orders and, except for a few individual complaints on the part of the third estate, they took a common cahier to the national assembly at Paris.[8]

For the elections prior to 1614 one can glean only a few isolated facts. In 1576, through a mistake made by the officials at Paris, orders were issued to have deputies elected in the bailiwicks rather than by the provincial estates. The bailiff of Vienne quickly seized this opportunity and directed the estates of his jurisdiction to assemble. He was halted by the Parlement of Grenoble on the petition of the procureur of the provincial estates. Later, the Parlement directed him to continue his plans to hold his estates, but to summon both the Protestants and the Catholics and to send the deputies elected to the provincial estates of Dauphiné at Grenoble — not to the Estates General at Blois. At Grenoble a single cahier was to be prepared and deputies chosen in the customary manner to go to the national assembly.

The bailiff had enjoyed his brief taste of independence and did not forget that he had received a commission from the king to have representatives sent to Blois. As a result he saw to it that his estates elected deputies to go straight to the Estates General as well as to Grenoble. The bailiff, himself, had to permit one departure from the normal procedure in his own assembly. At their request, the consuls of the towns who stood for the third estate were granted permission to deliberate separately. Several other bailiwicks acted with equal independence. The meeting at Grenoble was quarrelsome. The provincial estates annulled the bailiwick elections, and the deputies of the bailiwicks annulled, in turn, the elections made at Grenoble. The result, of course, was an appeal to the royal council. The council seated the representatives from Vienne because they had been elected on the orders, albeit issued in error, of the king and because the bailiwick claimed a semi-independent position in regard to Dauphiné. The deputies of the other bailiwicks were denied seats.[9]

The two convocations of the Estates General during the Fronde are also of some interest. By this time the estates of Dauphiné had ceased to be regularly convoked, and the crown was anxious to prevent a possible revival. Hence, in 1649 crown officials ordered that elections be held by bailiwick. The nobility especially sought to use the occasion to bring about a revival of the provincial estates. The provincial governor worked out a compromise that was put into effect when the Estates General was again convoked in 1651. It called for the bailiwick estates to meet and name deputies to assemble before the governor where in turn deputies to the Estates General were to be elected. Thus provincial unity was assured without a formal revival of the provincial estates.[10]

The provincial estates of Dauphiné were no more democratic than those of Brittany. The first and second estates were limited to those clergymen, ecclesiastical communities, and nobles who possessed rights of justice. The communes were generally represented by their consuls. This fact, coupled with the dominant role played by the ten most important towns, made the third estate more oligarchical than democratic. The lesser clergy, the nobles without fiefs, and much of the rural population were excluded.[11]

Provence

The picture is more confused in Provence than in Brittany or Dauphiné, for three types of provincial assemblies named deputies to the Estates General at one time or another. The assembly most frequently convoked was the three estates of Provence. To it came two archbishops, twelve bishops, eight abbots, one provost, and the nobles with fiefs. The canons, curés, vicars, and nobles without fiefs were excluded. The composition of the third estate varied.

At the close of the fifteenth century, representation was primarily by viguerie or bailiwick, but during the sixteenth century the principal towns sent deputies directly to the estates, and the other communities were represented by deputies chosen in assemblies of the vigueries and bailiwicks. In 1611 these preparatory elections were abandoned, and the communities took turns furnishing the deputy of the viguerie. Since the consuls represented those localities having direct access to the estates and also dominated the viguerie and bailiwick elections prior to their demise, the participation of the third estate was far from complete.

During the latter part of the sixteenth and the early part of the seventeenth centuries, the meetings of the three estates of Provence were slowly replaced by the assembly of the communities, an institution composed of the procureurs or syndics of the first two orders and the deputies, or rather the first consuls, of the same communities that were admitted to the provincial estates. The deputies of the vigueries were excluded. Historians have argued that the assembly of the communities was preferred by the crown because the virtual absence of the nobility made it less able to resist demands for taxes. The nobleman was almost as unwilling to have his peasants pay taxes as he was to make contributions himself. In 1596 and 1614 the assembly of the communities was used to elect some or all of the deputies to a national assembly.

A third way in which the government sometimes consulted the inhabitants of Provence was by convoking one or more of the three orders separately. The deputation to the Estates General in 1651 was to have been named in this manner, and the assembly of the nobility elected some of the deputies of their order in 1614.[12]

Provence first sent a delegation to a national assembly in 1484, but it is impossible to ascertain the electoral procedure used before 1561. The estates met at Aix in March of that year to decide what advice and aid to give the king concerning his debts. Each order voiced its opinion through a prominent spokesman, and then the three estates together named their deputies.[13]

Unfortunately the procès-verbal of the estates of Provence for 1576 is lost, but it is known that the clergy and third estates each sent a deputy to Blois. A syndic for the three estates was also present, so provincial unity was not entirely lost.[14] Luckily, it is possible to study the elections of 1588 with some care. The royal officials, instead of addressing the letters of convocation to the governor, sent them to the grand seneschal and to the lieutenants of the secondary jurisdictions. The lieutenants convoked the local estates to elect deputies to the Estates General. Shortly thereafter the grand seneschal of Provence summoned the three estates to meet in Aix to name deputies for the entire province. This assembly, to which only four of the sixty communities of the province sent deputies, nullified the elections made by the local assemblies as being contrary to the intentions of his majesty and to the usages of the province. Some of the secondary jurisdictions acquiesced, but Grasse and Draguignan refused, and their deputations were later seated with those of the province at Blois. The provincial estates then elected one deputy from each order to attend the Estates General. In addition, the communes of Forcalquier and Castellane were selected to send their first consuls or to name one delegate each. Castellane, at least, used this privilege and sent a deputy to Blois.

The royalist governor of Provence was not content to see the grand seneschal assume the authority to assemble the estates. He also convoked the estates of Provence, this time to meet in October at Pertuis. There two more deputies were named to go to Blois, and the earlier elections at Aix were declared null. The deputies from Pertuis, however, did not find their way into the Estates General.

The confusion of 1588 resulted from an error in the chancellery concerning the electoral procedure in Provence. Between 1493 and 1572 the offices of governor and grand seneschal had been held by one man, and he convoked the estates. The two offices were separated in 1572, and in 1588 the royal advisors did not study the precedents as carefully as they should have. Their error in sending the letter of convocation to the grand seneschal was to cost Henry III the vote of one of the twelve governments during the critical days ahead at Blois; for the seneschal's assembly at Aix was completely under the control of the League, while the able but ignored governor could have been counted on to try to insure the election of deputies devoted to the royal cause. Few instances illustrate more fully the ineptness of the Valois monarchy in the field of electoral manipulations.[15]

Twice in 1591 the three estates of Provence jointly named deputies to the Estates General of the League,[16] but in 1596 the assembly of the communities named two delegates to the meeting at Rouen ordered by the king.[17]

The crown's intention in 1614 was to follow the traditional practice of using the provincial estates to elect deputies to the Estates General, but the death of the brother of the governor made it impossible for him to attend at the appointed time, and the three estates proceeded as they pleased. The communities assembled with the syndics of the first two orders at Aix on August 1 to consider other matters concerning the province. Later, the clergy and nobility began to arrive, and on August 8 the members of the three estates who were present elected two deputies from the clergy to attend the Estates General. On August 9 over a hundred nobles chose four of their number to go to Paris. On the twelfth the assembly of the communities repeated the nominations of one of the deputies who had already been elected from each of the first two estates and named three members of the third estate as well. Thus some of the delegation of Provence were deputed by the three estates, some by the assembly of the communities, and three by the nobles alone.[18]

The peculiar circumstances surrounding the electoral assemblies of 1614 led Provence to submit its grievances by order rather than by province, although the three estates did find the opportunity to unite on some petitions. A cahier for the third estate exists which was presumably prepared in the assembly of the communities while that of the nobility was made in a special meeting in October. This was a departure from the customary procedure, for in 1560 the Bishop of Vence had stated in the Estates General at Orléans that Provence had a single cahier for the three estates and that he was bound by his instructions to act only in conjunction with his fellow deputies. No records survive for 1576, but in 1588 Provence again submitted a single cahier prepared by the three estates.[19]

The three estates of Provence, like those of Dauphiné, were discontinued before the convocation of the Estates General during the Fronde. The crown had little desire to revive the estates for this occasion, and as a result decided that the three orders should meet separately to name their deputies.[20]

Marseille and Arles did not participate fully in the estates of Provence during the sixteenth century because of their special status as terres adjacentes; both cities sent deputies directly to the Estates General on several occasions. The elections in Marseille were far from democratic, for the municipal council alone named deputies. To make matters worse the first consul dominated this small electoral body. In 1588 he virtually named the deputation, and in 1614 he successfully claimed that he and the assesseur of the town had the right to attend the national assembly for the town. Two notables from each quarter were consulted on the preparation of the cahier in 1576 and 1588. Some of the deputies elected by the towns of Marseille and Arles were nobles, and they sat with the second estate at the Estates General rather than the third where both the noble and nonnoble deputies elected by the other towns participated. To justify this unusual procedure, it was explained in 1593 that many nobles resided in the town where they occupied a special position. Then, too, both Arles and Marseille claimed special privileges in regard to Provence and the kingdom.[21]

Summary

As was true in other parts of France, the electoral procedures varied from election to election in Brittany, Dauphiné, and Provence, but the deputies were not usually delegated by their own order alone, and the cahiers they brought to the national assembly and the powers they bore were issued in the name of the province as a whole. Almost no friction existed between the three estates during the elections. The representative institutions of the three provinces were far from democratic, but during the last part of the sixteenth century there was a tendency toward the increased representation of the third estate and often toward the lowering of the barrier against the participation of nobles without fiefs. Only the clergy escaped this growing demand to be heard.

Other Jurisdictions

Not all jurisdictions can be conveniently classified under this or that government when they named deputies to the Estates General. Flanders, Tournai, Roussillon, and Cerdagne participated in the Estates General of 1484, but by 1560 when the Estates General began to be subdivided into governments, these territories had been lost to France. More often it was a question of what to do with newly acquired territory. The deputies from Bresse, Bugey, and Gex sat with those from Burgundy when they first attended a national assembly in 1614, and those from Brittany were accepted as a separate government in 1560. Frequently particularism was so strong in new territories that they declined to participate in the Estates General. Although Metz came under French domination before the outbreak of the Wars of Religion, the local estates refused to accept an invitation to participate in the Estates General of 1588 for fear of compromising local franchises and privileges. Not until 1789 did the area consent to take part in a national representative assembly.[22] Much the same sentiment was found in Navarre and Béarn. The two domains had been partially united with the crown by Henry IV, but in 1649 both proved most reluctant to take any step that would lead to their further incorporation into the giant kingdom to the north. Their continued refusal to participate irritated the royal councilors, but in 1789 Navarre was still unwilling to name deputies. In view of this desire for independence, it is surprising that in 1576 when the Marquisate of Saluzzo was temporarily under French control, it sent deputies to the Estates General, although its Italian inhabitants had even less historical and cultural affinity with France than the territories named above.[23]

12

OTHER PARTICIPANTS AND WOULD-BE PARTICIPANTS

General Considerations

The substitution of bailiwick elections in 1483 for the earlier practice of sending writs of summons to individuals and corporate groups was not accomplished without difficulty. The effort of the larger towns to retain the privilege of individual representation has been discussed in connection with the elections in the bailiwicks, for this situation is closely intertwined with the activities of the local royal officials and the third estate. It is necessary now to treat the individuals and other corporate groups who were denied seats under the new procedure.

The composition of the Estates General and the various consultative bodies varied so much before 1483 that it is impossible to say exactly who had a right to be summoned. The princes of the blood, peers of France, great officers of the crown, and royal councilors appeared on every list, and the archbishops, bishops, great nobles, and leading members of the sovereign courts had strong claims for consideration. As late as the Assemblies of Notables in 1617 and 1626, those summoned were selected from the above categories.

The role of these magnates is difficult to define. Prior to 1483 they had mingled with the lesser figures who came to the assemblies, but with the advent of deputation by bailiwick they were generally excluded from the deliberations. They were, however, in attendance upon the king when he appeared before the national assembly. Indeed, the great ceremonies at the opening and closing of the estates and at the other rare instances when the king made his appearance were regarded by the theorists as the only times that Estates General was in session. "All the deputies assembled before the king with the princes and peers make the estates,"[1] wrote Guy Coquille, himself a deputy from Nivernais, in 1560, 1576, and 1588. Elsewhere, he included the great officers of the crown in the same category. The deliberations of the individual orders that one is accustomed to think of as being the essence of the Estates General were only the outgrowth of the occasional brief withdrawal of the nobles, clergy, and deputies of the towns during the Medieval period to determine what aid to offer or advice to give the king. The length of these withdrawals became so prolonged during the Renaissance that historians have concentrated on them and forgotten the work of the peers and councilors. The surviving records of the royal council show that both the royal appointees and those who attended by right were kept busy answering the petitions of the deputies and settling quarrels between them. So closely did the council work with the estates that the Duke of Nevers, peer of France and royal councilor, has been mistaken for a deputy of the nobility at the Estates General of 1576. Guy Coquille, as we have seen, specifically stated that the magnates and important officials were part of the Estates General. Loisel was in agreement, and the Huguenot theorist, Philippe du Plessis-Mornay, considered the Estates General of 1588 null because Henry of Navarre, a prince of the blood, had not been summoned.[2]

The number of individuals who were princes, peers, great officers of the crown, or other royal councilors varied a great deal, but the maximum figure was never large. Only a limited number of persons who had once received individual writs continued to participate by virtue of holding these ranks or offices. Nevertheless, the new arrangement was satisfactory to the nobility. The great still participated, the middle nobility were happy to escape the trouble and expense of personal attendance, and the seigneurs who had previously been largely ignored now received a voice through their deputies. Indeed, the new mode of holding the Estates General provided further indication of the rising importance of this class.

The Prelates and the Chapters

The members of the clergy were less happy with the change. Either they were more interested in personally attending the estates or else fewer of them were admitted because of their birth or position. There were only six ecclesiastical peers. This left over a hundred archbishops and bishops who were excluded except for those who were elected by the bailiwicks and those few who might be princes of the blood or royal councilors. This situation was certain to lead to protests, especially when the estates were considering ecclesiastical matters.

In 1484 some prelates, described as "the archbishops and bishops of France," petitioned the king to grant them seats in the Estates General. They argued that in the past they had always been summoned and that their consent was necessary on issues concerning the church. The king referred the matter to the deputies, who decided that their assembly was one of the three estates and not a provincial synod. Therefore, it was no more necessary to summon all the bishops than all the archdeacons or curés. If the bishops insisted, they would be admitted to the assembly, but they would have to serve at their own expense. No one accepted this lukewarm invitation. The prelates preferred to meet separately to discuss the chapter of the cahier related to the church. There is no list of those who made up this group, but it is known that the Archbishops of Lyon and Tours played leading roles and "a large number" of other archbishops and bishops were present. On one occasion the deputies sent a delegation to them to discuss the chapter on the church, but to no avail. The prelates disapproved of the deputies' proposals and in the end were strong enough to prevent their acceptance by the crown.[3]

The bishops did not renew their effort to gain admittance to the assembly of the deputies in 1560, although the Cardinal of Lorraine, Archbishop of Reims and peer of France, was elected speaker for the clergy. He declined the honor because the deputies of the secular estates had not chosen him as well. In 1576 the Bishop of Montpellier unsuccessfully sought admittance to the chamber of the first estate by virtue of his episcopal office.[4] In 1614 four prelates who had not been elected deputies were given seats in the Estates General as the result of special invitations issued by the clergy. After the estates had opened someone noted that the deputies of the bailiwick clergy of Rouen had not yet arrived, and with this fact in mind suggested that Cardinal Joyeuse, Archbishop of Rouen, be asked to attend. Later, special delegations were also sent to invite Cardinal Bonsy, Bishop of Béziers, and the Archbishops of Reims and Toulouse. These prelates happened to be in Paris at that time and immediately joined the chamber of the clergy. Cardinal Joyeuse was asked to work with the Norman delegation, the Archbishop of Reims with that of Picardy, and Cardinal Bonsy and the Archbishop of Toulouse with that of Languedoc. No opposition is recorded in the procès-verbal to any of these additions to a chamber supposedly composed of the elected deputies of the clergy, and the king and council did not see fit to interfere.[5]

The chapters objected less to the substitution of bailiwick elections for the direct summons they had once received to elect deputies to the Estates General. Only the chapter of Saint-Martin of Tours continued to claim the privilege of sending deputies directly to the national assembly. In 1576, 1588, and 1614 the representatives of that chapter were given seats with the delegation from Touraine, but on the last named date it was decided not to permit this practice in the future.[6]

The Universities

The University of Paris made several efforts to obtain a seat in the Estates General. The faculty had often taken part in the assemblies of the estates during the Middle Ages and was anxious to have the same privilege when bailiwick elections were used. The rector of the university was a deputy in 1484 from the provostship of Paris. In 1560 the rector was ordered to attend the electoral assembly of the provostship, but failed to do so. Nevertheless, the regent and dean of the faculty of law was chosen as one of the deputies in the provostship elections. At the Estates General both the clergy and the third estate included a section on the universities in their cahier, but there is no evidence that the university sought separate representation or the right to submit an individual cahier on either of these occasions.[7]

The relative indifference of the University of Paris in the Estates General in 1484 and 1560 was replaced in 1576 by a determined effort to be heard. On December 10 a doctor in theology from that institution and a deputy from the University of Poitiers asked for seats in the chamber of the clergy at Blois. They were refused, but were invited to give their cahiers to the deputies of the clergy of their dioceses. A few weeks later deputies from the Universities of Paris, Poitiers, and Orléans also submitted a cahier to the third estate in the obvious hope that that order would support their demands. This lobbying was a monumental success. The section on the universities in the cahiers of the clergy and the third estate repeated many of the articles contained in a cahier submitted by the universities directly to the king. Furthermore, the nobility asked the king to carry out the requests of the institutions of higher learning. [8]

Only the University of Paris showed much interest in the Estates General of 1588. It sent one deputy to the assembly of the provostship of Paris and another directly to the Estates General at Blois where he was given a seat, with the understanding that it was not to establish a precedent.[9] In 1593 a professor of the university was chosen as one of the deputies of the provostship of Paris to the Estates General, but there was no attempt to have direct representation.[10]

A renewed effort was made by the university to secure a seat in 1614. The assistance of one of the deputies of the clergy of the provostship of Paris was secured, and on December 1 he asked his order to grant a seat to the university in accordance with "long possession, usage, and observance." A petition to this effect was also made to the king, but he referred it to the secular orders for their opinion. The third estate decided to turn the whole problem over to the clergy on the grounds that the university was not a separate jurisdiction with the right to elect deputies for the three estates, but rather an ecclesiastical corporation. The argument put forth by the university that it had been represented in the assembly of 1412 was disallowed on the grounds that at that time there had been another method of holding the estates. A few days later, the royal council handed down a decision denying the right of the university to have a seat in the Estates General and directing that its petitions be turned over to the deputies of the clergy of the provostship of Paris. This rebuff caused the university to return to the tactics it had used so successfully in the Estates General of 1576. The rector, accompanied by members of the faculty, appeared before each of the three orders and asked them to support the university's cahier. This cahier was criticized in the chamber of the clergy because it had not been approved by three of the four faculties or by three of the four nations into which the university was divided. No one was surprised when the syndic of the university appeared before the clergy to disavow that document in the name of the majority of his corporation. This dispute destroyed what little chance the university had of winning a position in the Estates General comparable to that held by Oxford or Cambridge in the English Parliament. [11]

The Crusading and Monastic Orders

The Knights of Saint John of Jerusalem were also interested in being heard at the Estates General. They sent an ambassador to submit a cahier directly to the king in 1576, and in 1588 their representative was given a seat by the clergy, but for some reason their cahier was presented to the crown as a part of that of the nobility. [12] The orders of Saint Benedict and Saint Augustine were less fortunate when they sought special representation in the Estates General of 1614 on the grounds that very few of their number had been chosen as deputies in the bailiwick elections. The council would do no more than direct them to turn their petitions over to those of their order who had been elected in the regular manner. [13] No difficulty arose, however, over the seating of the two general agents of the clergy in 1614. They were the permanent representatives of their order and had the duty of protecting its interests when the assemblies of the clergy were not in session. Theirs was an important role and from beginning to end their presence was unchallenged. They arranged the chairs and benches in the ecclesiastical chamber before the session began and were charged with the duty of pressing for the adoption of the cahier of the first estate by king and council after the assembly had terminated. [14]

The Parlements

Another corporate body which was often given direct representation in the national assemblies was the Parlement of Paris. The court normally took part in the medieval assemblies of the estates, the assemblies of the notables, and other advisory meetings; but the advent of bailiwick elections opened the question of whether its members ought to continue to receive writs to participate, be content with taking part in the municipal elections of Paris, or remain haughtily aloof until it became time to register the ordonnances based on the cahiers of the deputies. The Parlement adopted all three of these positions at one time or another. In January, 1484, it named a deputation to the Estates General, but for some reason none of those chosen attended. Only the procureur of the king in the Parlement appeared at Tours; and he had been individually mandated, a practice which was also followed in the meetings of the Estates General during the sixteenth century. [15]

At the assembly of the estates in 1558 the delegations from the Parisian and provincial Parlements were so large that a fourth estate was created for them and other royal officials, but in the meeting of the Estates General in 1560 those members of the Parlements who served did so only as deputies of the third estate of their geographical jurisdiction. The officers of the Parlement of Paris were not happy at this loss of prestige. When the king later complained at the slowness of their discussion of the Ordonnance of Orléans, they stated pointedly that they had not participated in the Estates General and therefore had had no part in the preparation of the cahiers on which the ordonnance was based. Hence, it was necessary to take time to study each article carefully.[16] This none too subtle hint had no effect, and the Parlement was not asked to depute to the Estates General until 1593. By that time the leaders of the Parlement had become so content with their role of reviewing and registering the ordonnances based on the cahiers of the deputies that they were loath to participate. They feared that their presence in the estates would be interpreted as giving approval to the cahiers, and therefore limit their right to make remonstrances on the ordonnance when it was submitted to them. Nevertheless, the Duke of Mayenne needed their support against the Spanish faction in the League and insisted that the Paris and some of the provincial Parlements name deputies along with the Chambre des comptes. He even tried to organize a fourth estate composed of these magistrates on the model of the assembly of 1558.[17]

In the elections to the Estates General of 1614 the Parlement adopted a new position. It not only made no effort to win direct representation in the Estates General, but it even refused to send deputies to participate in the elections of the town of Paris on the avowed reason that "the cahiers which will be decreed in the said estates would be presented to them for registration and verification."[18] Thus the position of members of the Parlement had changed from anxiety to participate in the Estates General in 1561 to refusal to name a delegation to the municipal electoral assembly in 1614, either for fear that to do so would put them in a subordinate position in regard to the national assembly or for more justifiable legal grounds.

The Assistants and Advisors

In addition to the prelates and representatives from the various corporate bodies who managed to win seats in the Estates General in spite of the rule for bailiwick elections, there were a few individuals who were appointed by important deputies to serve as their assistants. In 1576 the Archbishop of Lyon and the Bishop of Nîmes and in 1614 the Cardinals of Perron and Sourdis had assistants who were admitted to the ecclesiastical chamber, although with certain limitations as to their speaking rights in the 1576 meeting. In every known instance, these assistants were appointed by the deputy they were to help, or replace in event of absence, but sometimes the constituents had given their representative permission to take this action. A somewhat similar case occurred at the Estates General of Pontoise in 1561. The regular deputy of the third estate of Languedoc was replaced during a brief absence by the syndic of the province, although the syndic had not been elected deputy by the inhabitants of Languedoc or formally accepted by the third estate.[19]

Sometimes deputies brought advisors to the Estates General who made no effort to be seated. In 1588 the deputies of the nobility of Vermandois took to Blois a consultant who served as their advisor and at the same time rendered clerical assistance to the second estate as a whole. He was paid for his services by the nobility of Vermandois.[20]

If we omit those who participated in the Estates General by virtue of being members of the king's council and those who were dispatched by the towns, the number of exceptions to the requirement of election by province and bailiwick was not large. However, the intrigues of prelates, chapters, universities, and religious orders and the casual introduction of substitute deputies and advisors add further evidence of the haphazard, unsystematic nature of Renaissance government and point to the highly individualistic attitude of the leaders of the French people.

13

THE ELECTIONS IN RETROSPECT

Procedural Disputes[1]

The great variety of ways in which bailiwick assemblies could be held and the confused administrative structure of Renaissance government led to many procedural disputes during the elections. Among the sources of argument was the practice of choosing deputies in some subordinate jurisdictions to attend the bailiwick estates. In the provinces and larger bailiwicks it was inconvenient for the clergy and nobility to attend the bailiwick assemblies in person, and it was a hardship for the smaller towns and villages to send deputies. This situation made advisable the practice of holding meetings in the castellanies, viscounties, dioceses, and similar jurisdictions in which one or more of the estates selected deputies to attend the bailiwick estates. In Languedoc, Normandy, Provence, and parts of the Île-de-France and Champagne, preparatory elections were held before 1500. Additional localities adopted this procedure during the sixteenth century, but others abandoned it, and no definite trend can be established.

Simple and logical as this procedure may appear at first glance, it was filled with inherent difficulties. The nobility of Orléans pointed out in 1614 that some of the inferior jurisdictions of the bailiwick had only two or three members of their order as residents, others contained thirty, forty, or fifty gentlemen. But the deputies from each were given the same voting power in the bailiwick assembly. In other bailiwicks some of the first two orders attended in person, while others held local assemblies to name deputies, or simply gave their proxies to someone to attend the meeting and cast their ballot. For example, the nobility of Châteaudun held a preparatory assembly in 1576 and sent a deputy to the meeting of the bailiwick at Blois. Here it was decided that he should have only one vote, the same as the other nobles who attended in person without being elected by anyone. Vigorous protests against the injustice of equating all the nobles of a subordinate jurisdiction with a single noble from another locality were in vain. The nobility and clergy of Vitry had disputes within their respective orders on the same question, and similar situations arose in Chaumont-en-Bassigny and other places. Quarrels developed where there were rival candidates, but no debate occurred if the deputy of the subordinate jurisdiction and the various individuals who attended could agree on candidates.

The willingness to accept procurations when there were no rival candidates was also apparent in those bailiwicks where there were no subordinate assemblies, but where many members of the first two orders escaped the inconvenience of personal attendance by giving their proxies to someone to go in their stead. In jurisdiction after jurisdiction the votes of those absent — especially among the nobility — were counted without question, but when there was a bitter rivalry between candidates, the reverse was likely to be true. In the elections in Boulonnais in 1588, the proroyalist governor and lieutenant general got their candidate chosen by refusing to count the proxies of the supporters of the League, only to have the king's council later annul the election. The bailiff of Berry acted in a similar manner in 1614, but his candidate was rejected anyway. The resourceful official was by no means defeated, and declared both candidates elected despite the protests of the majority that the king had specified that there be only one deputy for their order. Again in Chaumont-en-Bassigny in 1649 the bailiwick officials refused to accept procurations or to give special consideration to the deputy of the nobility from a subordinate jurisdiction.

Another procedural difficulty centered on the problem of what weight to give the deputy of a large town in comparison to that allowed the proctors of the lesser towns and villages in the bailiwick assembly. The most famous quarrel on this score occurred in Amiens in 1576 when the royal officials gave one vote to each village in the bailiwick and only one to that important town itself. Tours was about to be overrun by the influx of deputies from the parishes of the other towns and villages of Touraine in 1614, and other great towns were faced with similar situations.

Far more often it was the municipal officials and bourgeois of the principal town who swamped the deputies of the lesser communities, an operation which required no great effort on their part because the elections were usually held in their town hall. To the assembly of the bailiwick of Orléans in 1588 were convoked the municipal officials and two proctors from each of the twenty-seven parishes of the capital city, but only one deputy each from seventeen castellanies. At Blois in 1576 the principal citizens of the town swarmed into the bailiwick assembly, and each cast a vote that carried the same weight as the deputy of any one of the eight other places in the jurisdiction that were represented. The protests of the lesser towns were again to no avail in 1588 when they held nineteen votes altogether as opposed to the ninety-four for the inhabitants of Blois who saw fit to attend.[2]

Sometimes there were disputes over where the bailiwick estates should meet. The king only directed that the electors be summoned to the principal seat of the jurisdiction, but here and there two or three towns claimed this honor. Rival electoral assemblies were often held. Once more there were disputes to be carried to the king in council.[3]

A final procedural difficulty grew out of the confusion as to the nature of the various jurisdictions and their relations to each other. In many instances neither the crown nor the local officials were certain which bailiwicks were subordinate and which independent. Letters of convocation were sent in error to the subordinate jurisdictions of Dauphiné and Brittany in 1576, of Provence in 1588, and to the seneschal of Auvergne at Riom in both years rather than only to those who had the traditional right to assemble the estates of these localities. In other cases, it was the local officials who were confused. The barony of Châteauneuf-en-Thymerais had exercised the undisputed right to choose deputies in 1560 and 1576 when it was an appanage, and not unnaturally her officials sought to continue to do so after it had come into the hands of the Duke of Nevers on the death of the king's brother in 1584. The bailiwick of Chartres successfully maintained in 1588 and 1614 that the barony had again become subordinate to her after it passed from royal hands. Saint-Pierre-le-Moutier offered a similar argument to support its claim to convoke the duchy of Nevers, but without favorable result because of the special privileges of the duchy. Newly created bailiwicks were likely to be pictured as dependent by the older jurisdictions from which they were formed. This happened to Beauvais, La Flèche, Amboise, and other localities.

Sometimes the ambitions of the officials of clearly subordinate jurisdictions led them to try to have deputies elected to go directly to the Estates General. Normandy, Poitou, and Vermandois, where assemblies preparatory to the bailiwick estates were often held, were especially troubled by this tendency. With the individuals and proctors legally convoked, it was too much for some officials to forbear bypassing the bailiwick estates and sending deputies to the national assembly. Occasionally too, local royal officials led the lesser communities in a break from a bailiwick assembly which they could not control, and again more deputies were named to go to Orléans, or Blois, or Paris.[4]

Amid all this confusion, the kings were content to assume the role of arbitrators of the disputes that arose. They made no effort to establish a uniform procedure for all of France, or to assure a more favorable position to any political faction or social class. The crown left almost everything to its local officials. No elaborate explanations of procedure were given in 1483 when bailiwick elections were generally utilized for the first time. The bailiffs were simply told to assemble the three estates of their jurisdiction to elect deputies with sufficient powers to attend the Estates General. In 1560 when bailiwick elections were held again after three quarters of a century of neglect, the crown was equally brief, except to add the phrase "in the accustomed manner." Again in 1649, after the lapse of a generation, no detailed instructions were given.

When one compares this cavalier attitude to the elaborate efforts made by the crown on the eve of the Estates General of 1789 to gather information on how elections had been held in the past and to issue detailed directives on who was to be summoned to the bailiwick assemblies, how voting was to be done, how cahiers were to be prepared, and how other duties were to be carried out, one cannot help but realize how much the climate of opinion had changed. From the Renaissance willingness to accept the decentralization of authority and infinite variation in procedure that accompanied leaving local officials so much to their own devices, the French had developed a desire for uniformity and order based on universal principles of morality and law that could be imposed on the populace only by the most minute instructions.

Only when disputes were appealed over the heads of the bailiwick officials to the king did he then interfere. On these occasions, decisions were rendered on the basis of tradition and privilege, with utility and justice playing secondary roles. Seats were given to deputies who could prove that representatives from their jurisdiction had been accepted in the past or that their bailiwick had become independent. If they were unable to do so, an independent vote was denied, but the deputies were usually permitted to attend the estates with the delegation of the locality to which the jurisdiction was judged to be a part, or at least to submit their cahier for consideration. Thus when the deputies of the third estate of Langres were denied a separate seat in 1576 at the request of the parent bailiwick of Sens, they were permitted to attend with that deputation. In 1588 they were only allowed to submit their cahier to the deputies of Sens. In both cases, the traditional superiority of Sens was preserved, but in the interests of justice the inhabitants of Langres were permitted to have their cahier considered by the Estates General. Similar decisions were rendered in regard to the claims of many other places.

The crown had no preferred method for holding bailiwick elections and was apt to offer several different solutions for solving the same problem. For example, one of the perennial arguments was over the weight that should be given to the deputies of the countryside as opposed to the large towns which had traditionally spoken for the third estate. To give the village representative the same voting power as the deputy of a great town was obviously unjust, but the Renaissance Monarchy was not so bound by tradition and privilege that it was willing to stand in the way of all change. It came to regard the denial of any voice to the inhabitants of the villages as unfair. Where there was no dispute, the crown took no action, but where an appeal was made to the king in council, any one of three solutions might be given. The government might institute a system of indirect suffrage with the villages naming deputies to assemblies of the subordinate jurisdictions where in turn representatives were elected to the bailiwick estates. Here the vote of the principal town was equated with that of an entire subordinate jurisdiction. A second solution was to permit the addition of a few of the lesser towns and communities to the localities traditionally convoked. The thirteen "good towns" of Basse-Auvergne became nineteen and the control of elections of Touraine was given to the mayor, échevins, and deputies of eight parishes of Tours in conjunction with the representatives of the seven royal seats and six selected villages. In both cases the privileged towns were protected from the influx of village representatives, but at the same time some extension of the suffrage was allowed. A third possibility was to give seats in the Estates General to the deputies so often angrily dispatched by the principal towns when they had been outvoted by the lesser localities.

If the situation was reversed and the inhabitants of the principal town attended the bailiwick estates in such numbers as to swamp the deputies of the other communities, the crown was willing to accept a delegation from the latter also. More than one participant in the Estates General styled himself as deputy of the plat pays of this or that bailiwick.[5]

Where no disputes arose over the handling of town and village voting, the crown remained aloof. No attempt was made to impose any of the above solutions on the country as a whole. The only general directive on how the bailiwick elections should be held was issued in July, 1614, to settle the question of the use of proctors in the bailiwick estates by those who owed personal attendance. This practice, which had been almost universally followed in the elections to previous Estates Generals, was forbidden; but the decree was largely a dead letter. Local officials did cite it in Berry in 1614 and in Chaumont-en-Bassigny in 1649 to justify their refusal to count proctors' votes, but elsewhere proctors continued to be accepted and the crown, as usual, surrendered. In 1651, procurations were specifically authorized in the letters of convocation.[6]

The Suffrage

The procedural problems in connection with the election of deputies to the Estates General were closely related to the decision of who was summoned to participate in the bailiwick estates. Here again there was a great variation from one part of France to another, and once more the crown had no definite rules to impose on each jurisdiction. The initiative was left with the bailiwick officials, who were expected to proceed "in the accustomed manner." In one place every ecclesiastical corporation might be told to send a proctor and every holder of a benefice told to appear in person, as often happened in the north; or the bishops alone might be convoked, as in Languedoc, where only eight ecclesiastics voted in the large seneschalsy of Carcassonne in 1614 and six in Toulouse in 1576 and 1649. Even where all or many of the abbots, priors, and deputies of the chapters and monasteries were summoned, the number who were present at the elections was apt to be exceedingly small. Six clergymen attended the assembly in Mâconnais in 1560, nine in Blois, and sixteen in Maine in 1576. Only in those places where the curés of the rural parishes were convoked was there a large attendance for the first estate. These relatively insignificant persons therefore claim our attention.

There is no known instance of the widespread convocation of the curés in any bailiwick in 1484, but they took part in assemblies to ratify treaties or to codify customs in Meaux in 1496, in many parts of Normandy by 1529, and in Valois and Clermont-en-Beauvaisis in 1539. By the time of the elections to the Estates General of 1560 their presence can be documented for parts of Picardy, the Île-de-France, Normandy, Champagne, and Orléans, although in several places in this northern tier of France they were certainly absent. Outside these five governments, the convocation of the lower clergy was less frequent and occurred later. The first traces of curés in the elections elsewhere were on the border of this region; by 1614 the movement towards increased representation of the first estate had spread eastward into the fringes of Burgundy to include the bailiwicks of La Montagne, Auxerre, and possibly Autun, and southward into central France. During the Fronde the parish clergy was consulted in Agenais, Armagnac, Marennes, and perhaps other localities in Guyenne, but in Brittany, Languedoc, Dauphiné, Provence, and scattered localities elsewhere the upper clergy was strong enough to prevent any radical departures even at this late date.

Suffrage among the nobility was more extended than in the other orders. The usual rule was for all nobles with fiefs to be convoked, including women and minors who sent proctors in the rare instances they chose to exercise this right. From the close of the sixteenth century there was a tendency in some places to include nobles without justice. They appeared in Périgord in 1614 and in Brittany and other localities at about the same time.[7]

Languedoc and parts of Guyenne provide a notable exception to the procedure described above. Here the great majority of the nobles with fiefs were excluded from the electoral assemblies. The Wars of Religion and the troubles which followed the death of Henry IV did provide an opportunity for several more nobles to gain admittance to the estates of Velay and Foix, and during the course of the sixteenth century the number of nobles convoked in Quercy increased from twenty-five to twenty-nine. In the Fronde the unfranchised nobles of Languedoc sought the privilege of naming deputies to the provincial estates in diocesan assemblies, but the movement failed, and the magnates who held the twenty-two seats of the second estate in the provincial assembly were more firmly entrenched than ever by the end of the Renaissance.

Royal and municipal officials who were nobles of the robe deliberated with the third estate even when they held fiefs. A few exceptions to this rule are known, but in general the second estate was composed only of those who wore the sword. By 1789 this situation had changed and the two types of nobility voted together for the deputies of the second estate, a fact which clearly marks the acceptance of the robe by the old nobility during the course of the century prior to the Revolution.

Suffrage among the members of the third estate must be considered under two headings — the municipality and the countryside. Voting rights varied widely from town to town. In some places, such as Amiens, Lyon, Dijon, Marseille, Vienne, Agen, Saintes, Limoges, Toulouse, and indeed, in most of the towns in southern France, the municipal officials controlled the election of the deputies. In other localities, such as Paris, Villefranche-sur-Saône, Bourges, and Rouen, important bourgeois or selected notables from each quarter were also summoned. Parishes in the towns of Melun, Le Mans, Chartres, Orléans, Angers, Poitiers, and Tours sent deputies to the bailiwick estates. This procedure was very common in the Loire Valley. Still other places such as Troyes, Langres, and Blois made definite efforts to secure larger attendance at the assemblies during the sixteenth century. In general, the towns in the north permitted far wider suffrage than those of the south, and even where there were rigid limitations, those who desired to make suggestions to be included in the municipal cahier were free to do so. In Amiens, Beauvais, and Lyon, the guilds were specifically requested to submit their complaints. In Paris, Nantes, Lyon, and Blois, boxes were set up to receive petitions from anyone. Too often it was the oligarchy who decided which of these suggestions would find their way into the cahier and which would be forgotten, but at least an opportunity for self-expression was given.

Contrary to the increase in suffrage among the clergy and nobility, the number convoked to the electoral assemblies of the towns tended — with some exceptions — to decrease. During the sixteenth century the bourgeois oligarchy slowly strengthened its hold over many municipalities and assumed more and more the right of selecting deputies to the Estates General. Henry IV did little to change this situation. The popular party had usually been pro-League, and on coming to power Henry interfered only to strengthen the position of the local representatives of the crown, and not to bring about a return to the larger more popular assemblies of an earlier day.

On the other hand, suffrage in the rural areas increased during the Renaissance. As early as the fourteenth century there were isolated incidences of the participation of the plat pays, but it is doubtful if the term plat pays should necessarily be interpreted to include more than the small unfortified towns without charters of privileges. No absolutely certain evidence has been found of a large number of peasants being consulted in any jurisdiction in the Middle Ages or in the Estates General of 1484. In that year the typical assembly of the third estate of a bailiwick was composed of deputies from a few of the larger towns. Only four municipalities sent representatives to the electoral assemblies of Senlis and Touraine, and six to that of Amiens. Shortly thereafter villages in large numbers began to establish rudimentary municipal administrations with assemblies of the inhabitants and elected syndics to look after their interests. They thus became legally and administratively capable of participating in the estates.

In 1560 the villages were included in assemblies in Boulonnais, the provostship of Paris, and in some or all of the preparatory elections in Normandy, Vermandois, and Lyon. Judging by the widespread convocation of rural communities to assemblies to codify the customs in the north during the previous decade, this list of bailiwicks would be much longer if more documents had survived. The villages were summoned to at least one preparatory election in Vitry-le-François in 1561, and deputies of some of the parishes in Lannes and Haut-Limousin were also consulted in that year. In the elections of 1576 the bailiwicks and governments of Troyes, Montdidier, Amiens, Sens, Perche, and Chartres definitely permitted the peasants a voice. By the time of the Fronde, the electoral jurisdictions of Ponthieu, Péronne, Chaumont-en-Vexin, Chaumont-en-Bassigny, Provins, Melun, Nemours, Touraine, Anjou, Étampes, Orléans, Gien, Loudun, Poitou, La Rochelle, La Montagne, Auxerre, Basse-Marche, and Bas-Limousin may be joined to the list. Even where the rural population continued to be excluded, there was usually an increase in the number of towns consulted.

There is a striking similarity between the jurisdictions in which the peasants were convoked and those in which the curés were called. The parish priest and the peasants in his spiritual charge were summoned in most localities in the governments of Picardy, Champagne, Normandy, the Île-de-France, and Orléans by the time of the Fronde. The adjoining jurisdictions in western Burgundy and northern and western Guyenne may be added. Only in Brittany and the southeast did the curés and the peasants make little or no progress towards suffrage during the Renaissance.

There are four possible explanations for the increased suffrage. It may have taken place on orders of either the king, the judges of the Parlements, or the bailiwick officials, or it may have been brought about by the initiative of the inhabitants themselves. If the king had been the controlling factor, there ought to have been a uniform change in procedure in the various bailiwicks. This was not the case. The crown was content to decide whether the towns and chapters or the bailiwicks were to name deputies to the Estates General. However, so many of the details were left to subordinates who were so willing to stretch or even to violate royal directives that the orders issued by the king were not a major factor in causing the increased suffrage in the bailiwicks.

The possibility that judges from the Parlements influenced the extension of the suffrage must also be considered. During the Renaissance selected judges supervised the codification of the customs by the bailiwick estates in many parts of France. If they got the suffrage extended for this purpose, it would have served as a precedent for meetings of the bailiwick estates to name deputies. Circumstantial evidence indicates, however, that initially the judges did not exercise any more control over the suffrage than the king, for a wide variety of procedures were employed in these assemblies during the first half of the sixteenth century. In 1521 the parishes sent deputies to the assembly of La Marche presided over by Roger Barme of the Parlement of Paris, but these deputies were excluded from an assembly at Blois in 1523 that was presided over by the same jurist.[8] In August, 1539, Francis I directed the same officials from the Parlement to supervise the codification of the customs of the neighboring bailiwicks of Clermont-en-Beauvaisis and Senlis. In the former, the curés and deputies of the villages attended, but in the latter they were excluded from the bailiwick assembly.[9] Clearly other factors were more important.

Of the members of the Parlement, only Christofle de Thou may have exercised a real influence on the extension of the suffrage. In 1555 he was given the mission of presiding over bailiwick assemblies in the jurisdiction of the Parlement of Paris to codify and reform the customs. The bailiwick officials issued the writs of summons, but attendance of the curés, lesser seigneurs, and villages was so common in these assemblies that Thou may have been the guiding force leading to their summons. For nearly three decades the eminent jurist presided over assemblies and by his death in 1582 the participation of these once excluded classes had become commonplace in northern France.[10] Their convocation to the assemblies to codify the customs was cited to justify their inclusion in electoral assemblies to the Estates General. Outside the jurisdiction of the Parlement of Paris this influence was not felt; the provinces in the south and on the borders of France more successfully resisted the expansion of the suffrage.

The work of Thou was not the only factor that brought about the growing list of those who were summoned, for in north and south alike there were jurisdictions in which the suffrage was increased, even though the meetings to codify the customs had been restricted. In Boulonnais, for example, both the curés and the villages were absent from the assembly to reform the custom in 1550, but participated in the election to the Estates General ten years later.

The local royal officials exercised the greatest influence on the suffrage. It was they who were charged with the convocation of the bailiwick estates. Their authority was limited only by the royal proviso that they proceed in "the accustomed manner." Sometimes "the accustomed manner" was not known or was in dispute, on other occasions the officials acted on their own initiative in spite of protests of well-informed persons. Whatever their excuse, their directives promoted the extension of the suffrage during the sixteenth century.

Two motives lay behind their actions. The first was the sincere belief that since the interests of the curés, lesser nobles, and peasants were at stake, they ought to be consulted. This belief was implied in the Roman law principle, quod omnes tangit, debet ab omnibus approbari, but it had not been taken as a justification for universal suffrage during the medieval period. At that time the practice was to emphasize the quality more than the quantity of those consulted. Wherever a limited number of people were summoned then or in the Renaissance, the clerk was likely to record that "the larger and wiser part" of the inhabitants was present.

Perhaps the increased interest in Roman law during the sixteenth century led to a more literal interpretation of quod omnes tangit, and with it, an increase in suffrage. The actual phrase, quod omnes tangit, was not used to justify an extension of the summons during the Renaissance, but over and over again statements were made to the effect that this or that group should be consulted because its interests were involved. This argument emerged clearly in Châlons-sur-Marne in 1651 when the cathedral chapter protested against the inclusion of the curés in the bailiwick estates. The case was brought before the Parlement of Paris instead of the king's council because a fine was involved. Here, after the usual arguments based on precedents, the chapter took the stand that it was contrary to reason to give the curé who was merely a "cadet" a voice equal to its own. This position was attacked by a spokesman of the procureur of the king who took the stand that since the curés' interests were involved in the Estates General, it would be unjust to deny them any voice. His opinion was accepted by the Parlement. In 1593 the provost of the merchants of Paris recommended that the suffrage be extended because the elections "concerned everyone and were of such consequence that the deputation should be made by everyone and in as large a company as possible."[11]

The belief that all concerned should be consulted was undoubtedly behind the efforts of Thou to include the curés, lesser nobles, and peasants in the assemblies to codify and reform the customs, and must have influenced many of the bailiwick officials as well; but a second and less worthy motive also explains their actions, especially in regard to the third estate. Many officials found in the deputies of the lesser towns and villages allies in their struggle against the bourgeois oligarchies of the great municipalities. To extend the suffrage was to increase their voting strength in the bailiwick elections. A victory there was apt to mean a trip to court as deputy, and this post was coveted more by the officer class than by any other. More important, the control of the electoral assembly assured that in the cahier the bailiwick submitted to the king a friendly attitude would be taken towards their activities. Indeed, the cahier might be used as a popular petition for changes that would further their designs against the bourgeoisie.

One of the best examples of the devious activities of bailiwick officials occurred in Amiens in 1576 when they convoked the villages and then proceeded to give the proctor of each village a voice equal to that of the town of Amiens. This situation produced the expected victory. The cahier that was prepared included a request for changes designed to give the royal officials control over the municipality, and two of their number were elected to take it to Blois. The lieutenant general of Anjou added deputies from eighty to a hundred rural parishes to those ordinarily convoked in order to defeat the powerful bourgeoisie of Angers. The royal officials at Riom summoned the communities of the plat pays to the estates of Basse-Auvergne in 1576 and 1588 in the hope of supplanting the powerful position of thirteen privileged towns. In La Montagne, in usually conservative Burgundy, the presence of village proctors who voted for the lieutenant general gives rise to the presumption that they had been summoned for that very purpose. The outraged bourgeois of Châtillon-sur-Seine were consequently defeated. They appealed to the Parlement of Dijon and the provincial estates of Burgundy to reverse the elections on the grounds that the lieutenant general would not press the petitions they intended to make against the government. When these appeals failed, they dispatched their own deputy to the Estates General.

How often the towns sent representatives to the Estates General when they had been defeated in the bailiwick elections by the machinations of the local officials is difficult to say, but at least twenty-five municipalities were given seats on one or more occasions in the Estates Generals of 1576, 1588, and

1614.[12] In some instances this desire for separate representation from the bailiwick may have had nothing to do with the activities of the local officials, but there were many cases in which towns dispatched deputies to the Estates General to protest against actions of local officials only to have their envoys refused seats. Amiens was rebuffed time and again.

The crown did not support the questionable activities of its officials, but rather upheld the privileged towns by either severely limiting proposed increases in the number of localities convoked or by ordering the use of preparatory assemblies to reduce the voting power of the lesser communities. Where their position can be ascertained, we find that the nobility generally supported the bourgeois against the royal officials. While the Estates General of 1576 was in session, several deputies of the nobility of Picardy brought the representatives of the town of Amiens into contact with the king when they wanted to protest against the unfair electoral practices of the bailiwick officials. Again, it was the nobility who thwarted the efforts of the lieutenant criminal of Ponthieu to gain precedence over the mayor of Abbeville in the elections of 1588. That same year the three estates of Burgundy, in answer to complaints like those of Châtillon-sur-Seine described above, ordered that in the future no bailiwicks in the province elect royal officials to the national assembly. The nobility of Maine supported the third estate against the aspirations of the royal officials in 1651, and in that same year the Duke of Rohan sought to perform a similar service for the inhabitants of Angers. Thus the nobility closed ranks with the bourgeoisie to save them from the machinations of the local royal officials, who alone were seeking to upset the long established privileges of the elite of French society.[13]

Another factor which made for an expansion in the suffrage was the insistence of the inhabitants of some of the smaller towns and villages that they be given representation in the electoral assemblies to the Estates General and in the provincial and local estates. This demand became particularly strong during the Wars of Religion. The number of towns convoked in Forez was increased from 13 to 19; in Berry the number went from 6 in 1561 to 31 in 1614; and in the estates of Foix, from 28 in 1520 to 45 in 1693. Similar figures could be cited for Brittany, Agenais, Périgord, and elsewhere. The lesser towns of central and southern France, angered at heavy taxation, the sufferings of civil war, and the overbearing attitude of the larger towns, were determined to be included in the local estates and in the electoral assemblies. Sometimes the smaller towns managed to persuade the peasants to give them support in their search for recognition, but by and large the rural population was indifferent. In the north, where the small towns were already represented, they had no need to solicit the aid of the peasants, and the rural population was content to remain aloof unless summoned by the local crown officials.

The forces that worked for a limited suffrage must also be taken into account when one considers why the number of persons summoned increased more rapidly in one locality than in another. Clergymen, noblemen, and burghers who were consulted opposed the extension of their privilege to the lesser members of their respective orders. The chapter clergy fought moves to include the curés in the summons in Chaumont-en-Bassigny, Maine, and elsewhere. The prelates and great seigneurs resisted any increase in those who attended the estates in Languedoc. Large towns opposed the inclusion of smaller towns and villages. These conservative forces were especially successful in those places where there were regularly convoked estates. Here it was clear who had the historic right to be summoned, and the privileged were better organized to oppose any move to fulfill the ambitions of the disqualified classes. In Burgundy, Auvergne, Dauphiné, Provence, Languedoc, Guyenne, and Brittany, the suffrage expanded slowly, if at all.[14] Where there were no regularly convoked estates — in Picardy, Champagne, the Île-de-France, Orléans, and parts of Lyonnais — the traditional procedures were not well known and the upper classes were poorly organized. Here it was easier for the local royal officials to introduce changes, and they were not afraid to take advantage of their opportunity.

Thus far we have dealt with those who attended and those who sought to attend the electoral assemblies to the Estates General, but what of those who did not want to participate? Their number was by no means insignificant, and figures could be cited indefinitely to prove that only a minority of those who could vote went to the bailiwick assemblies. Often officials had to resort to the threat of heavy fines when they desired a large attendance.[15] One noble and the proxy of another represented their order in Touraine in 1484, 3 nobles attended in Berry in 1561, 12 in Rouen in 1588, 10 in Guyenne in 1560, and 12 out of the 27 summoned in La Montagne in 1588. The record of the upper clergy was a little better, but in those jurisdictions where they were convoked, a majority of the curés was usually absent. No less than 53 missed the electoral assembly in La Montagne in 1588. Towns and other subordinate jurisdictions were more likely to obey a summons. At Orléans in 1588, 15 out of 17 castellanies were represented, in Maine in 1576, 17 out of 27 communities answered the summons, but in the same year at Blois only 8 out of 20 did so. For Bas-Limousin in 1588 figures for the three orders reveal that 97 were present and 184 absent for the clergy, 90 nobles attended or sent proctors, 75 did not, 73 communities were represented, 93 failed to honor the summons. When there was rivalry among several candidates, the turnout was sometimes much larger. Over four hundred nobles were reported to have attended the estates of Anjou in 1588, but it is surprising how many absented themselves during the Wars of Religion when there were so many disputes. Attendance increased during the seventeenth century. The bailiwick elections in Rouen, which had been insignificant affairs during the Wars of Religion, were so well attended in 1614 that not everyone could get into the hall reserved for the meeting. During the Fronde over 200 ecclesiastics and 174 nobles were present, a far cry from the 12 who had deigned to vote for the latter order in 1588. Two hundred and eight nobles attended in Basse-Auvergne in 1651.

The growth in attendance indicates an increased interest in the Estates General and in the local and provincial assemblies; this points to the rising importance of men of secondary rank. Too often emphasis has been on the disappearance of many of the great noble houses near the close of the Middle Ages, and there has been a failure to recognize that this vacuum was replaced in the countryside less by the crown than by the seigneurial nobility whose ambition and sense of public responsibility were felt in many ways. Local royal officials showed little inclination to threaten their position before the beginning of the seventeenth century, preferring to limit their efforts to a struggle against the bourgeoisie of the towns. The increased political consciousness of the middle clergy and the lesser towns and communities is still more noteworthy.

The Relations Between the Estates

During a period which saw the growing political importance of some groups and the decline of others, one might expect to find a bitter class struggle, but the elections provide little evidence that this was the case. It is true that the three estates ceased to deliberate together in many places during the latter half of the sixteenth century. In 1484, deputies were generally elected in the name of the bailiwick as a whole and not of a particular social class. In 1560 the best available evidence indicates that all, or at least a majority, of the deputies from the governments of Brittany, Dauphiné,

Provence, Champagne, Languedoc, Normandy, and Guyenne were elected by the three orders voting together. In the Île-de-France, Picardy, Orléans, Lyonnais, and Burgundy the three orders acted apart in a majority of the jurisdictions. By 1614 there had been a marked change. The three estates had ceased to act together in a majority of jurisdictions in Champagne and Guyenne. Even Provence showed a tendency to slip into this category since only part of her deputation was chosen by the three orders together. But as in Marseille, and probably Arles, voting continued to be in common, the government should be classified as being about evenly divided.

Since each government was given one vote in the Estates General after 1484, this change meant that in 1560, seven ballots were cast by deputies representing the three orders and five by those standing for a single order; but that in 1614 the votes of only four governments were cast in the name of the three estates, seven were voted by those chosen by a single estate, and the remaining government was divided. Was this change brought about by a royal policy of divide and rule, the machinations of local crown officials, a growing social cleavage, or did it result from other causes?

There is no evidence to suggest that the king sought to divide the orders.[16] The letters of convocation directed that the three estates be assembled together, and nothing was included to suggest that they separate when it came time to vote. In the surviving archives of the hundred-odd jurisdictions that named deputies to the Estates General, no secret directives have been found telling royal officials to divide the estates. Furthermore, the decisions rendered in the royal council in disputed elections offer no indication prior to the Fronde that the crown had any desire to interfere in this matter.

Local royal officials played an important part. It was they who planned the bailiwick assemblies, and often it can be shown that they directed the orders to separate and name their deputies. What is not clear is the motives that lay behind this policy. Perhaps the officials divided the estates in order to avoid the confusion of having too large a number of persons meeting in one place; it will later be shown that the increased suffrage was accompanied by the separation of the orders in many localities. Perhaps they sought to pattern the bailiwick estates after the Estates General, where in 1560 and thereafter the estates deliberated apart. Very likely there were times when the local officials separated the three estates in order to further their own designs. This ambitious group could hardly hope to challenge successfully the clergy and nobility until they had won the towns. It was to their interest to separate the three orders and capture the control of the third estate. From this position they could push their claims at court and eventually win the great towns themselves. Only then would they be ready to compete with the nobility. By the time of the Fronde there were signs that they felt prepared for the struggle.

Various developments may have led the members of the three estates to prefer to deliberate apart during the late sixteenth century. A review of the elections reveals that in Vitry-le-François and Troyes the three estates voted together in 1560, but that soon thereafter the orders began to act separately in both places. In each instance this change was marked by the introduction of a large number of villages to the bailiwick assemblies. To have continued to deliberate together would have exposed the nobility to being outnumbered by the peasants of their own manors, and they could have regarded this possibility with little pleasure. Further circumstantial evidence of the effect of the extension of the suffrage is offered by the inability to find a single instance where the villages were summoned in 1614 in the three governments of Champagne, Picardy, and the Île-de-France or in the border regions in Burgundy and Orléans, that the three orders still voted together. The noble and the deputy of his village might vote together occasionally, but in the long run such practices tended to die; for though there is little evidence of a conscious class struggle during the sixteenth century, the age was far from equalitarian. In Normandy alone did the three orders continue to vote together when the peasants were consulted, but it had a relatively complete system of preparatory elections, and only the principal viscounty of each bailiwick had more than one representative at the electoral assembly to stand for the smaller towns and villages. The nobles, who usually attended in person, were in little danger of being overrun by so few. Their only problem was to attend in large enough numbers to outvote the delegations from such cities as Rouen.

The bailiwick of Alençon provides a further example of the difficulties of voting by head when large masses from the third estate were admitted. There during the Fronde the nobles turned out in large numbers for preparatory assemblies to elect deputies to the bailiwick estates. For reasons not too difficult to imagine, the lieutenant general permitted the inhabitants of Alençon, including artisans, to attend and vote individually in the bailiwick estates, thereby completely overwhelming the handful of proctors of the second estate. The two candidates desired by the nobility of all the subordinate jurisdictions were defeated, and the lieutenant general was chosen. The king's council sustained the nobility and ordered that in the future the third estate not be allowed to vote with the nobility. This is the only known instance in which the crown encouraged a separation of orders in the elections, and this step was undertaken to protect the privileged from a royal official, yet the deputies of the nobility were far less likely than the lieutenant general to have supported the royal government if the Estates General had been held. One reason, then, for the separation of the estates in northern France was the desire of the first two orders to avoid being overpowered by the ever-growing number of voters from the third estate. Where few members of the third estate attended the bailiwick assemblies, the three estates often continued to vote together. Even where the peasants were convoked, the clergy and nobility sometimes retained the practice of acting in the same chamber, as in Sens and Ponthieu in 1614.

Other considerations may have had some influence in causing the three estates to deliberate separately. In parts of Guyenne and in Auvergne the practice developed for only the third estate to attend local assemblies that dealt primarily with tax matters. As this was the most frequent cause of meetings, that order became accustomed to acting alone and often preferred to continue to do so when the clergy and nobility attended.

The anticlerical attitude of the lay estates exerted some influence. Animosity between the two groups was great enough to lead to a separation of the orders in Lyon in 1468 and in Paris in 1483. The reform movement of the sixteenth century made Catholic and Protestant alike still more critical of the clergy. When the king convoked the three estates in 1561 to offer advice on how he ought to solve his financial difficulties, the lay orders seized the opportunity to recommend that part of the goods of the clergy be confiscated. An unusual electoral procedure was followed on this occasion: The bailiwick estates chose deputies to attend assemblies of their government or province, where in turn deputies were chosen to attend the Estates General. It was in these governmental assemblies that there is evidence of the unfriendly attitude of the lay orders. In Languedoc and Champagne, where the three estates had usually deliberated together, the clergy found itself ostracized, while the secular estates continued to act as one. Perhaps some bailiwick assemblies were divided for the same reason, and once the new procedure was accepted, it was difficult to change.

Another possible factor was the example set by the three estates deliberating separately in the Estates General in 1560 and thereafter. It must have been difficult for a deputy, chosen to represent three orders and armed with the cahier of their complaints, to find himself thrown into a national assembly in which his fellow deputies, chosen by the same constituents, deliberated elsewhere. This specific problem troubled the Bishop of Vence in 1560, and at that Estates General the ecclesiastical deputies of Guyenne, Auch, and Brittany insisted that the deputies from their order consult the representatives from the other estates of their provinces so as "to be better instructed."[17] They and others may have reported their difficulties upon their return home with the result that in the future, the estates were more inclined to give separate instructions to their deputies.

Whether the three orders voted together or separately is in itself no proof of whether they were friends or enemies. Co-operation was possible when they met in different chambers, and bitter feuds could take place when they acted together. We must go further to explain the conflicts that took place in meetings of the estates. In 1561 there were places in which the secular orders co-operated against the first estate. This situation resulted from the great unpopularity of the clergy at that time, but it can give little comfort to the advocates of a class struggle, for the clergy was drawn from both the lay estates. By 1576 and 1588 many lay Catholics had rallied to the side of the Church and still others to the side of the crown. The struggle was one between the two Catholic groups, and the Protestants often boycotted the assemblies. In 1614 and during the Fronde the issue was between royal and antiroyal factions. Such quarrels were deeply intermixed with family alliances, local personalities, and local issues. They cut across class lines to such an extent that few disputes between the orders during the elections can be found, except during the anticlerical elections of 1561.

Most of the quarrels that can be cited grew out of the activities of the local royal officials, and usually it was the municipal leaders who formed the opposition. Occasionally there were disputes over precedence between the estates. In 1576 the provost of Paris gave the nobility seats on the right side of the chamber, and this led to protests from the clergy. Even such a quarrel between the first two estates had few if any counterparts. The same year there were two disagreements; one between the councilors and the chapter of Rouen over the location of the seats of the clergy, and a second more significant one between the townsmen and noblemen concerning how many persons should be admitted to the assembly; this was an important point where voting was by head.

The activities of the local royal officials rarely brought them into direct conflict with the clergy and nobility during the sixteenth century, but by the time of the Fronde they had won control of most of the towns and had turned their attention towards winning equality with the first and second estates. In 1649 the lieutenant general of Angoulême claimed the seat immediately to the right of the seneschal, but was successfully challenged by the clergy aided by the nobility. It was also during the Fronde that the lieutenant general of Alençon packed the assembly with his henchmen from the third estate so as to outvote the nobility and win the election. Certainly the most serious quarrel was at Chartres at the same time, when the bailiwick officials sought seats in the chamber of the nobility and were ejected by that order with some bloodshed.

These episodes, however, can hardly be considered as symptoms of an underlying antagonism among the three estates. With the rarest exceptions the ecclesiastics, nobles, and burghers respected the privileges of others just as they defended their own. Only the local royal officials showed any tendency to instigate change. Motivated by the sincere belief that all who were concerned should be consulted and by the desire to win control over the bailiwick elections and the municipalities, this group of men did much to extend the suffrage. Most often their actions brought them into difficulties with the third estate and occasionally, with the other orders. Except for these clashes, it is amazing how few and how petty were the disputes that can be found in the vast number of accounts of elections that have survived. The three estates may have had different views on certain matters in this or that bailiwick, but they stood together as defenders of their mutual privileges, and in this they had the unfailing support of the king in council.

14

THE DEPUTIES

Requirements for Election

The crown was as vague in its directives on who should be elected to the Estates General as it was on how they should be chosen. In 1484 the government was content to ask that "notable personages" be named, in 1560 they were to be "good persons," and in 1576 and 1588 "some of the most notable persons from each province, bailiwick, and seneschalsy," the latter request being later modified by the provision that only Catholics full of zeal be chosen. In 1614 the deputies were to be "competent and honest."[1]

Although local officials had no hesitation in tampering with the electoral procedure to secure the choice of their candidates, they rarely established rules to bar the election of anyone because of age, sex, place of residence, or social position. The lack of official instructions did not mean that the voters had no guide, for custom and prejudice played a major role. In no instance was a woman chosen as a deputy in a bailiwick election.[2] Minors, who were defined as persons not yet twenty-five, fared a little better. The only deputy who was challenged because of his age was Jacques Chavaille of Bas-Limousin in 1614. Bas-Limousin was one of those jurisdictions in which there was bitter rivalry among the local royal officials, and at the Estates General the lieutenant generals at the seats of Brive and Tulle questioned the right of Chavaille of Uzerche to serve on the grounds that he was only twenty-one or twenty-two years old. Chavaille replied that those who had elected him had known his age and that minors could be the proctors of those who had reached their majority. The bulk of the deputies accepted this argument, but others pointed out that while the voters of Bas-Limousin might have the right to give their power of attorney to a minor, the entire order was affected if he were seated. The vote of Bas-Limousin might be the deciding one in the government of Guyenne, and the vote of Guyenne could be decisive in the assembly.[3]

In other instances minors were accepted without question. Philibert Venot was scarcely twenty-one when he sat for the third estate of the bailiwick of Autun in the Estates General at Blois in 1588.[4] Louis de Nogaret de La Valette, Archbishop of Toulouse, was only twenty-two in 1614 when he was invited by the clergy to assume a seat in the Estates General.[5]

Church affiliation was generally no more of a serious hurdle than age. In 1484 there was no problem on this score, but the advent of the Protestant Reformation did bring the matter to the fore. Protestants were accepted without question in 1560, 1561, and 1576, but as has been indicated above, Henry III ordered that only zealous Catholics be elected in 1588. This directive was carried out with rare obedience, since most Protestants boycotted the elections and the League held sway in much of Catholic France. One interesting case did arise. Two deputies of the third estate chosen by the lesser localities in the seneschalsy of Bordeaux questioned the right of Fronton Duvergier, a deputy elected by the town of Bordeaux, to a seat. The ambitions of local royal officials may have led to the attack, for the two deputies of the seneschalsy were members of the local Parlement, while Duvergier was a jurat. The justification for the refusal to seat Duvergier was that he was a heretic. The League-dominated third estate sided with the two royal officials, but Duvergier won the support of the king's council. This assistance was not effective until after the assassination of the Duke of Guise; only then was Duvergier able to take his seat.[6]

By 1614 the worst of the religious hatred had passed, and Protestants were admitted to the Estates General without question. The new situation was clearly indicated in that year when a Catholic from Montpellier claimed a seat in the chamber of the third estate on the grounds that the recognized deputy from his jurisdiction was a Protestant. The nobility, he pointed out, had both a Catholic and a Protestant delegate and this division of authority was practiced elsewhere in Languedoc. The king's council refused to accept this argument and ordered the Catholic claimant to give his cahier to the deputies from the seneschalsy of Toulouse.[7]

Whether residence, or at least the ownership of property, or the holding of an office in a jurisdiction was required of a deputy is a more difficult problem. It is virtually impossible to say categorically that a man had no connection with the locality that elected him, for one can rarely feel sure that all of the records have survived. In most instances, the location of the benefice of a clergyman, or the seigneury of a noble, or the office held by the deputy of the third estate quickly reveals him to have been from the jurisdiction which chose him. Our suspicions are aroused most often when a man was elected by two or more jurisdictions. In such cases the clergy can be investigated with the greatest facility. One ecclesiastic represented two jurisdictions in 1484; two stood for two, and two for three localities in 1576; one for three or perhaps four in 1588; one for three in 1593; and five for two, and one for four in 1614.[8]

Most striking about this list is that in every instance except one, the electoral jurisdictions were close to each other. Often, though not always, they lay at least partly in the same diocese. It was not a case of electing a stranger, but rather a neighbor who had already undertaken the inconveniences of a trip to the national assembly for another jurisdiction. Such a man was likely to accept a second mission willingly, and the cost of his services was less than that of a separate delegation. Only Jean de Bertier, Bishop of Rieux, served from two far-removed localities. No doubt his bishopric and his family connections won him the nomination of his native seneschalsy of Toulouse in 1614, but his election by the bailiwick of Valois seems strange until we learn that he was also Abbot of Saint-Vincent in nearby Senlis and chancellor of Queen Marguerite, Duchess of Valois.[9]

The election of nonresidents did occur in instances other than in the case of multiple elections. Arnaud de Pontac, Bishop of Bazas, illustrious scholar and member of a prominent family of Bordeaux, was deputy of Bazadois in 1576, but in 1588 he served for neighboring Armagnac. The three estates of Rouen elected the Bishop of Lisieux in 1588, but the clergy of the diocese was unhappy at the choice of an outsider and met separately to name its own archbishop. Renaud de Beaune, Archbishop of Bourges, was deputy for Chartres in 1588, but he then held an abbey in that diocese. In at least two other cases a bailiwick elected a deputy whose principal benefice was not in a neighboring jurisdiction. Claude de Coquelet, Bishop of Digne, was chosen by the bailiwick of Meaux in 1593, but his election can readily be explained by his also being dean of the cathedral chapter of that town. Robert de Pellevé, Bishop of Pamiers, served for the bailiwick of Sens in 1576, but he held an abbey in the diocese of Sens, and his uncle was at that time the local archbishop.[10]

Thus the election of one clergyman by several jurisdictions did occur. Some localities chose men whose principal benefice lay elsewhere, but the deputy concerned either resided in a neighboring locality or else had an official position, and perhaps family connections in each and every electoral district that named him. Residence was not required, but there was a strong prejudice against voting for an outsider. This prejudice was clearly reflected by the successful opposition of the clergy of Vitry-le-François in 1649 to the candidacy of the Bishop of Châlons-sur-Marne on the grounds that the bulk of his diocese, including the episcopal seat, lay outside the bailiwick.[11]

Election by several localities was less frequent in the second estate and except for the closely associated provostships of Montdidier, Péronne, and Roye, no deputy of the nobility was named by three or more jurisdictions. Indeed, the election of a noble by a second locality was rare, and in every such instance the two jurisdictions were close together. Only Haute- and Basse-Auvergne in 1560, Agenais and Condomois, Chaumont-en-Vexin and Senlis, and Bas-Limousin and Basse-Marche in 1576, Berry and Gien in 1588, and Paris and Meaux, Laon and Reims, and Orléans and Berry in 1593 made the choice of the same deputy. If the candidate did not hold land in both jurisdictions, we may rest assured that he was at least well known in each.

The property of the middle class was not as widely scattered as that of the other orders, and the members of the third estate were less likely to be known beyond their homes. As a result the election of an outsider was exceptional, unless the dangers of travel prevented local inhabitants from seeking office, as occasionally happened in turbulent 1593. Only the closely associated bailiwicks of Senlis and Chaumont-en-Vexin shared the same deputy of the third estate in other years. Even the desire to save the expense of separate delegations did not lead to joint elections, although a proposal was unsuccessfully made by a member of the estates of Comminges in 1576 to choose the deputy from the third estate of the seneschalsy of Toulouse as an economy measure.[12]

Another suggested disability was that of being a royal official. No difficulty arose on this question in the first two estates, but the crown denied royal officials and later lawyers the right to represent the Norman viscounties and bailiwicks in the provincial estates. A protest was made against the election of a royal official in Maine in 1576, and the idea that this group should be excluded was pressed vigorously in Burgundy by Châtillon-sur-Seine in 1588 after the lieutenant general of the bailiwick had been elected deputy. The mayor and échevins appealed to the Parlement of Dijon and to the provincial estates. The latter finally ruled that royal officials would not in the future be elected to the Estates General, an order that was forgotten by 1614. The town of Poitiers protested in 1614 against the predominance of royal officials who were serving as deputies, but to no avail.[13]

The influence of class must also be investigated. It will be remembered that the letters of convocation directed that members from each estate be elected, but could and did the electors ignore royal directives and choose someone from another estate? If one excludes from consideration those provincial and bailiwick assemblies where the three orders voted together, there is no evidence that anyone who did not hold an ecclesiastical benefice sat for the clergy after 1560 though, of course, some of these benefice holders were not priests. The possession of benefices by laymen made it possible for Georges de La Trémoille to serve for the clergy of Poitou in 1560 in his capacity of Abbot of Chambon and Saint Laon de Thouars, and for the nobility in 1576 as the Seigneur of Royan. The second estate did not stray from its ranks when it came to choosing deputies to the Estates General, but the third estate was apt to prefer a nobleman. Most often when the third estate turned to the holder of a title, it was to honor the office-holding nobility who, as we have seen, were classified as members of the third estate for voting purposes. Even men whose ancestors had been nobles of the sword in the Middle Ages

joined their fellow members of the robe in the electoral assemblies if they
became royal, legal, or administrative officials. Thus Henri de Mesmes,
lieutenant civil of the provostship of Paris, was deputed by the third estate in
1614, even though his family dated back to the thirteenth century in Béarn and
the ancestor who had established himself at Paris a century earlier had held
five seigneuries. His great-grandfather and grandfather had married into the
powerful Hennequin family and his mother was the daughter of the Viscount of
Vandeuil. He himself married Jeanne de Monluc, widow of Charles d'Amboise,
Marquis of Reynel and Bussy, and daughter of the famous Jean de Monluc,
Prince of Cambrai and Marshal of France. Henri de Mesmes was to become
a marquis, and his daughter married Louis de Rochechouart, Duke of Vivonne,
Peer and Marshal of France. Yet this scion of a great family was elected as
a deputy of the third estate because he himself wore the robe.[14]

Lesser seigneurs maintained their gentility with more difficulty when they
became officeholders. The Coquilles claimed nobility dating back to 1391, but
on more than one occasion members of the family found it necessary to have
their title verified. The great jurist, Guy Coquille, was deputy to the Estates
General in 1560, 1576, and 1588, but was elected by the third estate because
he was an official of the Duke of Nevers.[15] Séraphin Thielement, Seigneur of
Guyencourt, was of an old Luxemburg family, but determined on an administrative career and became a secretary of the king in 1576. In 1593 he was
elected secretary of the chamber of the third estate, an office which he accepted with the stipulation that it would be "without prejudice of his status as
a noble."[16]

Deputies from the old seigneurial families who sat for the third estate
were not limited to those who then wore the robe, for more than one representative of that order claimed no office and simply styled himself seigneur
of this or that place. In 1576 a deputy of Provence, Louis Lévêque, Chevalier
of the Order of the King, was forbidden to wear his sword into the chamber of
the third estate because he had threatened someone.[17]

It seems clear, then, that although anyone the electors desired could be
made a deputy, the prejudices of the age prevented the election of women,
minors, Protestants, and nonresidents except on rare occasions. The clergy
and nobility selected only men from their respective orders, but the third
estate was willing to reach above itself and elect a nobleman of the robe and
even of the sword.

Social Background and Experience of the Deputies

The fact that nearly anyone could legally serve as a deputy did not prevent
the establishment of definite patterns. Most of the representatives of the first
estate were members of the secular clergy. The benefice or position of every
ecclesiastical deputy to two meetings of the Estates General is known. In the
assembly of 1588, 80 per cent and in the assembly of 1614, 75 per cent of the
deputies held their principal benefices with the secular clergy. Since members of chapters and others of the secular clergy who were abbots or priors
in commendam were classified with the regular clergy, the proportion of secular to regular clergy was really much larger. Incomplete figures on the
representation at the earlier meetings of the Estates General indicate that
about the same division between the two branches of the clergy held true.[18]

The division between upper, middle, and lower clergy is of greater significance. In Table 1 the archbishops, bishops, and abbots are classified as
upper clergy, the vicars-general, members of chapters, archdeacons, archpriests, college and university professors, provosts, priors, etc., as middle
clergy, and the curés and brothers as lower clergy.

Table 1. — Membership of the First Estate

Deputies	1484	1560	1576	1588	1593	1614
Upper Clergy	51.3%	20.5%	32.7%	28.4%	37.5%	55.3%
Middle Clergy	12.8	52.0	54.5	63.4	47.9	37.6
Lower Clergy	3.8	7.1	3.6	8.2	12.5	7.1
Unknown	32.1	20.5	9.1	0.0	2.1	0.0
Total	100.0%	100.0%	99.9%	100.0%	100.0%	100.0%

One is struck by the decline in the membership of the higher clergy from about one half in 1484 to one fifth in 1560, and then by its rise to over 50 per cent in 1614. The initial decline may be explained by the widespread distrust of the higher clergy on the eve of the Wars of Religion and by the indifference of many important clergymen to their responsibilities. The rise in the number elected from higher clergy thereafter reflects the power of the Catholic Reformation. The great ecclesiastics became so respected that they were elected in increasing numbers in spite of the simultaneous extension of the suffrage to include the lower clergy in many places. The prelates' interest in serving is also proven.

The record of the higher clergy in 1614 is even more striking when realizes that in that year the fourteen archdioceses in France furnished ten archbishops to the Estates General, and the one hundred and one dioceses gave fifty bishops. It is true that four of the archbishops and bishops attended on the invitation of the assembled clergy rather than by virtue of election by a bailiwick, but an equal number of bishops were chosen by from two to four electoral jurisdictions. Furthermore, the absence of most of the other prelates is readily explained. All the missing archbishops and most of the missing bishops came from southern France where the lay orders frequently had a voice in selecting the deputies of the clergy and where there were many prelates to choose from. Indeed, nearly a fifth of the archdioceses and dioceses in France lay in Languedoc, but the province regularly furnished deputies from only four jurisdictions. There were no less than ten archbishops and bishops in the seneschalsy of Carcassonne alone, of whom one and only one was elected to go to the Estates General in 1614. Moving to the north away from the ancient center of Christianity, the dioceses became larger, but at the same time the bailiwicks became smaller, so small indeed that many did not contain an episcopal seat. Here the elections of prelates could hardly be expected. Furthermore, no elections were held in the three recently acquired dioceses of Metz, Toul, and Verdun, and many prelates must have been too old and infirm to make the difficult journey to the national assembly or too deeply engaged in governmental or church affairs to be able to serve. The record of the clerical magnates in 1614 was therefore a remarkable one.

That the number of prelates who were elected deputies increased with the extension of suffrage after 1560 does not mean that the lower clergy always preferred to be represented by their superiors. This is brought out clearly by comparing the status of the deputies elected where the curés participated with those chosen in places where they were not summoned. About half the deputies of the first estate sent to the Estates General of 1560, 1576, 1588, and 1614 by the aristocratic governments of Brittany, Burgundy, Dauphiné, Guyenne, Languedoc, Lyonnais, and Provence were archbishops, bishops, and abbots, but only 30 per cent of the deputies whose status is known from the five less undemocratic governments can be so classified. On the other hand, twenty-seven of the thirty-four curés and brothers who won election came

from these areas. The bishop, the abbot, and the canon were everywhere preferred, but in the few instances when a curé was elected, his peers almost
always had the right to vote. The curés who won election were not half-
literate priests of tiny villages. Over a third can be identified as doctors of
theology and almost as large a percentage had a parish in the principal town
of the bailiwick. There were a few, however, from the little towns and communities. Most often the curés were elected by the small bailiwicks in which
there was no bishop's seat, such as La Montagne, Dreux, Montfort l'Amaury,
Caux, Gisors, and Montargis.

If the nobility are subdivided into three classes: the higher nobility consisting of the princes, marquises, and counts; the middle nobility including
the viscounts and vidames; and the lesser nobility including the barons, seigneurs, and écuyers; Table 2 showing the status of the deputies of the second
estate can be prepared.

Table 2. — Membership of the Second Estate

Deputies	1484	1560	1576	1588	1593	1614
Higher Nobility	2.5%	0.0%	1.2%	2.9%	4.2%	16.9%
Middle Nobility	3.8	1.9	2.3	5.9	0.0	5.1
Lower Nobility	65.0	67.0	83.7	90.2	95.8	77.9
Unknown	28.7	31.1	12.8	1.0	0.0	0.0
Total	100.0%	100.0%	100.0%	100.0%	100.0%	99.9%

Since the great majority of those who did not designate their rank undoubtedly belonged to the lower nobility, the numerical preponderance of the
seigneurs was indeed overwhelming. The growing attendance of counts, marquises, and the like after 1576 reflects both the increased political consciousness of the upper and middle nobility and the willingness of the crown to satisfy the craving of the second estate for new and higher titles. The number
of lay peerages more than doubled between 1547 and 1600, and in the century
preceding the death of Henry III twelve marquisates, twenty-six duchies, and
five principalities were created. [19]

The families that furnished deputies were among those who profited.
Antoine de Brichanteau was content to style himself simply as the "Sieur of
Beauvais-Nangis" when he served as deputy of Melun in 1588, but in 1614 he
was the "Seigneur and Marquis of Nangis." René du'Bellay was simply the
Baron de la Lande when he acted as deputy of Anjou in 1588, but when his son
Martin attended the Estates General of 1614, he was Prince of Yvetot and
Marquis of Touarsy. Alof de l'Hôpital, Sieur of Choisy, was deputy of the
bailiwick of Orléans in 1560. His son became a count, and his grandson was
a marquis when he sat for Provins in 1614. A grandnephew, who also became
a marquis, was deputy from Meaux in 1593.

That the marquis, the count, and the viscount were rare figures at the
Estates General does not mean that the nobility elected only their most insignificant colleagues as their representatives. Almost invariably a member
of one of the most distinguished seigneurial families of a bailiwick was chosen. Often veritable dynasties were established: the Beaufremont, father,
son, and grandson served as deputies for Chalon-sur-Saône; the Rabutin usually sat for Autun; the Malain or Damas for Auxois; the Lenoncourt for Bar-
sur-Seine; and there were many others. [20]

Younger sons or cadet lines of ducal or near ducal families also served.

This list includes several Montmorencies, Brissacs, La Trémoilles, Foix, and Saulx-Tavannes, a La Marque, a Bourbon-Rubempré, a Grammont, and several others. Some families had far-flung possessions which made their members likely candidates from several jurisdictions. The Damas family sat for three different Burgundian bailiwicks after 1576; the Pot served for Berry, Orléans, and the duchy of Burgundy; the Hôpital for Orléans, Provins, Dourdan, and Meaux; the Illiers for Blois, Vendôme, Sens, and Chartres; and additional examples could be given. In short, just as the knights of the shire in England were drawn from the great county families and were sometimes related to the peers, so in France the deputies of the nobility were from families of local distinction. Furthermore, just as the English peers did not become candidates in the shires, so no French prince of the blood or lay peer tried to win a bailiwick election.

The status of the deputies of the nobility may also be ascertained by the court positions they held. One fourth were gentlemen ordinary of the king's chamber, members of the king's household, or else held similar positions for other persons in the royal family in 1588. Nearly 40 per cent of the deputies that same year were chevaliers of one or both orders of the king. Twenty-eight per cent held the title of councilor in the conseil d'état in 1614, and 16 per cent in the conseil privé. Also in 1614, one fifth were bailiffs or seneschals and a few others held important administrative positions. It was as soldiers, however, that the deputies of the nobility were best known. Exclusive of the governors of towns and châteaux, about a third of the deputies of 1588 and 1614 held military rank, most often captain of fifty men at arms. Unfortunately, our data for the earlier meetings of the Estates General is less complete, but it seems probable that such offices were less frequently held by the deputies at that time. There was a tendency to multiply the titles of chevalier, councilor, and captain just as that of marquis. The best indication of the improved status of the noble deputy may be found in the percentage who were bailiffs and seneschals. The number of these posts changed slowly, and whenever one was added, it meant that a new electoral jurisdiction had been created thereby increasing the quantity of deputies. In 1484, 6 per cent of the noble deputies were bailiffs or seneschals; in 1560, 5 per cent; in 1576, 4 per cent; in 1588, 12 per cent; and in 1614, 19 per cent. These figures, along with the increased attendance of the nobles in the bailiwick and provincial estates around the turn of the century, point to the growing interest of the second estate in representative assemblies.

As with the clergy, the jurisdictions where the suffrage was narrowly restricted tended to elect a higher percentage of the upper nobility. A third of the deputies of Languedoc to the Estates Generals of 1576, 1588, and 1614 were marquises, counts, and viscounts, and a third were seneschals. Four out of ten were councilors in both the conseil d'état and the conseil privé in 1614.

The deputies of the third estate were as aristocratic as those of the other two orders. Two deputies were classified as farmers and one as a merchant and farmer in 1576, one deputy was listed as a farmer, merchant, and receveur in 1588, and one as a farmer in 1593. Except for these five men, there is no evidence of the agricultural classes serving in the third estate. Even these men were not poverty stricken, ignorant peasants. One, Odet Soret of Caux, kept a journal of the estates of 1593 and had sufficient resources to serve from January 12 to August 23 before he received an order for financial compensation.[21] The typical deputy was either a royal official or a member of the bourgeois oligarchy. The two groups that fought for control of the bailiwick elections renewed their rivalry in the Estates General.

If the deputies are classified into six groups: royal officials, municipal officials, other inhabitants of towns (advocates, bourgeois, merchants, doctors, etc.) officials of provincial estates, officials of nobles, and farmers, Table 3 showing the status of the deputies of the third estate can be prepared.

Table 3. — Membership of the Third Estate

Deputies	1576	1588	1593	1614
Royal Officials	35.8%	43.8%	47.3%	49.5%
Municipal Officials	17.6	24.3	29.1	25.8
Other Inhabitants of towns	23.0	19.4	16.4	9.1
Officials of Provincial and Local Estates	2.7	2.0	1.8	6.6
Officials of Nobles	0.5	0.5	0.0	1.5
Farmers	1.1	0.0	1.8	0.0
Unknown	19.3	10.0	3.6	7.6
Total	100.0%	100.0%	100.0%	100.1%

These figures reveal the growth of the power of the royal officials in the Estates General. Their electoral successes were most conspicuous in Champagne, the Île-de-France, Orléans, and Picardy where there were no provincial estates. Where the estates existed, they protected the bourgeois oligarchy; not a single royal official was elected by Dauphiné or Provence in 1614. The provincial estates, controlled as they were by the upper clergy, nobility, and the deputies of the towns, provided a potent check on the inroads of the officer class into the municipalities and the countryside, and this fact does much to explain the bureaucracy's desire to weaken representative assemblies during the seventeenth century.

The great majority of royal officials who served as deputies held important judicial and administrative posts. Tax collectors were rarely chosen by the electorate. The municipal officials were usually mayors or échevins, while the advocates were the most numerous group who held no governmental position at all. Those who styled themselves as being simply bourgeois, merchants, or doctors of medicine were not numerous, and the unavoidable conclusion is that the third estate was composed almost entirely of officials and lawyers.

Another striking aspect of the social background of the deputies of the third estate was the large number who claimed to be nobles. In 1614, 38 per cent were seigneurs, sieurs, or écuyers, and an additional 14 per cent stated that they were noblemen. Surviving figures are incomplete for the earlier meetings of the Estates General, but the available evidence suggests that fewer nobles then served as deputies of the third estate. Just as the seigneurs were winning higher titles, the members of the third estate were acquiring nobility.

No satisfactory equation between the extent of the suffrage and the percentage of noble deputies of the third estate can be established. In 1614 over two thirds of those elected were nobles in the governments of Champagne, the Île-de-France, and Picardy where the suffrage was generous, but the same fraction applied to the governments of Brittany, Dauphiné, and Provence where the provincial estates controlled the elections. In the first group, the high percentage of nobles may be attributed to the tendency of the rural population to elect royal officials, who nearly always claimed noble status. In Brittany, Dauphiné, and Provence the other two orders had much to say about who was elected for the third estate. These electors, and the municipal leaders who comprised the third estate, naturally preferred to choose men with a high social position. Elsewhere in France, where the suffrage for the third estate was neither excessively broad nor excessively narrow, only a little over 40 per cent of the deputies were nobles in 1614.

There was, however, a geographical distinction between those regions in which nobles were chosen as deputies of the third estate and the places where men without this claim were preferred. With the exception of Dauphiné, not one of the seven eastern and southern governments elected a majority of noble deputies in 1614. Half the deputies from central France — that is, from the government of Orléans — were nobles, but 80 per cent of the deputies from the four northeastern governments of Brittany, Île-de-France, Normandy, and Picardy had the distinction. We can offer no satisfactory explanation for this phenomenon.

When the towns, rather than the bailiwicks, served as the electoral jurisdiction for a national assembly, deputies of an equally prominent background were chosen. The one striking difference between the town and the bailiwick selections was the number of royal officials who were elected. Out of the forty-five deputies named by seventeen towns to attend the assembly of 1517, only five were royal officials and two more combined a royal with a municipal post. The remainder were town officials, lawyers, or merchants, with the exception of three canons and five noblemen, including a viscount and a baron.[22]

The deputies of the third estate, like those of the other orders, were the leaders of their localities. There was the same tendency for certain families to dominate the jurisdictions in which they resided, although not as frequently as in the case of the nobility. Three members of the Venot family sat for the third estate of the bailiwick of Autun in the Estates Generals of 1576, 1588, 1593, and 1614, and another Venot served for the clergy in the last named year. The Vigniers of Bar-sur-Seine, the Belins of Troyes, and the Godets of Vitry-le-François were among those that furnished two or more deputies to the Estates Generals of 1560 and thereafter.[23]

The high status of the deputies of the three estates ensured that they were also men of considerable administrative experience. Holdsworth's argument that the members of the English Parliament had a greater practical knowledge of government than their continental counterpart has no validity.[24] A large percentage — sometimes even a majority — of the deputies of the clergy were archbishops, bishops, or abbots. These men, through their ecclesiastical duties, had achieved considerable administrative experience, and many had also held governmental posts in France and served abroad on diplomatic missions. The priors and the deputies from the chapters had also held positions of responsibility. Most of the administrative experience that the deputies of the nobility had received was drawn from service in the army, at court, or as bailiff, a post which had lost much of its real importance. However, it must not be forgotten that the seigneur still played an important role in local government, and though he seldom personally exercised his rights of justice, he was both the administrator and leader of his seigneury. The deputies of the third estate were usually crown or municipal officials, and most of those who were not had held public office or were lawyers. Certainly the deputies to the Estates General did not lack experience.

The common problems which confront those who serve in representative assemblies also had been faced by many of the deputies. No less than seven of the twelve governments of France had provincial, and often local, estates during the sixteenth century. In an eighth government, Lyonnais, there were several local assemblies. Those who had the political aspirations or the prestige to be elected to the Estates General were likely to have already been honored by public trust in the smaller estates nearer home.

The great lack was a group of deputies in the Estates General who had the experience of working together; in this the English Parliament held a decided advantage. Less than 7 per cent of the deputies in 1576 had participated in the Estates Generals of 1560 and 1561. Eleven per cent of the deputies in 1588, 15 per cent in 1593, and under 4 per cent in 1614 had had prior service in the national assembly.[25]

One cause of the failure of the deputies to serve on more than one occasion was the large number of years which separated the meetings of the Estates General. Only the Estates Generals of 1561 and 1593 followed soon after other national assemblies, and over 40 per cent of the deputies in 1561 had served at Orléans in 1560. Perhaps because of the revolutionary character of the meeting, relatively few representatives in 1593 had been present at previous meetings of the Estates General. Still other causes must be sought, however, because 30 per cent of the deputies elected to the English Commons in 1584 had also sat in earlier Parliaments, though the lapse between this and the previous elections was twelve years.[26] After a similar time interval, the Estates General of 1588 counted only 11 per cent of its deputies who had served before. Service in the French Estates General was less popular, and during the Wars of Religion many men could not spare the time. It is worth noting that the nobility — the bulwark of the armies — was least likely to be able to return the same deputy a second time until the relatively peaceful year of 1614. But whatever the cause, the small number of old members put the Estates General at a serious disadvantage, and partially explains the failure of the French assembly to develop a more efficient procedure.

No Frenchman ever obtained the vast parliamentary experience of many Elizabethans, four of whom sat at Westminister on twelve or more occasions.[27] Only nine deputies attended three meetings of the Estates General, and seven of them were from the third estate. Edmond Réymond served for La Montagne in 1576, 1588, and 1593. His control of the seat came from his office of lieutenant general of the bailiwick and from the assistance of a large number of relatives who were also local officials. The support they brought him from the rural areas in 1588 won the election over the opposition of the échevins of the bailiwick capital. Michel Boissonade, often consul of Agen, sat for Agenais in 1560, 1561, and 1576. Ponthieu favored the mayor of Abbeville, Jean de Maupin, who was elected in 1560, 1588, and 1593. Robert Choquel, advocate and finally mayor and procureur général of the king, served for Péronne in 1576, 1588, and 1614. Bazadois turned to Jean de L'Auvergne, a jurat of Bazas, in 1560, 1576, and 1588. Quercy sent the syndic of her estates, Paul de la Croix, in the same years, but Guy Coquille of Nevers was the only deputy for three meetings who ever achieved more than local notoriety, and even that great jurist failed to play an important part at the Estates General. Antoine Regourd, Archdeacon of Cahors, and Antoine de La Sayette, Dean of Poitiers, sat for the clergy in 1560, 1561, and 1576. The parliamentary leaders of the Estates General were nearly always serving for the first time and no forceful personality sat on more than two occasions. Much of the confusion that attended the meetings of the Estates General is hereby explained.

The scholarly training of the members of the Estates General should also be investigated. The deputies of the clergy were all educated men, and it seems necessary only to point to some of its most famous members. Any list must include François Arnault, Chancellor of the University of Bordeaux, canon lawyer, and author of such works as Traité des anges et démons; François de La Béraudière, Bishop of Périgueux, writer of poetry and prose, and funeral orator of Henri IV; Jean Pierre Camus, Bishop of Belley, leader of the Catholic Reformation, prolific writer, and friend of Saint François de Sales; Pierre Du Val, Bishop of Séez, teacher of the children of Francis I, member of the Council of Trent and the Colloquy of Poissy, translator of Plato and other writers; Cardinal Jacques Davy Du Perron, Archbishop of Sens, a great ecclesiastical statesman whose speech against the divine right of kings in the Estates General of 1614 was translated into several languages and provoked a reply from no less a person than James I of England; Claude de Sainctes, Bishop of Évreux, theologian and philosopher who wrote several works including one on the Eucharist and another to justify the assassination of Henry III; and Pontus de Thiard, Bishop of Chalon-sur-Saône, humanist, author, and above all astronomer.[28]

The scholar was a rarer figure in the second estate where the pursuit of arms was the most common occupation. But illiteracy was certainly rare, and there was only one recorded instance of a deputy — from Brittany — who could not sign his name to the cahier.[29] There were, of course, a few writers among the nobility. We may cite Adrien de Boufflers; François de Racine, Seigneur de Villegomblain; Bertrand de Salignac, Seigneur of La Mothe-Fénelon; and Anne, Count d'Urfé, brother of the great Honoré d'Urfé, and himself the composer of 140 sonnets by the time he was eighteen.

The third estate, dominated as it was by men of law, included a galaxy of the greatest jurists and political theorists of the age. We need name only Jean Bodin, Louis Charondas Le Caron, Guy Coquille, Claude Le Brun de La Rochette, Antoine de Murat, Louis d'Orléans, and Jean Savaron. Scholars in other fields were more rare, but among the deputies were the poet Gabriel Bonnyn; the doctor and humanist, Jean Lalemant; and Guillaume Du Vair. There was no lack of talent; only lack of experience in working together handicapped the deputies to the French Estates General.

15

THE DEPUTIES AT THE ESTATES GENERAL

The Journey to the Estates General

The deputies were free to journey to the Estates General in any manner they saw fit. Sometimes the representatives of the three estates of a bailiwick traveled together. On other occasions a noble or ecclesiastic went with the deputies of his order from neighboring jurisdictions. Others traveled alone or only with a servant, and there were many instances of deputies from the same locality arriving at the Estates General a day or more apart.[1] The traveling companions of Jacques Decasalmartin, deputy of the third estate of Gévaudan in 1588, may be taken as typical. Decasalmartin journeyed to Blois with two deputies of the clergy from his jurisdiction and shared the same room with them during the Estates General. At the end of the session he went to Tours and then home in the company of several ecclesiastics and members of the third estate from Languedoc, from whom he found it necessary to borrow money.[2]

The highways were full of danger during the Hundred Years War and the Wars of Religion, and many deputies were waylaid on their travels to and from the Estates General. In 1576 a representative from Provence was kidnapped by his enemies as he was going to Blois, and he never reached his destination. It was reported that the Governor of Lyonnais arrested the deputies from Provence and Auvergne on their way to the Estates General of 1593, but the delegation from Provence managed to appear at the session. Only one of the five deputies elected by Périgord to the same assembly was able to overcome all difficulties and attend.[3] On his return from the Estates General of 1588, the royalist deputy of Langres was arrested at Brie by the League and held for 300 écus ransom. The municipal council of Langres raised the sum to free their delegate by taxing local inhabitants not favorable to the king and by seizing the goods of some merchants of pro-League Troyes who were then in their town.[4]

Occurrences like these sometimes caused armed guards to be furnished to protect the deputies in their travels. This was especially true in 1593 when the kingdom was in greater turmoil than during any earlier meeting of the Estates General. The assembly was originally scheduled to be held at Reims, and when it was transferred to Paris at the last moment, the Spanish army provided an escort for the deputies who had already gathered at the former city. That same year the deputies of the three orders from the Burgundian bailiwicks met at Dijon where they were joined by four hundred horsemen who conducted them to Paris. The two deputies of the third estate of Troyes were unwilling to make the relatively short journey to the capital without a large escort, the danger being thought so great that a guard of sixty horsemen was refused. At length it was decided to ask the Burgundian troops mentioned above to come through Troyes and pick them up. This was apparently done, for a Burgundian deputy reported that other representatives joined their party at Troyes, and the deputations from Burgundy and Troyes arrived at the

143

Estates General the same day.[5] The war also caused some difficulty at Lyon.
The first two deputies elected to go to the Estates General of 1593 sought to
evade attending because of the long journey, family affairs, health, old age,
and every other excuse that came to mind. One of them was given a reprieve,
and a third deputy was then named in his place, but he and his colleague still
refused to go until the municipality promised to reimburse them if they were
robbed and to ransom them if they were made prisoner on their trip to and
from the assembly.[6]

Many journeys to the estates were uneventful. The deputies of the town of
Orléans in 1588 reported no unusual difficulties in their short trip down the
river to Blois. Decasalmartin and the two deputies of the clergy of Gévaudan
made the longer journey from Mende by horse and boat without mishap. Six
deputies of the clergy and third estate of Brittany were able to turn their trip
to Paris in 1614 into a very enjoyable outing. Hardly had they gotten out of
the suburbs of Rennes before they produced pâtés and wine from their baggage
which one deputy reported "begat no melancoly." At Angers they inspected
the churches and convents, at La Flèche one of the travelers saw his son, at
Chartres they visited the cathedral and the episcopal garden, and when at
length they arrived at Paris they had taken thirteen days to encompass a
journey of less than 220 miles.[7]

Life at the Estates General

The deputies rarely found security and comfort after their arrival at the
Estates General. The presence of the king, the court, the deputies, and their
servants undoubtedly brought many people of questionable character to the
towns where the Estates Generals were held. The unfortunate mayor of
Périgueux purchased a complete new outfit at a cost of 4 livres, 10 sous to
make himself presentable at the estates of Tours in 1468, only to have his hat
stolen from the council chamber.[8] Nor, indeed, were the courtiers or the
deputies themselves immune from committing acts of violence. The king and
his councilors found it advisable to require the municipal officials of Tours
to take a special oath to enforce law and order in the town during the meeting
of the Estates General of 1484. A watch was to be kept at the city gates by
day and on the walls at night. No one was to go out after dark without a light,
and lanterns were to be hung along the streets. A large guard was to patrol
the various quarters between 10 P.M. and 6 A.M. and arrest all unruly persons, including the people of the king and the princes. Somewhat similar
precautions had been taken by Louis XI when the three estates had been held
in the same town in 1468.[9]

The presence of several thousand extra persons in the small Loire Valley
towns where the Estates General was so often held undoubtedly taxed their
rooming facilities. Blois did not have a population of over 16,000 in 1600,[10]
and one suspects that the château and taverns were strained to provide for
the court and its followers during the frequent periods of royal residence.
The addition of about four hundred deputies usually accompanied by servants
must have added greatly to the congestion.

Even in 1561 when the number of deputies was greatly reduced by convoking the governments rather than the bailiwicks, the king thought it advisable
to avoid confusion by forbidding anyone except the deputies to go to Pontoise
where the meetings of the estates were to be held.[11] At the larger meetings
of the Estates General the problem was much worse, and in 1560 the crown
transferred the location of a meeting of the Estates General from Meaux to
Orléans, where there were more and better accommodations for the deputies.[12]
In 1483 the captain of the town of Amboise was charged with the duty of finding

in 1651 the mayor and échevins of Tours were given this duty in anticipation
of the Estates General scheduled to meet in their city.[13] The deputies were
the Estates General scheduled to meet in their city.[13] The deputies were
anxious to avail themselves of royal assistance; and in 1588, on the day after
their election, the Brittany delegation told one of its number to ride to Blois
as rapidly as possible to ask the king's maréchaux des logis to reserve lodging for them.[14]

It is not known how the deputies of Brittany fared that year, but they may
not have done too badly. Two clergymen and a deputy of the third estate from
Gévaudan managed to find a room together, although they arrived months late,
and the two delegates of the town of Orléans also shared a furnished chamber.
We are best acquainted with the activities of the Breton deputies of 1614.
They were introduced to the king and the queen mother shortly after their arrival at Paris, found time to frequent the churches as good Christians, and
managed to dine exceedingly well on several occasions.[15]

The deputies who were left at the mercy of the inns fared worse. This
statement is amply supported by numerous complaints put in the cahiers to
be submitted to the king. The representatives, fresh from their journey to
the national assembly, painted an unattractive picture of loafers, gamblers,
blasphemers, and thieves, who frequented the inns and taverns hoping to profit
from the legitimate traveler, and of innkeepers who overcharged their guests.
Sometimes the kings were content to include an article or two on the matter
in the general ordonnance which followed the Estates Generals, but in March,
1577, at the request of the deputies, Henry III published a special decree intended to correct the abuses found in such establishments.[16]

Food was also a problem, and the crown took special measures to ensure
that there was sufficient quantity to satisfy the deputies and their horses. In
1560 when the Estates General was held in Orléans and in 1651 when the assembly was to meet at Tours, the mayor and échevins of nearby Amboise
were directed to speed the delivery of supplies. Only in 1593, when Paris was
being beseiged by Henry IV, did the deputies complain of cold or hunger, and
even then the chief cause for unhappiness was high prices.[17]

Indeed, lack of money was one of the most persistent problems that plagued
the deputies. As proctors they were entitled to financial compensation, but
payment was usually made after the close of the Estates General. Sometimes
the deputies, especially those of the third estate, did not have sufficient personal resources to finance themselves at the estates, or else underestimated
the duration of the meeting or the cost of living in the crowded towns where
the assemblies were held. It was not unusual for them to write their constituents for advance payments.[18]

The hardships of travel and the uncomfortable quarters in which so many
deputies were forced to reside probably contributed to some deaths. Take the
clergy in 1614 as an example. The Bishop of Rodez died on his way to Paris
to attend the Estates General, and the Archbishop of Tours and the deputies
of Boulonnais and Sézannes died during the session. Sézannes was especially
unfortunate because her deputy for the third estate also died, leaving only the
representative of the nobility to report what took place at Paris.[19]

It is not surprising that many persons sought to avoid election to the Estates General. Pierre Martin served in 1576 for Brittany, but begged to be
excused from acting as deputy in 1588. The first nobleman elected by the
estates of Dauphiné in 1614 was excused from attending. It was so doubtful
whether the second choice would accept that an alternate was named who was
already at court on business, and presumably would have no objection to attending. A deputy elected by Provence to go to the estates in 1596 begged to
be excused because of his health and even refused the responsibility of naming someone to go in his place. Étienne Bernard, who had been one of the

most prominent deputies of the third estate in 1588, sought to avoid attendance in 1593, and finally consented to go only at the insistence of the Duke of Mayenne.[20] Such examples could be multiplied without end. Most often sickness was given as the reason for refusing. Sometimes this must have been the most readily available excuse, but on other occasions it was certainly valid. In 1614 both the deputies elected by the third estate of Maine refused the assignment on the grounds of ill-health. At length they were prevailed upon to accept, but one of them died at Paris.[21]

There were, of course, compensations which partially repaid the deputies for their trouble; not the least of these must have been the discussions at the end of the daily session. Often the deputies of the three estates of a province stayed together in a house to facilitate these meetings. The Normans had their common lodging in 1484; so did the Picards. The Bretons in 1614 developed the practice of meeting in the town house of the Bishop of Rennes, or less frequently, in that of the Dukes of Brissac or Rohan, where they had the opportunity to associate with the great figures in their province in the most pleasant surroundings.[22] Here they exchanged views on the events of the day in spite of the rule of secrecy adopted by the estates. The deliberations show clearly that on any given morning the deputies in each chamber knew what had happened in the other two chambers the day before.

More important, the Estates General provided an opportunity for family reunions. This fact may be illustrated by arbitrarily taking the Hôpital family and tracing its connections. The house was of Italian origin and had settled in Orléanais during the fourteenth century. The first of the line to concern us was Adrien, Seigneur of Choisy, a gentleman who had among other children, two sons. The eldest, Alof, was deputy of Orléans to the Estates General of 1560, and one of his grandsons, Jacques, was a deputy from Provins in 1614. This same Jacques married Magdelène de Cossé, and was thus connected with the great House of Brissac, which furnished deputies in 1588 and 1614 from Normandy and Brittany. A second grandson, Anne, Seigneur of Sainte-Mesme, was deputy of the bailiwick of Dourdan in 1614. Another son of Adrien de l'Hôpital was Charles, Seigneur of Vitry. A daughter of Charles married into the D'O family. The D'O, in turn, was allied to many of the most important houses in France, including the Illiers, who furnished deputies for the nobility or clergy in 1484, 1560, 1576, 1588, and 1614. A son of Charles, François, married Anne de La Châtre. Her brother was deputy of Orléans and Berry in 1593, and her cousin, Henri de La Châtre, served for Berry in 1614. A son of François and Anne, Louis, Marquis of Vitry, was a deputy in 1593 and married Françoise de Brichanteau. The Brichanteaus furnished deputies for the first two orders in 1588 and 1614 and were allied to such houses as the Beaufremont who sat in the Estates Generals of 1561, 1576, 1588, and 1614; the Lenoncourt who served in 1588, 1593, and 1614; the Rochefoucauld who furnished two deputies of the clergy in 1588 and in 1614; and the Hennequins, from whose house came one representative of the clergy in 1576, one in 1588, two in 1593, and one in 1614. A son of Louis and Françoise was deputy of Orléans in 1614. There is no need to push the matter further though one is tempted to show how the Beaufremont, the Lenoncourt, and the Rochefoucauld were related, in turn, to still more families that often furnished deputies to the Estates General. Thus the Estates General brought together brothers, uncles, nephews, near and distant kinsmen who, perhaps, had not had an opportunity to see each other in many years. We may rest assured that much of their free time was spent together. Such meetings, though social in nature, provided further opportunities to exchange information and ideas on the developments in the Estates General and to plan the strategy for future sessions, strategy which certainly took into full account family alliances and interests. They also help explain why an event that occurred in the assembly of one of the estates was known by the other two the following day.[23]

The clergy and royal officials provided the best links between the estates because their ranks were filled from the nobility and third estate. There were even instances of a single family sending representatives at one time or another to all three estates. Take the Villars of Lyon, for example. A certain Pierre de Villars had three sons who are of interest. The first was François, lieutenant civil and criminal of Lyon. A son of François served as deputy of the clergy of Dauphiné in 1593, and another relative served for the town of Lyon that same year. A second son of Pierre became Archbishop of Vienne and sat for Dauphiné in 1576. A third son became a noble of the sword, and this line furnished a deputy of the clergy in 1588, the nobleman who prepared the cahier of the nobility of Lyonnais in 1614, and the Marshals and Dukes of Villars so famous in the seventeenth century. Further examples of families who were connected through marriage to deputies of all three estates could be found by investigating the nobles of the robe, men who sat for the third estate but who often originated from the seigneurial nobility or intermarried with that class. They used their influential position to place their relatives and children in high ecclesiastical posts. The L'Huillier, Mesgrigny, Hennequin, and Mesmes are only a few of those who could be mentioned. Cardinal Richelieu's mother was from a parliamentary family, but his grandmother was a Rochechouart and his great-grandfather had married into the equally distinguished House of Laval.[24]

In short, it was an age of social change. The Gouault were seigneurs in Brittany in the fifteenth century, but during the sixteenth one of their number became a procureur at the Parlement of Rennes. He in turn begat sons who sat for the clergy and the third estate of Brittany in 1614. On the other hand, Antonio Gondi, one of fifteen children of a well-known Florentine family, settled in Lyon between 1505 and 1510 where he became a merchant and a bourgeois. In 1521 he began the family's rise by purchasing the first of several seigneuries, and still later he became an échevin in his adopted city. This Italian of good but predominantly bourgeois origin had nine children. One became an abbot; another, the wife of a president of the Parlement of Toulouse; and a third, Albret de Gondi, became a duke, peer, and marshal of France. He was among those invited to attend the estates of Rouen in 1596, and his son was deputy of the clergy in 1614 and later a cardinal. A fourth child of Antonio was a bishop, a deputy of Paris to the Estates General of 1576, and finally a cardinal. A fifth became a marquis. We need go no further to show the rise of this family which was to become one of the most illustrious of France. Thus, though a hierarchical conception of society existed, it did not bar the elevation or degradation of a family and the clergyman, seigneur, noble of the robe, and bourgeois patrician could be related. These family alliances were a determining factor in the deliberations and did much to tie the three estates together as well as to add social enjoyment to the meetings of the Estates General.[25]

To see the king, the princes, and the great figures of the court undoubtedly incited the curiosity of many; one deputy in 1614 wrote that he would not have surrendered his place in the opening ceremony of the Estates General for a hundred pistoles. Such exuberance was short lived, however, and this same deputy, as well as those few others who have left a record of their feelings, ended their sojourn at the Estates General in sadness and disappointment.[26] Their risks and discomfortures could have been effaced permanently only by a feeling of the success of their mission, and this feeling was almost universally lacking. There remained of pleasant memory only the pageantry of the opening and closing ceremonies and evenings spent with long unseen kinsmen and friends.

16

THE PAYMENT OF THE DEPUTIES[1]

The Method of Payment

The difficulties the deputies encountered in securing payment for their efforts must have removed any pleasant memories of the Estates General. As legal representatives of their jurisdictions they were entitled to financial compensation; only those who were individually summoned were ever expected to serve without pay. Simple as was this principle, few matters connected with the Estates General caused more quarreling; and expense was one of the most frequent reasons given by the crown for not calling the estates or for dismissing the deputies at the earliest possible moment.

Prior to 1484 there was no great difficulty in regard to salaries. The magnates came in person or paid proctors. The towns, chapters, and other corporate groups elected and paid their representatives from common funds held by the community. The quarrels that did take place were over the amount to be paid, and not over who was to contribute or how the money was to be collected. These disputes led to appeals to the royal council, but the crown was anxious to keep the peoples' financial burden to a minimum and usually did no more than direct that a reasonable compensation be given.[2] This policy of trying to keep the salary of the deputies at a low figure was followed by all the Valois and gives support to the statement of Charles VII in 1442 that he stopped calling the Estates General in order to ease the burden on his poor subjects.

The convocation of the estates by bailiwick in 1484 created new problems. Should the deputies of the clergy and nobility be paid now that the policy of individual summons had ceased? If so, should they be compensated by their respective orders, or should the entire burden be placed on the third estate? In either case, how was money to be collected? The bailiwicks, unlike the towns, had no treasuries, and special assessments were necessary. A member of the clergy opened the discussion at the Estates General by pointing out that they had already spent two long and expensive months at Tours and should be given financial compensation. A deputy of the third estate from Troyes said that he, too, favored an indemnity, but asked that the people not have to pay the wages of the nobles and ecclesiastics. Should the poor give alms to the rich? Should they pay the costs of those who did not represent them? The clergy of Poitiers had agreed to compensate the deputies of their order before their departure for the Estates General. This praiseworthy action should be followed by all jurisdictions.

A deputy of the nobility of Troyes replied with great eloquence and vehemence: "I would like the orator to tell me, my lords, if he thinks that the ecclesiastics and nobles of this assembly have brought no relief to the people, and if he imagines that his services and those of the deputies of the third estate have profited them more than the work of the clergy and the nobility. I strongly believe that he would not have audacity enough to affirm what to the eyes of all is most obviously false."[3] Furthermore, the nobleman argued, why should the nobility be expected to pay the representatives of their order while the people pay for those of the third estate? The deputies of the three estates had generally been elected and empowered by the same assembly. They were responsible to the same group. Those who served for the third estate were no more tallageable than the deputies of the nobility because they had been ennobled, or were bourgeois of free communes, or had privileges attached to their offices. The clergy were to pray for all, to advise, and to preach. The nobility were to protect everyone with their arms, and the people were to nourish and support the first two orders by their taxes and their agriculture. This arrangement was not devised to the advantage of anyone in particular, but to make it possible for everyone to advance, not in accordance with his own interests, but as the servant of the entire community. Did not the people always pay the deputies of the three orders in the provincial estates of Normandy and Languedoc? Let the natural order of things be followed and direct the people to pay all the representatives.

Some wished to reply, but the chancellor interposed, saying that the council had spoken much on the indemnity of the deputies and would announce its decision before the end of the session. At this point in the conversation the deputies of the first two orders left the room, and the chancellor remarked that he wished they would either surrender their wages or be content to collect from their respective estates, because of the poverty of the people. Nearly all the deputies of the clergy and the nobility were rich enough to make this sacrifice without difficulty. Still, he confessed, the law sided with them, and the people would have to bear the entire burden.[4]

The few surviving documents indicate that in 1484 the deputies of the three estates were generally paid from the taille. Where there were provincial estates, consent had to be given before the sum could be collected, and in Languedoc, Burgundy, and Haute-Auvergne, the receveur of the estates made the payments.[5] Where there were no estates, the royal receveur of the tailles assumed the task.[6] Sometimes the privileged towns resisted efforts to make them contribute, and in Périgord and Armagnac the seneschals had to take strong action to bring results.[7]

There were exceptions, especially in the north, where the deputies of the third estate were sometimes paid by the more important towns and communities of the bailiwicks. Six municipalities reimbursed the representatives of the bailiwick at Amiens. Laon contributed twenty livres toward the salary of a man described as the deputy of the town, but the small amount suggests that other municipalities paid something. Troyes consented to give an advance to the deputy of the third estate of the bailiwick, but refused a similar request made by the representative of the clergy, with the suggestion that he refer his petition to his fellow ecclesiastics. No wonder the representatives of Troyes played the leading role in the debate on the payment of the deputies during the estates.[8]

The next national assembly in which deputies were elected by bailiwick took place in 1560. On January 30, 1561, the day before the final meeting of the estates, Charles IX issued a decree for payment of the deputies; this transferred the burden from the unprivileged to all three orders. Bailiwick assemblies were to be convoked to name deputies to a new meeting of the Estates General and to choose six persons from each estate to apportion a tax levied to pay those who had served at the earlier meeting. This tax was to be divided among the clergy in accordance with the décimes, among the nobility according to the arrière-ban, and among the third estate according to the taille, except that the free towns were to be included. Thus the tax for the payment of the deputies was based essentially on income, for the décime was levied on the revenue of the benefices, the arrière-ban on the revenue of the fiefs, and the taille took into consideration the revenue of the individual.

The procès-verbal of the division of the tax was to be sealed and sent to the royal council within two months.[9]

Approximately the same procedure was requested during the remainder of the century, and for that matter until 1615. On March 26 of that year the king in council issued an order for the payment of deputies who had just departed from the meeting of the Estates General at Paris. The clergy was told to determine the amount to be given the representatives of its order, and arrangements were made to assess the benefice holders in each bailiwick in accordance with the décimes they paid. All fiefs, including those held by ecclesiastics, were to be taxed to pay the deputies of the nobility. The trésoriers of France and the receveurs of the tailles were directed to assess and collect a tax based on the taille from the towns and plat pays in each bailiwick to pay the deputies of the third estate.[10] The only important change was that since 1576 the local magistrates instead of the bailiwick estates, had chosen the members of the three orders to help divide the tax. Only in 1560 and 1561 did the two meetings of the Estates General come so close together that the electoral assembly of the second could be used to take up the question of the payment of the deputies to the first.

It is necessary to turn to the bailiwicks to see how the royal directives were implemented. The most detailed information available is for the payment of the deputies of the bailiwick of Vermandois to the Estates General of 1560. For some reason Vermandois did not take the necessary steps to pay its deputies in the electoral assembly for the Estates General of 1561 as directed, but rather held a special assembly for this purpose in April, 1562. The total amount that had to be raised was 2,393 livres, a figure which included not only the payment of the deputies of the three orders, but also the costs of holding the bailiwick assembly. The latter involved compensation for some of those who attended the meeting, pay of messengers, and clerical fees. Each order was assigned the task of paying its own deputies and a part of the common electoral expenses. The amount levied on the clergy was subdivided among the five archbishoprics and bishoprics of the jurisdictions in accordance with the wealth of each. The amount levied on the secular estates was subdivided among the provostships. Unfortunately, it is not known what further subdivisions were made of the charges on the ecclesiastics, but each holder of a fief was assigned a share of the sum levied on his provostship for the nobility. The charges for the third estate were further subdivided among the deaneries and finally among the individual communities.[11]

In pursuing the matter further, each estate will be considered in turn. As has been indicated, the royal orders directed that the costs of the deputations of the clergy be divided among the benefice holders in proportion to the décimes paid by each. In the bailiwick of Orléans many curés were excused from making payments for the delegation of 1560, but in 1588 and 1614 the costs were divided among all those who paid the décimes. In Mâcon in 1614 several hundred curés were among those who contributed toward the payment of their bishop, in spite of the fact that none of them had been permitted to participate in the assembly which had elected him to attend the Estates General. All ecclesiastics in Bas-Limousin were called upon to help pay their delegation for that year.[12]

The roll of the ban and arrière-ban in each bailiwick, that is, the list of the fief holders who owed military service directly or indirectly to the crown, was the basis of the tax on the nobility. By the sixteenth century it had become customary for a vassal to pay, in lieu of military service, a sum of money varying in accordance with the estimated income from his fief. To facilitate this levy, rolls had frequently been prepared giving the estimated revenue of the fiefs in a particular jurisdiction. From 1560 the rolls formed the basis for the division of the tax to pay the deputies of the nobility.

The rolls of Bas-Limousin and Vermandois for the Estates General of 1560, of Ponthieu and La Montagne for 1576, of Rouen for 1588, and of Périgord and Maĉon for 1614 indicate that noblemen who held fiefs were not the only ones who were assessed. Widows and unmarried women who held fiefs also paid. Neither ecclesiastics nor princes of the blood were excepted. The Cardinal of Bourbon and the Prince of Condé paid for fiefs held in Ponthieu, and the Cardinal of Lorraine and the King of Navarre did not escape the tax collectors in Vermandois.[13]

Foreigners were not exempted, and the Genevese who held fiefs in the bailiwicks of Gex were charged with part of the expenses of the delegation in 1614. Henry III specifically ordered that the costs of the Burgundian nobles in 1576 be divided among nobles and commoners who held fiefs. But under the old regime exceptions can always be found: A few months earlier, as the result of an appeal by the mayor and échevins of Amiens, this same king revoked an order assessing the inhabitants in that town who held fiefs, on the grounds that among their privileges they numbered exemptions from the franc-fief and the ban and arrière-ban.[14]

The tax for the payment of the deputies of the third estate was divided among the parishes in accordance with the amount of taille levied on each and, theoretically at least, without regard to privileges or exemptions. Among the rolls that survive are those for Vermandois in 1560, where over four hundred communities were assessed, and for the various Burgundian bailiwicks in 1576 and 1614. No community, however small, was deliberately overlooked, even though it possessed no suffrage rights, as was so often the case in Burgundy and elsewhere. In addition to these rolls, documents from literally hundreds of communal archives indicate the amount paid toward the expenses of this or that deputy.[15]

There were many variations in the procedure used to pay the deputies in different parts of France, but only a few of the more important ones need be considered here. The first place to look for exceptions is in the jurisdictions where the three estates voted by head rather than by order. Here it would not be surprising to find the deputies compensated by a universal tax or the taille as in 1484. This surmise proves correct for Brittany, where the deputies of the three orders were paid by the provincial estates, which, of course, removed most of the burden from the clergy and the nobility. In other localities, however, where the three orders named their deputies together, each estate generally paid its own delegates. This was true in Provence in 1588, 1614, and was agreed on in principle in 1591, and in the seneschalsies of Languedoc in 1576, 1588, 1614, and in the government of Languedoc in 1561.[16]

On the other hand, in Burgundy where the three estates voted separately, the clergy and nobility persisted in the effort to place the burden on the third estate as had been done in 1484. A lively debate developed on this issue in 1561. The nobility argued that the delegation from their order would act for "the common good of the estates" and therefore should be paid by the estates. The third estate offered strong and successful protests against this point of view. In 1576 the difficulty arose again, and the king had to issue special orders for each estate to pay its own deputies. Apparently the directive was not fully carried out, for in 1588 a complaint was made that several deputies had not been paid half their wages, and the Burgundian delegation of that year asked that this time their salaries be raised by a special tax on salt, a request which was granted by the king. It is probable that the deputies to the estates of the League were compensated from the treasury of the provincial estates. In 1614 Burgundy and the adjacent territories returned to the system of each order paying its own delegation. Thus, in some parts of France where the three orders named their delegations together, each order paid its own deputies. In a few others, where the deputies were elected by their own estate, they were paid from a common fund.[17]

Frequently in those jurisdictions where the lower clergy, the lesser nobility, the unprivileged classes in the towns, or the rural communities were denied suffrage rights, they were made to pay part of the costs of the deputations. It is an oversimplification, therefore, to say that the deputies of the bailiwicks were paid by their constituents. Rather they were reimbursed for their services by a tax levied by royal command and, after 1484, generally falling on their order in their jurisdiction regardless of who had actually participated in their election. The fact that the representatives were paid by a special tax rather than from the usual revenue coming into the royal treasury made the people much more conscious of the costs of holding representative assemblies. They were likely to insist on large and specific benefits from the Estates General before being willing to advocate its frequent convocation, and the failure of the institution to provide many useful results must be considered when one seeks to explain its decay in France.

When the towns sent deputies to a national assembly, even one in which only the bailiwicks had been summoned, they paid the entire costs of the deputation. Lyon compensated her deputies to the numerous assemblies of Charles VII and in 1468, 1483, 1506, 1560, 1576, 1588, and 1614.[18] Amiens contributed toward the cost of the bailiwick deputations in 1560, 1561, and 1576, but in 1588 and 1593 the town reimbursed the deputies it had sent directly to the Estates General. Such independence was liable to prove costly, for in 1614 Amiens was ordered to pay 50 livres toward the expenses of the deputy of the bailiwick, even though the municipal officials had refused to participate in the bailiwick elections and had again sent their own deputy directly to Paris. Troyes paid for its individual deputations in 1468 and 1516. Marseille supported its municipal delegations in 1576, 1588, and no doubt on other occasions. Additional examples could be given in profusion.[19]

In the period following 1550 those who were sent individual summons also received financial compensation for their services, and it is not surprising that the crown tried to place this burden directly on the people. Henry II ordered that a tax be levied on every inhabitant in Burgundy to pay the first president of the Parlement of Dijon for his services at the estates of 1558, although he was either a royal appointee or at best authorized by the local Parlement.[20] In 1617 the crown attempted to levy a special tax to pay the magnates who attended the Assembly of Notables, although none of them had been elected. The trésoriers généraux of France in Provence asked the provincial estates to vote 9,000 livres toward the costs of this meeting. The estates refused, but the issue was raised again and again until 1622. Burgundy and Mâcon were no less displeased. Perhaps it was the opposition raised against this levy that led the king to assume the responsibility of paying most of the costs of the Assembly of Notables in 1626.[21]

The Amount of Payment

The controversy over who should pay the deputies indicates very clearly that the expense of having a delegation was regarded as serious. Provence complained about the cost of her participation in the Estates General of 1614. The clergy of the seneschalsy of Guyenne permitted the Archbishop of Bordeaux to have an assistant deputy in that year only when assured that they would not be charged for the costs of both representatives at any one time. Auxois was strongly opposed to the payment of the Burgundian delegation from a common levy in 1588 because the other bailiwicks had named more deputies. Foix decided to elect only one deputy from each estate in 1614 because of the poverty of the province. There were a few instances of two or more bailiwicks naming the same deputy as an economy, although local pride sometimes rebelled against this practice. Indeed, pride often so completely conquered avarice that bailiwicks named more than the requested number of deputies. The crown was well aware of the expenses required and used economy as an excuse to forbid the estates of Burgundy to assemble for the election of deputies in 1560.[22]

It is not easy to judge whether the deputies were justified in their complaints on the costs of holding the estates, and it is still more difficult to ascertain whether the expenses had anything to do with the small demand on the part of the people for holding the Estates General. The royal financial officials estimated the costs of indemnifying the deputies at more than 50,000 livres in 1484, but the assembly was willing to grant the crown a <u>taille</u> of only 1,200,000 livres per year. In 1614 Brittany paid her delegation to Paris 52,418 livres, 17 sous, but her provincial estates were not ashamed to offer the king a mere 200,000 livres for the year 1619. The amount of tax levied on individuals varied greatly. In Bas-Limousin in 1560, nobles paid anywhere from 2 sous to 25 livres, and in Vermandois, from 9 sous to 25 livres. In Ponthieu in 1576 fiefs were assessed from 6 sous to 206 livres. Here figures indicating the estimated revenue of each fief reveal that the noble was forced to surrender about 4 per cent of his annual income. The revenue of the fiefs may have been underestimated, but Ponthieu was not one of the small jurisdictions and had had only one deputy. The burden must indeed have been severe in those bailiwicks which had two or more delegates. By 1614 the assessment per fief varied from 3 to 300 livres in Mâcon and Périgord.[23]

The amount levied to pay the deputies of the third estate varied greatly. In 1421 Tours paid its deputies 300 livres for the thirty days they were absent to attend the estates at Clermont, but Lyon managed to escape with a bill of only 117 livres because her representatives were able to accomplish their mission in only thirteen days. The burden of supporting a delegation was evidently regarded as a heavy one, and by the spring of 1424 Tours found it advisable to try to reduce her deputies' allowance. The smaller towns summoned by Charles VII must, indeed, have suffered from his frequent convocations of the Estates General.[24]

The advent of bailiwick elections in 1484 brought considerable relief because the cost of the deputations began to be spread among the smaller towns and villages. Laon had to pay only 13 livres, 10 sous towards the cost of the delegation of Vermandois in 1560 because over four hundred communities in the bailiwick contributed an average of 2 livres each. Some rural parishes paid only 2 or 3 sous. Amiens was assessed only 120 livres to pay her share of the wages of the bailiwick deputies in 1576. Vitry-le-François paid about 50 livres towards the bailiwick deputation in 1588, and so it went. When one considers how inflated the late sixteenth century currency was and how much longer the Estates General remained in session at that time, one cannot help but recognize the advantages that bailiwick elections brought to the third estate.[25] In England the towns continued to be summoned, but only the wealthiest found that they were able to support the cost of their deputations in spite of the low wages paid in that country. Gradually the practice developed of electing nonresident gentlemen who were willing to serve without a fee, and the urban inhabitants lost much of their influence in the House of Commons as a result.

The salary scale fluctuated widely in France until the late sixteenth century, because the individual constituencies determined the amounts to be paid. Tours sought to reduce a deputy's allowance from 100 sous per day in 1421 to 40 in 1424, and large changes can be noted in other towns as well. The kings issued ordonnances for the payment of the deputies in 1560, 1561, and 1576, but they specified no precise wages, beyond directing that the deputies be paid as little as possible. Henry III set a maximum limit on the salaries of the delegates to the estates of 1588, and Louis XIII established a definite pay scale for 1614. [26]

If the salary scales established by the crown in 1588 and 1614 are accepted and the surviving documents utilized to determine the approximate amounts paid those who attended the other meetings of the Estates General, Table 4 can be prepared.

Table 4. — Pay Per Day of Deputies to the English Parliament and the Estates General in Sous Tournois

Deputies	1484	1560	1576	1588	1614
Knights of the shire (English)	18.8	32	34.3	38.4	41.7
Burgesses (English)	9.4	16	17.1	19.2	20.9
Archbishops	-----	-----	500.0	--------	540.0
Bishops	-----	200	400.0	--------	480.0
Abbots, priors, deans, canons of cathedral churches	40.0	150	160-300	300 max.	240-300
Curés, priests, and other ecclesiastics	-----	-----	120.0	--------	200.0
Nobles	60-75	150	?-400	300 max.	400.0
Lieutenant generals and other crown officials	-----	-----	-------	--------	300.0
Municipal officials of important towns	40-90	60-90	?-180	180 max.	260.0
Other deputies of the third estate	-----	-----	-------	--------	240.0

For the most part, the bailiwicks gave the deputies of 1588 and 1614 the amount directed by the king, but there were some exceptions. In 1588 the bailiwick of Orléans paid the deputy of the clergy 20 livres per day instead of 15, but in 1614 the same jurisdiction elected three deputies for the clergy rather than one and therefore felt compelled to be much less generous. Their combined salary ought to have been 9,180 livres, a tremendous burden, which was met by lowering the wage of the bishop from 24 to 12 livres per day and of the other two deputies from 15 to 3 livres per day. The injustices of this arbitrary action were compensated for by saving 6,120 livres. Other, though perhaps less extreme, examples could be given. [27]

Instead of giving a deputy a fixed sum for each day he spent away from home, a jurisdiction sometimes offered to pay a small salary and expenses. In 1588 Guy Hurault and Joachim Gervaise, two deputies of the town of Orléans, set out for Blois accompanied by two servants. Both Hurault and Gervaise were paid 30 sous a day for their services. In addition, they were allowed all their expenses, including transportation, wine for their boatmen on the Loire, a furnished room at Blois at 67-1/2 livres per month, a tip of 15 sous to the concierge of the hôtel de ville at Blois where the third estate met, 12 sous, 6 deniers for Masses celebrated for their souls, and the wages of their servants at 10 sous each per day. The total cost of the deputation

was about 1,420 livres, but the sum would have been greater had not Hurault
fled from Blois on the day of the assassination of the Duke of Guise, thereby
remaining away from home thirty-nine days fewer than his companion.[28]

Occasionally, a community made special gifts to their deputies. Lyon
provided her representatives with some big hams in 1588, and Nevers sent a
large cask of wine to Guy Coquille the same year.[29]

On the whole, the compensation given the deputies fluctuated violently
during the fifteenth century, but steadily increased with the inflation of the
sixteenth century. The increase continued after 1600, and the crown paid 600
sous per day to most of those who attended the Assembly of Notables at
Rouen in 1626. In England the legal wage of four shillings per day for knights
of the shire and two for the burgesses was established during the fourteenth
century and remained in effect throughout the Renaissance. As a result the
compensation paid the French deputies of the nobility and third estate increased from three to nine times that of their English counterparts in 1484,
to from ten to fourteen times in 1614, despite the greater decline in value of
French currency. It is difficult to explain the wide difference in the pay
scales between the two countries. Perhaps the cost of living was higher in
France; yet surely the basic factor must have been the ability of the English
constituencies to find deputies at a lower rate. This does not hide the fact
that the English salaries inflicted grave injustice on those who were elected
to go to Westminister, for they could not hope to live within their allowance.
Nevertheless, the cost of representation was so great that the boroughs gradually ceased to elect their own inhabitants in favor of the "foreigner" who was
willing to serve without compensation. The result was the highly aristocratic
Parliament of the sixteenth, seventeenth, and eighteenth centuries. This situation may reflect indifference on the part of the burgesses, but it could not
have developed if the English gentry had not been sufficiently interested in
Parliament to volunteer to serve without pay. The French gentleman had too
little belief in the importance of the Estates General to be willing to make a
comparable financial sacrifice. It was the royal official, and not the country
gentleman, who gradually supplanted the bourgeois in the national assemblies.

Indeed, the only case that has been found of anyone in France offering to
serve free in return for election was that of a royal official of La Rochelle
and Aunis in 1614. This official charged the sergeants who delivered the
messages to the parishes concerning the elections to say that he wished to be
chosen and in return would pay his own expenses. He was selected as one of
the three deputies of the third estate of the jurisdiction.[30]

There were several instances of deputies offering to serve free after
election. The royal ordonnance for the payment of the deputies to the Estates
General of 1560 stated that archbishops and bishops were not to be recom-
pensed because some of them had expressed willingness to forego pay, a
generosity which doubtless resulted from the strong feeling in many quarters
against the prelates at that time. A bishop who was a deputy from Brittany
was paid nevertheless, and perhaps others also. After their election in 1649,
two deputies of the clergy of the bailiwick of Chaumont-en-Bassigny announced
their intention to serve without pay because of the poverty of the local clergy.
Their offer was to cost them little because that assembly was never held.[31]

There are several instances of deputies who expressed willingness to
serve for less than the normal wage because they had to go to court anyway,
and even of someone who agreed to go for less than the usual wage in return
for election. In 1614 the procureur of the town of Lyon wanted to be named
assistant deputy to the provost of the merchants, and his request was granted
on the condition that he would be paid only his expenses and his usual salary
as procureur. He was denied only his special stipend as deputy — scarcely a
sacrifice to be compared with that made by every deputy who made the trip to

Westminster. But even such cases were extremely rare.[32] The deputy in France remained essentially the representative of his locality, where he was, with very few exceptions, a prominent resident paid for his service. He almost never thought that a seat in the Estates General was so desirable that he offered to go at his own expense. The result was that the French deputy never broke from his locality, as his counterpart did in England, or came to think of himself as representing the nation as a whole. The practice of free service, which had already begun in Tudor England and became universal after 1695, never really appeared in France.

The French deputies may have been more fortunate than those of England in the amount they were supposed to be paid, but they often had difficulty collecting. Generally a year or more was needed after the Estates General had closed to assess the special tax to pay the deputies even when there was no dispute. The bailiwick assembly to divide the tax to pay the deputies of Vermandois to the Estates General of 1560 did not meet until April, 1562. In 1589 it was reported that several Burgundian deputies to the Estates General of 1576 had not been paid half their wages. Compiègne delayed ten years before paying her share of the salary of the deputy of the bailiwick of Senlis to the second estates of Blois. The deputy of the nobility of the bailiwick of Rouen in 1588 had to wait until 1608 for payment, and the representative of the nobility of Provence to Blois in 1576 was still seeking payment in 1581. Ten years elapsed before the heirs of the deputies of the nobility of Vermandois in 1588 could collect the salaries due them. These examples could be multiplied almost without end.[33]

No doubt the difficulty of collecting salaries influenced many men to avoid election. Several courses could be followed by those who were named deputies. They could insist on an advance payment of part of what was likely to be owed them by the end of the assembly. This method was most successful where the provincial estates or the towns were to pay the deputies. In either case there was a local treasury which usually contained the necessary funds. The deputies of the third estate of Provence got advances in 1588 and 1591. The delegates of Périgueux did likewise in 1468; and those of Lyon, in 1576. The delegate of Amiens to the estates in 1593 was absent so long that the town made several payments to his wife who remained at home. Sometimes deputies found it necessary to write the échevins of their municipalities during the Estates General asking for funds, saying that they had reached the end of their personal resources. Such recourse was not open to the deputies of the bailiwicks, since the special tax to pay them was levied only after their service was complete. Fortunate indeed were the representatives of the clergy of Péronne in 1576 who wrangled a small advance from those who assembled to elect them. By and large, the deputies were forced to provide for the costs of their services from their own funds with only the hope of eventual reimbursement to comfort them.[34]

Frequently, deputies found it necessary on their return to apply forceful persuasion to secure payment. In 1484 a deputy of the bailiwick of Senlis refused to show his constituents a copy of the cahier the Estates General had submitted until he had been paid. Before they left the Estates General, deputies usually took the precaution of getting a writ from the chancellery ordering their payment, although there was a heavy fee for this service. A deputy from Ponthieu to the Estates General of 1576 paid 10 livres, but in 1614 the protests of the estates led the chancellor to reduce the charge to 3-1/2 livres. Frequently royal officials showed no haste in honoring the crown's directives. It took four years and numerous orders before the deputy of the provostship of Paris in 1614 could get his salary.[35]

These episodes were discouraging to those who had braved the dangers of a journey to court and had suffered the inconveniences of living away from home in the crowded little towns where the French kings all too often assembled the nation. Their sacrifices could have been compensated for only by the feeling that they had accomplished much at the Estates General and that the people were grateful for their efforts. Instead, they were frequently greeted on their return by complaints of the cost of their expedition, and neither they, the people, nor the crown found much cause for rejoicing in their work. Little wonder there were few demands for holding the Estates General.

This situation did not result from a diabolical plot on the part of the kings. They had had no fixed preconceived ideas on how the elections to the Estates General should be held and had made almost no rules defining who was eligible to be deputies. The royal officials and the leading inhabitants of a locality had been left to their own devices. Only when disputes had been appealed to the king in council had the crown intervened. On these occasions the government's decisions had favored the privileges of the clergy, nobility, and urban patricians at the expense of the local royal officials who had been attempting to expand the crown's, and incidentally their own, authority at the expense of the traditional leaders of society.

Perhaps it was the very unwillingness or inability of the crown to intervene effectively that led to the difficulty. Detailed, precise, uniform instructions that were enforced would have removed the infinite variations in the electoral procedures of different jurisdictions and prevented many disputes. If the bailiwicks and seneschalsies alone had been allowed to elect deputies and if they had always chosen the same number, much of the confusion that took place in the Estates General would have been avoided as will be shown in a later volume. If a more regular procedure had been adopted for the payment of the deputies, they would have been spared worry, inconvenience, and quarrels with their constituents. But it does little good to speculate in this manner; for if the state had been absolute, rational, and ordered, if it had been "the fruit of reflection and careful adaptation,"[36] it would not have been the Renaissance Monarchy.

REFERENCE MATTER

APPENDIX A

Towns Convoked to Assemblies

Town	1483[1]	1485[2]	1506[3]	1517[4]	1596[5]
Abbeville	A	. . . .	A	. . . .	C
Amiens	A	. . . .	A	A	CA
Angers	A	C	A	. . . .	C
Arles	. . . .	. . . .	. . . .	. . . .	C
Arras	A	. . . .	. . . .	. . . .	. . . .
Auxerre	A	. . . .	. . . .	. . . .	. . . .
Bayonne	. . . .	. . . .	. . . .	A	. . . .
Bordeaux	A	C	A	A	CA
Bourges	A	C	A	A	CA
Boulogne-sur-Mer	. . . .	. . . .	. . . .	A	. . . .
Caen	A	. . . .	. . . .	. . . .	. . . .
Châlons-sur-Marne	. . . .	. . . .	. . . .	. . . .	C
Chartres	A	. . . .	. . . .	. . . .	. . . .
Clermont in Auvergne	A	. . . .	. . . .	. . . .	CA
Cremeaux	. . . .	C	. . . .	. . . .	. . . .
Dijon	. . . .	C	A	A	C
Grenoble	. . . .	. . . .	. . . .	A	C
Laon	A	. . . .	. . . .	. . . .	. . . .
La Rochelle	A	C	. . . .	A	C
Le Mans	A	. . . .	. . . .	. . . .	CA
Limoges	A	C	. . . .	A	. . . .
Lyon	A	C	A	A	CA
Mâcon	. . . .	C	. . . .	. . . .	. . . .
Marseille	. . . .	. . . .	. . . .	. . . .	C
Mirabel	. . . .	C	. . . .	. . . .	. . . .
Montpellier	. . . .	C	A	A	. . . .
Moulins	. . . .	. . . .	. . . .	. . . .	CA
Orléans	A	. . . .	A	A	C

Town	1483	1485	1506	1517	1596
Paris	A	C	A	A	CA
Perpignan	....	C	....	....	....
Poitiers	A	C	....	....	C
Reims	A	....	A	....	C
Rennes	....	....	....	....	C
Riom	....	....	....	....	CA
Romans-sur-Isère	....	C	....	....	....
Rouen	A	C	A	A	CA
Saint-Lô	....	C	....	....	....
Sainte-Menehould	....	C	....	....	....
Saint-Pourçain	....	C	....	....	....
Saint-Quentin	....	C	....	....	....
Sens	....	....	A	....	....
Thérouanne	A	....	....	....	....
Toulouse	....	C	A	A	....
Tournay	....	C	....	....	....
Tours	A	C	A	A	C
Troyes	A	C	A	A	C
Total	23	24	16(20)	17	C=24 A=10

A Attended
C Convoked

[1]Thierry, II, 410-11. This is the complete list of the towns represented.

[2]Procès-verbaux des séances du conseil de régence du roi Charles VIII. CDI, ed. Adhelm Bernier (Paris, 1836), p. 211. The wide difference between the localities summoned in 1485 and those called on other occasions is explained by the decision to convoke towns with mints in that year because coinage problems were to be considered. This indicates how the composition of the Renaissance assemblies was varied with their purpose.

[3]About twenty towns attended. IAC, Rouen, I, 94. The sixteen towns listed are compiled from a variety of sources.

[4]BN, MS. n.a. fr. 7,144, fols. 5v-7v. This is the complete list of the towns that sent deputies. The estates of Brittany and Provence were also represented.

[5]Mayer, XVI, 1-8.

THE DEPUTIES TO THE ESTATES GENERAL

Deputies of the First Estate (Clergy)

Deputies	1484	1560	1561	1576	1588	1593	1614
Secular Benefices							
Archbishops	2	1	1	4	5	3	10[3]
Bishops	19(-1)	10	5	20	20	12(-2)	55[4](-6)
Vicars-General and Grand Vicars	2	5	1	1	5	1	1
Chapters	8	41	13	41(-2)	52	16	27
Archdeacons and Archpriests	0	6	1	13(-1)	9	0	4
Other important Benefices	0	7	1	5	6	2	6[5](-1)
Curés	1	6	1	3	11	6	9
Total	32(-1)	76	23	87(-3)	108	40(-2)	112(-7)
Regular Benefices							
Abbots	20	15	2	15(-3)	15(-2)	5	19
Priors	0	7	0	3	11	4[2]	16(-1)
Other important Benefices	0	0	0	0	2[1]	0	1
Brothers	2	3	0	1	0	0	1
Total	22	25	2	19(-3)	28(-2)	9	37(-1)
Unknown	25	26	0	10	0	1	0
Total Elected	79(-1)	127	25	116(-6)	136(-2)	50(-2)	149(-8)
Number Present	78(+)	127	25	110	134	48	141

(-) Indicates the number of deputies counted more than once because they had been elected by two or more jurisdictions.

(+) Indicates a meeting in which additional deputies are known to have been present.

[1] Includes a representative of the Knights of Saint John of Jerusalem.

[2] Includes a representative of the Order of Cluny.

[3] Includes three archbishops who were invited to take seats by the clergy after the Estates General had begun to meet.

[4] Includes one bishop who was invited to take a seat by the clergy after the Estates General had begun to meet.

[5] Includes two general agents of the clergy of France who had not been elected by a bailiwick.

Deputies of the Second Estate (Nobility)

Deputies	1484	1560	1561	1576	1588	1593	1614
Princes and Marquises	0	0	. . .	0	0	1	9
Counts	2	0	. . .	1	3	0	14
Viscounts	3	1	. . .	2	6	0	6
Vidames	0	1	. . .	0	0	0	1
Barons, Seigneurs, Écuyers, and Sieurs	52	72(-1)	. . .	74(-2)	94(-2)	26(-3)	109(-3)
Unknown	23	33	25	14(-3)	1	0	0
Total Elected	80	107(-1)	25	91(-5)	104(-2)	27(-3)	139(-3)
Number Present	80(+)	106(+)	25	86	102	24	136

(-) Indicates the number of deputies counted more than once because they had been elected by two or more jurisdictions.

(+) Indicates a meeting in which additional deputies are known to have been present.

Deputies of the Third Estate

Deputies	1560	1561	1576	1588	1593	1614
Royal Officials						
Lt. Generals, Civils, Particulars, or Criminals, and Presidents of Presidial Seats	6	4	24	28	6	61
Provosts and Judges of Subordinate Seats	1	2	24(-1)	27	2	15
Procureurs and Advocates of the King	3	5	10	20	5	16
Tax Officials	1	0	4	8	2	2
Other Royal Officials	4	2	6	5	11	4
Total	15	13	68(-1)	88	26	98
Municipal Officials						
Mayors, etc.	4	1	9	7	4	13
Échevins, Councilors, etc.	4	1	20	32	8	31
Other Town Officials	2	2	4	10	4	7
Total	10	4	33	49	16	51

Deputies	1560	1561	1576	1588	1593	1614
Other Inhabitants of Towns						
Advocates and Lawyers	4	6	27	21(-1)	7	12
Bourgeois and Merchants	6	0	12	14	3(-1)	6
Doctors of Medicine	1	0	3	2	0	0
University Professors	0	0	0	3	0	0
Merchants and Farmers	0	0	1	0	0	0
Total	11	6	43	40(-1)	10(-1)	18
Others						
Officials of Provincial and Local Estates	1	2	5	4	1	13
Officials of Nobles	0	0	1	1	0	3
Farmers	0	0	2	0	1	0
Unknown	184	3	36	20	2	15
Total	185	5	44	25	4	31
Total Elected	221	28	188(-1)	202(-1)	56(-1)	198
Number Present	221(+)	28	187	201	55	198

(-) Indicates the number of deputies counted more than once because they had been elected by two or more jurisdictions.

(+) Indicates a meeting in which additional deputies are known to have been present.

The tables above showing the rank and status of the deputies to the Estates General are an approximation only. In the first place, any classification is arbitrary, for many deputies held more than one position or office. Each deputy has been assigned in accordance with his highest title or most important function except that those who were both royal and municipal officials have been classified with the latter, and members of chapters who held abbeys or priories have been counted as abbots or priors even though they held these benefices in commendam. A second difficulty grows out of the incomplete nature of the documents themselves. For some meetings of the Estates General almost nothing survives; for others there is only a list of those who signed the cahiers, but for still others we have the clerk's record of those who attended. The statistical tables above were formed by comparing and compiling the various lists. Additional names have been added when documents from the local archives show conclusively that someone attended. Mere election to the Estates General provided no assurance of actual participation. Local histories, manuscripts, and other documents have been used to determine the status of a given deputy and the Gallia Christiana and Gallia Regia have been of assistance. These tables could be further refined, especially for 1484 when I was not always sure of the estate from which a deputy came, but it is doubtful if additional research would provide enough information to alter the basic conclusions reached.

Deputies with Prior Service in the Estates General [1]

	Clergy			Nobility			Third Estate			Total		
	Total	Prior Service		Total	Prior Service		Total	Prior Service		Total	Prior Service	
Year	No.	No.	%	No.	No.	%	No.	No.	%	No.	No.	%
1561	25	15	60.0	25	8	32.0	28	12	42.9	78	35	44.9
1576	110	10	9.1	86	3	3.5	187	13	7.0	383	26	6.8
1588	134	16	11.9	102	9	8.8	201	23	11.4	437	48	11.0
1593	48	9	18.8	24	3	12.5	55	7	12.7	127	19	15.0
1614	141	4	2.8	136	6	4.3	198	7	3.5	475	17	3.6
Total	458	54	11.8	373	29	7.8	669	62	9.3	1500	145	9.7

[1] No deputy has been counted more than once regardless of the number of jurisdictions that elected him. I have excluded the restricted assemblies in 1558, 1575, and 1596 from consideration. The first two were very brief, and the procedure followed in the three meetings differed somewhat from that used when there were bailiwick elections.

NOTES

Abbreviations

AC	Archives Communales
AD	Archives Départementales
AN	Archives Nationales
BEC	Bibliothèque de l'École des Chartes
Bernard	Procès-verbaux des États généraux de 1593. CDI, ed. Auguste-J. Bernard (Paris, 1842)
B. Mun.	Bibliothèque Municipale
BN	Bibliothèque Nationale
BN, MS. fr.	Bibliothèque Nationale, Manuscrits françaises
BN, Ms. n. a. fr.	Bibliothèque Nationale, Manuscrits nouvelles acquisitions françaises
BR	Charles-A. Bourdot de Richebourg, Nouveau Coutumier général (Paris, 1724), 4 vols.
CDI	Collection de documents inédits sur l'histoire de France
Dumont	Corps universel diplomatique du droit des gens..., ed. Jean Dumont (Amsterdam, 1726-31), 8 vols.
FGC	Forme générale et particulière de la convocation et de la tenue des assemblées nationales ou États généraux de France, eds. Lalourcé and Duval (Paris, 1789), 3 vols.
HL	Claude de Vic and Jean Vaissete, Histoire générale de Languedoc (Toulouse, 1874-1905), 16 vols.
IAC	Inventaire sommaire des archives communales antérieures à 1790
IAD	Inventaire sommaire des archives départementales antérieures à 1790
Isambert	Recueil général des anciennes lois françaises depuis l'an 420 jusqu'à la révolution de 1789, eds. François-A. Isambert and others (Paris, 1821-33), 29 vols.
Masselin	Jehan Masselin, Journal des États généraux de France tenus à Tours en 1484. CDI, ed. A. Bernier (Paris, 1835)
Mayer	Des États généraux et les autres assemblées nationales, ed. Charles J. Mayer (Paris, 1788-89), 18 vols.
RCG	Recueil des cahier généraux des trois ordres aux États généraux, eds. Lalourcé and Duval (Paris, 1789), 4 vols.
RPO	Recueil de pièces originales et authentiques, concernant la tenue des États généraux, eds. Lalourcé and Duval (Paris, 1789), 9 vols.
SHF	Société de l'histoire de France
Thierry	Recueil des monuments inédits de l'histoire du tiers état. CDI, ed. Jacques Augustin Thierry (Paris, 1853-70), 4 vols.

NOTES

Chapter 1

[1] Johan Huizinga, The Waning of the Middle Ages (London, 1924).

[2] For an account of the various types of representative institutions see J. Russell Major, Representative Institutions in Renaissance France, 1421-1559 (Madison, 1960).

[3] Letters of convocation have been published in many places. For the reign of Charles VII, see especially A. Thomas, "Les États généraux sous Charles VII. Étude chronologique d'après des documents inédits," Le Cabinet historique, ser. 2, II (1878), 212-21. For the reigns of Louis XI and Charles VIII, see P. Viollet, "Élections des députés aux États généraux réunis à Tours en 1468 et en 1484," BEC, XXVII (1866), 24-25, 33; Lettres de Louis XI, SHF, eds. Étienne Charavay and Joseph Vaesen (Paris, 1883-1909), 11 vols.; and Lettres de Charles VIII. SHF, ed. Paul Pélicier (Paris, 1898-1905), 5 vols. For the sixteenth and seventeenth centuries see FGC, II, and Mayer, VII, 302-57.

[4] A. Thomas, "Le Midi et les États généraux sous Charles VII," Annales du Midi, IV (1892), 17. Roland Delachenal, Histoire de Charles V (Paris, 1927), I, 251. C. H. Taylor, "The Composition of the Baronial Assemblies in France, 1315-20," Speculum, XXIX (1954), 433-59; and "Assemblies of French towns in 1316," Speculum, XIV (1939), 275-99. Henri Hervieu, Recherches sur les premiers États généraux (Paris, 1879), pp. 57-60. See Appendix B.

[5] See Appendix A for towns participating in meetings in 1483, 1485, 1506, 1517, and 1596.

[6] Mayer, IX, 204-10. R. Charlier-Meniolle, L'Assemblée des Notables tenue à Rouen en 1596 (Paris, 1911), pp. 52, 129-34. Georges Picot, Histoire des États généraux (Paris, ed. of 1888), IV, 256, 275-76.

[7] See Major, pt. I, chap. iii, sect. iii. Large bailiwicks or provinces were also sometimes ordered to send two deputies from each estate, e.g., Vermandois in 1484. G. Hérelle, "Documents inédits sur les États généraux tirés des archives de Vitry-le-François," Mem. de la soc. des sciences et arts de Vitry-le-François, IX (1878), 198-200.

[8] G. Post, "Plena Potestas and Consent in Medieval Assemblies," Traditio, I (1943), 355-408; and "Roman Law and Early Representation in Spain and Italy, 1150-1250," Speculum, XVIII (1943), 211-32. Thomas went so far as to deny the title of Estates General to assemblies in which full powers were not required in the letters of convocation; A. Thomas "Les États généraux sous Charles VII," Revue historique, XL (1889), 79-80.

[9] Thomas, Le Cabinet historique (1878), 212. FGC, II, 49.

[10] Paul M. Viollet, Droit publique. Histoire des institutions politiques et administratives de la France (Paris, 1903), III, 197-99.

[11] C. H. Taylor, "An Assembly of French Towns in March 1318," Speculum, XIII (1938), 299, n. 2.

[12] FGC, II, 21-26.

[13] Thierry, II, 830-34.

[14] FGC, II, 28-31. The full description of the powers to be granted was "avec amples instructions, et pouvoirs suffisans, pour, selon les bonnes, anciennes et louables coutumes de ce royaume, nous faire entendre de la part des dits états, tant leurs dittes plaintes et doléances, que ce qui leur semblera tourner au bien public, soulagement et repos d'un chacun, ensemble les moyens qui leur sembleront plus propres et moins dommageables pour entretenir notre état, et délivrer notre dit royaume de la nécessité en laquelle ils le voyent réduit, à notre très grand regret. . . ."

[15] BN, MS. fr. 8,277, pp. 551-53.

[16] As examples of procurations during the Renaissance, see Bernard, pp. 578-79, 581-84, 598. For the verification of powers, see as examples, RPO, III, 148-82; IV, pt. II, 3-37; VII, 13-35; VIII, 16-17.

[17] For some different interpretations of these problems see, Post, Traditio, I (1943), 355-56, 383-408. R. H. Lord, "The Parliaments of the Middle Ages and the Early Modern Period," Catholic Historical Review, XVI (1930), 138; Owen Ulph, "The Mandate System and Representation to the Estates General under the old Regime," Journal of Modern History, XXIII (1951), 225-31; and Edmond Charleville, Les États généraux de 1576 (Paris, 1901), pp. 70-90 should be added.

[18] Taylor, Speculum, XIII (1938), 299-300.

[19] Charles de Grandmaison, "Nouveaux Documents sur les États généraux du XV siècle," Bul. de la soc. archéologique de Touraine, IV (1877-79), 144-48.

[20] Archives historiques du département de la Gironde, VIII (1866), 537-38. Mayer, XI, 169-85.

[21] Post, Traditio, I (1943), 358, 364.

[22] For example, the deputies of the third estate of Berry in 1614 were "donné plein pouvoir, puissance et mandement spécial de comparoir auxdits Etats qui seront tenus en ladite ville de Sens, le dixième de septembre prochain, faire les remontrances, requêtes et déclarations contenues par les cahiers dudit pays, résoudre et adhérer à la pluralité des voix dudit tiers-état qui sera assemblé suivant ladite convocation, et généralement faire et procurer pour le bien et utilité dudit pays, décharge et soulagement dudit tiers-état, tout ce qu'ils verront bon être, jaçoit qu'il ne soit particulierement exprimé esdits cahiers, et que le cas requiert mandement plus spécial." FGC, II, 157. However, in extreme cases the minority might insist on recording its position in the procès-verbal. This occurred in 1561. J. R. Major, "The Third Estate in the Estates General of Pontoise, 1561," Speculum, XXIX (1954), 469. For an explanation based on Roman law of why unanimity was not necessary see G. Post, "A Roman Legal Theory of Consent, Quod Omnes Tangit in Medieval Representation," Wisconsin Law Review (1950), pp. 71-78.

[23] Thus in 1576 the third estate of Agenais prepared "un cayer des plainctes générales et autre cayer des plainctes particullières et porra celluy qui faira le dict voyage adjouster ny diminuer aulcune choze auxdits cayers." G. Tholin, "Les Cahiers du pays d'Agenais aux États généraux," Revue de l'Agenais, IX (1882), 507. Post equates the "full powers" with the "sufficient instructions" requested in the letters of convocation, but he recognizes the existence of a second kind of instructions given to proctors by their constituents. These were the cahiers. Post, Traditio, I (1943), 396.

[24] As examples of this correspondence, see Gaston Du Fresne de Beaucourt, Histoire de Charles VII (Paris, 1885), III, 501-9; and Correspondance de la Mairie de Dijon. Analecta Divionensia, ed. Joseph Garnier (Dijon, 1868-70), especially vol. II.

[25] Lord, p. 138.

[26] Hippolyte Abord, Histoire de la Reformé et la Ligue dans la ville d'Autun (Paris, 1855), I, 140-41.

[27] RPO, II, 85-87; III, 293-94. Saint-Quentin also wished to disavow Bodin. G. Lecocq, "Cahiers de doléances de la prévôté de Saint-Quentin aux États généraux de Blois de 1576," Le Vermandois, IV (1876), 133-35.

[28] Gustave Dupont-Ferrier, Les Officiers royaux des bailliages et sénéchaussées (Paris, 1902), pp. 53-229. Roger Doucet, Les Institutions de la France au XVIe siècle (Paris, 1948), I, 251-70.

[29] RPO, VI, 144-45.

[30] Mayer, VII, 386-87. FGC, II, 53. In 1521 the use of proctors was forbidden in the assembly of the estates of Saintonge to codify the custom, but individuals sent proctors anyway. BR, IV, 864-65.

[31] André Bossuat has recently dealt with this problem at the local level. See his Le Bailliage royal de Montferrand, 1425-1556 (Paris, 1957).

[32] See Doucet, I, 360-402, for a good discussion of town and village government.

[33] Antonin Debidour, La Fronde angevine, tableau de la vie municipale au XVIIe siècle (Paris, 1877), pp. 176-77. HL, XIV, 237.

[34] B. Mun., Blois, MS 89, fols. 12-13. FGC, II, 265-66.

Chapter 2

[1] Thierry, II, 816-26, 923-24, 998-1003, 1007-8, 1038. Bibl. du Sénat, MS. 379, fol. 174. IAC, Beauvais, ed. Renaud Rose (Beauvais, 1887), p. 16. IAC, Amiens, ed. Georges Durand (Amiens, 1897), III, 94.

[2] Studies on the elections in Amiens are M. Lavernier, "Mémoire sur ce qui s'est passé à Amiens à l'occasion des divers États généraux de France," Mém. de la soc. des antiquaires de Picardie, V (1842), 275-314; L. Fournier, "Mémoire être joint au recueil des actes trouvés aux archives de la ville d'Amiens concernant les États généraux," Bul. de la conférance littéraire et scientifique de Picardie, II (1881), 48-65; and more important, Édouard Maugis, Recherches sur les transformations du régime politique et social de la ville d'Amiens, des origines de la commune à la fin du XVIe siècle (Paris, 1906), pp. 202-13. The bulk of the relevant documents have been published in Thierry, II-III, and IAC, Amiens, I-V.

[3] Thierry, II, 403.

[4] Ibid., 422-23.

[5] Thomas Rymer, Foedera, Conventiones, Literae (The Hague, 1741), V, pt. 4, 92-93, 103. BR, I, 113-17. Dumont, IV, pt. II, 41-42.

[6] Thierry, II, 418. BR, I, 118-19. Dumont, IV, pt. II, 41-42.

[7] Maugis, pp. 78-156. Thierry, II, 88-90, 124-25, 407.

[8] Thierry, II, 504-39.

[9] AC, Amiens, BB 31, fols. 28-29v. Thierry, II, 655-56.

[10] AC, Amiens, BB 33, fols. 177 and 182v. Thierry, II, 668-73.

[11] BN, MS. fr. 3,953, fol. 2; MS. fr. 4,812, fols. 8-19v. Thierry, II, 673-77.

[12] BR, I, 200-219.

[13] Thierry, II, 816-26; 830-34.

[14] Ibid., 851-63.

[15] AC, Amiens, AA 16, fols. 170v-71. Adrien Huguet, Histoire d'une ville picarde, Saint-Valery, de la Ligue à la Révolution (Paris, 1909), I, 291, n. 2.

[16] Thierry, II, 972-73, 1016-17, 1036-41. RPO, IV, pt. II, 154. BN, MS. n. a. fr. 7,755, fols. 347-53v. Bernard, pp. 580-81.

[17] AC, Amiens, BB 55, fols. 20 bis, 49, 51v, 57, 59, 87, 89, 96, 97.

[18] Thierry, III, 5-10.

[19] Ibid., 86-90.

[20] Ibid., II, 862-63.

[21] When the bailiff or the lieutenant general of Amiens received orders to convoke the bailiwick, he met with other officials to determine the procedure to be followed. BR, I, 113. Dumont, IV, pt. II, 41. IAC, Amiens, II, 438. Thierry, II, 670.

[22] Émile Coët, Histoire de la ville de Roye (Paris, 1880), I, 259. Victor de Beauvillé, Histoire de la ville de Montdidier (Paris, 1875), I, 167-68.

[23] BR, II, 593-94.

[24] BN, MS. Moreau 1,427, fol. 192v. RPO, I, 6, 26-27.

[25] Coët, I, 280.

[26] BR, II, 642-58.

[27] BN, MS. fr. 3,329, fols. 20-47v. Beauvillé, I, 220.

[28] J. Gosselin, "La Ligue à Péronne," La Picardie, XVI (1870), 271. RCG, II, 121, 183. Coët, I, 294.

[29] Beauvillé, I, 231-32. Mayer, XIV, 340-41. RPO, IV, pt. II, 29-30.

[30] Beauvillé, I, 248-49. BN, MS. fr. 7,525, fols. 44v-45.

[31] BN, MS. Moreau, 1,427, fols. 188-89. RPO, V, pt. II, 25, 53, 76; VI, 71; VII, 22. Mayer, XVI, 152. Bibl. de l'Arsenel, MS. 4,255, fol. 13. Eustache de Sachy, Essais sur l'histoire de Péronne (Péronne, 1866), p. 272.

[32] BN, MS. Moreau, 1,427, fols. 190-91.

[33] BR, I, 81-82. BN, MS. Mélanges de Colbert, 366, no. 317.

[34] Thierry, IV, 404-22. Albéric de Calonne, "Réparation entre les gentilshommes tenant fiefs nobles en Ponthieu de l'idemnité allouée à messire André de Bourbon Rubempré, délégué aux États généraux de Blois en 1577," Mém. de la soc. des antiquaires de Picardie, XXIII (1873), 71-98. Ernest Prarond, La Ligue à Abbeville, 1576-1594 (Paris, 1868), I, 142-44, extract from Mém. de la soc. d'émulation d'Abbeville, XI-XII (1861-72).

[35] Thierry, IV, 455-57. Prarond, II, 9-14.

[36] Bernard, pp. 47 and 58. Prarond, III, 27-37.

[37] Thierry, IV, 497-98.

[38] IAC, Abbeville, ed. Alcius Ledieu (Abbeville, 1902), p. 24.

[39] BR, I, 25-26. Rymer, V, pt. IV, 104. BN, MS. Mélanges de Colbert, 366, no. 316.

[40] BR, I, 70-78.

[41] Auguste d'Hauttefeuille and Louis Bénard, Histoire de Boulogne-sur-Mer (Boulogne-sur-Mer, 1860), I, 303-13, 337-38. Joseph-Hector de Rosny, Histoire de Boulonnais (Amiens, 1868), III, 341-44, 382-83. AD, Pas-de-Calais, IX B 2, fols. 150-202v.

[42] Hauttefeuille and Bénard, I, 375-83, 397-98. Rosny, III, 442-45. BN, MS. fr. 18,186, fols. 52v-53. AD, Pas-de-Calais, IX B 5, fols. 22-34v.

[43] Rosny, III, 382. Abbé Lefebvre, Histoire générale et particulière de la ville de Calais (Paris, 1766), II, 385, names only two deputies for 1576. RPO, III, 172; IV, pt. II, 29; V, pt. II, 52, 76. BR, I 18-22.

Chapter 3

[1] Auguste Lognon, "L'Île-de-France, son origine, ses limites, ses gouverneurs," Mém. de la soc. de l'histoire de Paris et de l'Ile-de-France, I (1875), 1-43. Bibl. du Sénat, MS. 379, fols. 181v-82.

[2] Georges Hérelle, "Documents inédits sur les États généraux tirés des archives de Vitry-le-François," Mém. de la soc. des sciences et arts de Vitry-le-François, IX (1878), 195-98. IAC, Châlons-sur-Marne, ed. Paul Pélicier (Châlons, 1903), p. 48.

[3] Hérelle, pp. 198-200. IAC, Châlons-sur-Marne, p. 48. IAC, Laon, ed. Victor Dessein (Laon, 1885), ser. CC, p. 74.

[4] BN, MS. Mélanges de Colbert 370, no. 374. BR, II, 539-81.

[5] Amédée Combier, Étude sur le bailliage de Vermandois (Paris, 1874), pp. 86-88, 144-62. AC, Châlons-sur-Marne, BB 11, fol. 34v; AA 16, fols. 1-36. An extract from the cahier of the third estate of Vermandois, 1560, has been published by Georges Hérelle in La Réforme et la Ligue en Champagne (Paris, 1892), II, 11-14.

[6] G. Lecocq, "Cahiers de doléances de la prévôté de Saint-Quentin aux États généraux de Blois de 1576," Le Vermandois, IV (1876), 124-70. RPO, II, 72, 74-75, 85-87; III, 162, 293-94. Mayer, XIII, 224.

[7] AC, Châlons-sur-Marne, AA 16; BB 13, fol. 110. RPO, II, 110, 118-19.

[8] Bernard, pp. 9, 778-79, 792-95. Louis Paris, "Procès-verbal de l'élection des députés de Reims, pour les États généraux d'Orléans, 18 dec. 1590," Bul. du comité historique des monuments écrits de l'histoire de France, I (1849), 150-52.

[9] Mayer, XVI, 2-3. AC, Châlons-sur-Marne, AA 16; BB 16, fols. 150, 154.

[10] Combier, pp. 92-100. AC, Châlons-sur-Marne, AA 16. B. Mun., Reims, MS. 1,700, fols. 1-25v. Bibl. de l'Arsenel, MS. 4,255, fols. 5-7. V. Suin, "Pièces concernant les frais remboursés à des députés aux États généraux de 1614," Bul. de la soc. archéologique, historique et scientifique de Soissons, XX (1866), 196-97.

[11] Combier, pp. 100, 162-64.

[12] AC, Châlons-sur-Marne, AA 16. G. Hanra, "Élections des députés aux États généraux de 1651," Mém. de la soc. d'agriculture, commerce, sciences et arts du département de la Marne, ser. 2, VIII (1904-5), 255-68.

[13] Jules Flammermont, Histoire des institutions municipales de Senlis (Paris, 1881), pp. 98-99, 276-78. P. Viollet, "Élection des députés aux États généraux réunis à Tours en 1468 et en 1484," BEC, XXVII (1866), 28, 41-42, 56. Arthur Bazin, Compiègne sous Louis XI (Paris, 1907), pp. 75-76. H. de L'Épinois, "Notes extraites des archives communales de Compiègne," BEC, XXV (1864), 126, 136.

[14] Dumont, IV, pt. II, 39-41. BR, II, 733-60.

[15] Adhelm Bernier, Monumens inédits de l'histoire de France, 1400-1600. Mémoires originaux concernant principalement les villes d'Amiens, de Beauvais, de Clermont-Oise, de Compiègne, de Crépy, de Noyon, de Senlis et leurs environs (Paris, 1835), pp. 53, 68-69, 147-49.

[16] Henri Prentout, Les États provinciaux de Normandie (Caen, 1925), II, 32-37, extract from Mém. de l'ac. nationale des sciences, arts et belles-lettres de Caen, NS., II. Dumont, IV, pt. II, 39-41. RPO, I, 3, 19; V, pt. II, 12, 53. Registre des délibérations municipales de la ville de Pontoise, 1608-1683, ed. Ernest Mallet (Pontoise, 1899), p. 14. BN, MS. fr. 18,186, fol. 9.

[17] John T. Dupont-White, La ligue à Beauvais (Paris, 1846), pp. xli-xlvi. IAC, Beauvais, ed. Renaud Rose (Beauvais, 1887), pp. 6, 19, 24. "Remonstrances, plaintes et doléances des habitants de Beauvais pour l'assemblée des états de

Blois, 1576," Mém. de la soc. académique, d'archéologie, sciences et arts
du département de l'Oise, I (1847-51),
264-77.
  [18]IAC, Beauvais, p. 25. For quarrel
between Beauvais and Senlis at the Estates General, see AD, Oise, MS. Bailliage de Beauvais. Organisation, limites, bâtiments, LXXX, Collection
Bucquet-aux-Cousteaux; RPO, IV, pt. II,
33-34, 157-60; and BN, MS. fr. 16,236,
fol. 264.
  [19]IAC, Beauvais, p. 25.
  [20]AD, Oise, B 51.
  [21]G. Monbeig, "Notes relatives aux
États généraux de 1614. Analyse des
doléances de la ville de Beauvais et des
cahiers d'aucuns du tiers-état du bailliage de Beauvais," Bul. de la soc.
d'études historiques et scientifiques de
l'Oise, IV (1908), 1-4.
  [22]IAC, Beauvais, p. 33.
  [23]Monbeig, pp. 26-28. BN, MS.
Clairambault 1,099, fols. 129-37v; MS.
Clairambault 742, fols. 17-39. AD, Oise,
B 51.
  [24]BR, II, 777-81, 811-18. BN, MS.
fr. 18,186, fols. 5-6.
  [25]BR, II, 741-42. RPO, II, 30; V, pt.
II, 10, 54; VII, 22. Mayer, XIV, 342.
  [26]The account of the elections in 1614
in Feuilloley, Notice sur le canton de
Magny-en-Vexin (Magny-en-Vexin,
1872), pp. 66, 71-72, is inaccurate. See
Abbé Desprez, Mémoire sur les États
généraux (Lausanne, 1788), pp. 176-79;
RPO, V, 12, 54; VII, 22. BN, MS. fr.
18,186, fols. 239v-40v.
  [27]Georges Picot, "Recherches sur
les quartiniers, cinquanteniers et
dixainiers de la ville de Paris," Mém.
de la soc. de l'histoire de Paris et de
l'Ile-de-France, I (1875), 132-66. Paul
Robiquet, Histoire municipale de Paris
(Paris, 1904), I, 443-76.
  [28]P. Viollet, "Textes relatives à
l'élection des députés du clergé de Paris
aux États généraux de 1484," Mém. de la
soc. de l'histoire de Paris, IV (1877),
157-58, 172-82.
  [29]BR, III, 16-19, 56-75.
  [30]Registres de délibérations du
bureau de la ville de Paris, eds.
François Bonnardot and others (Paris,
1883-88), I, 117-20, 229-30; IV, 516-17.
  [31]Ibid., V, 67-80. FGC, II, 243, 249-
58. Robiquet, I, 500-507.
  [32]Registres... de Paris, V, 84-87,

91-96, 99-100. Robiquet, I, 509-17.
FGC, II, 222-29. Négociations, lettres
et pièces diverses relatives au règne de
François II. CDI, ed. Louis Paris (Paris,
1861), pp. 833-34.
  [33]FGC, II, 229-31, 242-45, 303-23.
Registres... de Paris, VIII, 9-21.
Édouard Barthélemy, Journal d'un curé
ligueur de Paris, sous les trois derniers
Valois (Paris, 1866), pp. 176-78. Robiquet, II, 61-70.
  [34]M. Taillandier, "Élection du député
de la prévôté de Paris aux États généraux
de 1588," BEC, VII (1845-46), 422-59.
FGC, II, 258-69.
  [35]Registres... de Paris, X, 119-24,
129-31, 327-31. AN, LL 165, pp. 874,
876. Bernard, 689-96. Mémoires-
journaux de Pierre de L'Estoile, eds.
Gustave Brunet and others, (Paris, 1875-
96), V, 99.
  [36]Registres... de Paris, XI, 285-86,
317.
  [37]Ibid., XVI, 28-77.
  [38]Ibid., 78-98.
  [39]FGC, II, 236-41, 245-46, 269-87,
366-67. Registres de l'hôtel de ville de
Paris pendant le Fronde. SHF, eds.
Antoine-J. Le Roux de Lincy and Louis-C.
Douët-d'Arcq (Paris, 1846-48), 3 vols.
contains nothing on the elections.
  [40]RPO, II, 87-88; IV, pt. I, 112; pt. II,
34, 75. BN, MS. fr. 16,236, fol. 256v.
Bibl. de l'Institut, MS. 280, fol. 33. H. de
Clercq, "Notice historique sur Cerny,"
Annales de la soc. historique et archéologique du Gâtinais, VIII (1890), 31-36. B.
Mun., Reims, col. P. Tarbé, carton XIII,
no. 26. BN, MS. fr. 7,525, fol. 37-37v.
  [41]E. Grave, "Eustache Pigis, député
du bailliage de Mantes aux États d'Orléans
en 1560, et aux États de Blois de 1576,"
Département de Seine-et-Oise. Commission des antiquités et des arts, XXVI
(1906), 34-35. RPO, IV, pt. II, 73-75.
BN, MS. Vexin, 31, fols. 230-33. Alphonse
Durand and Victor-E. Grave, La Chronique
de Mantes (Mantes, 1883), pp. 342-43,
403-4. BR, III, 196-206.
  [42]BR, III, 427-32, 458-67. AD, Seine-
et-Marne, B 130. Gabriel Leroy, Histoire
de Melun (Melun, 1887), pp. 332-34.
  [43]BR, III, 132-39, 154-66. Joseph Guyot,
Chronique d'une ancienne ville royale,
Dourdan (Paris, 1869), pp. 81-82, 113, 417-
18. BN, MS. fr. 32,926, fols. 41-54. IAC,
Seine-et-Marne, ed. Côme Lemaire
(Fontainebleau, 1880), IV, 26.

Chapter 4

[1] Thomas Rymer, Foedera, Conventiones, literae (The Hague, 1741), V, pt. IV, 92, 96-100.

[2] BR, III, 403-5.

[3] RCG, I, 268-75. M. Bourquelot, "Plaintes et doléances de la ville de Provins aux États généraux d'Orléans, 1560," Bul. du comité historique des monuments écrits de l'histoire de France, I (1849), 271-80. IAD, Seine-et-Marne, ed. Côme Lemaire (Fontaine-bleau, 1880), IV, 322. The third estate of the bailliage prepared a separate cahier again in March, 1561. B. Mun., Provins, MS. 177.

[4] BR, III, 483-84, 530-45. Dumont, IV, pt. II, 26.

[5] C. Jolivot, "Recherches sur l'assemblée des habitants de Tonnerre," Bul. de la soc. des sciences historiques et naturelles de l'Yonne, XXX (1876), 217-47.

[6] FGC, II, 61-64.

[7] Th. Pistollet de Saint-Ferjeux, "Langres pendant la Ligue," Mém. de la soc. historique et archéologique de Langres, II (1861-77), 106. BN, MS. fr. 16,631, fol. 634; and MS. fr. 16,236, fol. 286v. Paul-M. Baudouin, Histoire du protestantisme et de la Ligue en Bourgogne (Auxerre, 1881), I, 136-38. RPO, II, 2, 6, 26; III, 189.

[8] BN, MS. fr. 16,236, fols. 248v, 253-53v, 286v. Saint-Ferjeux, p. 129. RPO, IV, pt. II, 166-67. IAC, Langres, ed. E. Jullien de La Boullaye (Troyes, 1882), pp. 46, 109.

[9] IAC, Langres, pp. 47, 48, 81, 111. BN, MS. fr. 7,525, fols. 41v-42.

[10] T. Boutiot and A. Babeau, "Documents inédits tirés des archives de Troyes et relatifs aux États généraux," Collection de documents inédits relatifs à la ville de Troyes (Troyes, 1878), I, 3-5, 7-25. Théophile Boutiot, Histoire de la ville de Troyes (Paris, 1873), III, 83-85, 238-42, 291-92, 437-38.

[11] Boutiot and Babeau, pp. 6-7. Boutiot, III, 169-74. BR, III, 255-57, 267-69, 277-79.

[12] Boutiot and Babeau, pp. 25-87. Boutiot, III, 462-81.

[13] Boutiot and Babeau, pp. 87-90. Boutiot, III, 483-87. AD, Aube, G 139, cahier of the clergy of Champagne, March 22, 1561, and procès-verbal of

clergy of Champagne, June 10, 1561; C 1,181, cahier of the nobility and clergy of the town of Troyes, May 10, 1561. Mayer, XII, 327-34. Arthur-É Prévost, Le Diocèse de Troyes (Dijon, 1924), II, 244-45. Bibl. du Sénat, MS. 279, fols. 173v-74.

[14] Boutiot and Babeau, pp. xxvi-xxxii, 90-171. Boutiot, IV, 76-89. Salomon, "États généraux de 1576 et 1614. Remonstrances et doléances de la ville de Saint-Florentin en Champagne," Bul. de la soc. des sciences historiques et naturelles de l'Yonne, XVIII (1864), 476-83. FGC, II, 73-75, 103-9, 115-20. AN, Ba 1, cahier of Méry-sur-Seine.

[15] Boutiot and Babeau, pp. 171-91. Boutiot, IV, 162-63. Prévost, II, 392-93.

[16] Boutiot and Babeau, pp. 171-91. Boutiot, IV, 199, 218-21. Bernard, 780-84, 802-4. Prévost, II, 400-401. There were plans to consult the estates of the town and other elements in the bailiwick in December, 1590, but the Estates General was not held.

[17] Boutiot, IV, 285-86.

[18] AC, Troyes, BB carton 16, liasse 2, contains documents on the elections in the subordinate jurisdictions. See nos. 14, 16-20, 31-34, 55-57, and 60 for election in Jaucourt. FGC, II, 58, 64, 75-79, 84-90, 92-99, 102-3, 110-15, 123-24. Salomon, 483-92.

[19] Boutiot, IV, 304-7, 321-25.

[20] Ibid., 395-98.

[21] Ibid., 398-401. AD, Aube, G 141.

[22] Boutiot, IV, 401-6.

[23] BR, III, 328-30. Dumont, IV, pt. II, 26-28.

[24] Georges Hérelle, "Documents inédits sur les États généraux tirés des archives de Vitry-le-François," Bul. de la soc. des sciences et arts de Vitry-le-François, IX (1878), 120-27, 200. Sources de l'histoire d'Épernay. Archives municipales d'Épernay (XVI siècle), eds. Raoul Chandon de Briailles and Henri Bertal (Paris, 1906), I, 154-58. Henri Jadart, Les Remonstrances des habitants de Rethel et du bailliage de Vitry-le-François aux États généraux de Blois en 1588 (Paris, 1905), pp. 6-8, extract from Revue historique ardennaise, XII (1905), 237-77. Chéri Pauffin, Rethel et Gerson (Paris, 1845), pp. 100-105.

[25] BN, MS. Champagne, 111, fols. 156-99v. Hérelle has published an extract from this procès-verbal in La Réforme et la Ligue en Champagne (Paris, 1892),

II, 86-96. The procès-verbal varies greatly from an account based on two memoirs published by Hérelle in his documents on Vitry. In the latter, no quarrel is reported among the nobility, and the three orders are said to have voted together after preparing individual cahiers, Bul. . . . de Vitry-le-François, IX (1878), 127-31.

[26] Hérelle, Bul. . . . de Vitry-le-François, IX (1878), 132-40, 209-22; and La Réforme et la Ligue en Champagne, II, 205-14. Jadart, pp. 9-43. B. Mun., Châlons-sur-Marne, MS. 469.

[27] Hérelle, Bul. . . . de Vitry-le-François, IX (1878), 253-69.

[28] BR, III, 362-64, 372-73. Émile Jolibois, Histoire de la ville de Chaumont (Paris, 1856), 110-11, 130-32, 157-61. BN, MS. n. a. fr. 2,808, fols. 1-10.

[29] Abbé Millard and Alphonse Roserot, "Procès-verbal de l'assemblée des trois ordres du bailliage de Chaumont (Haute-Marne) pour les États généraux convoqués à Orléans en 1649," Mém. de la soc. academique d'agriculture des sciences, arts et belles-lettres du département de l'Aube, XLVII (1883), 321-45.

Chapter 5

[1] Henri Prentout, Les États provinciaux de Normandie, extract from Mém. de l'ac. nationale des sciences, arts et belles-lettres de Caen, N.S. I-III (1925-27). Prentout undoubtedly overlooked the procès-verbaux of 1529 located at BN, MS. fr. 6,199 because the catalogue of manuscripts described them only as "procurations et autres pièces concernant la ratification du traité de Cambray, 1529." Actually 69 of the 72 pieces are related to the ratification in Normandy and provide at least one, and usually two, procès-verbaux of the elections in every viscounty and bailiwick in the province.

[2] Prentout, I, 147-50.

[3] Ibid., II, 44-82; III, 135-40, 206-8.

[4] BN, MS. fr. 6,199, nos. 58 and 35 for the bailiwick assemblies; and nos. 66 and 41 for the viscounty of Bayeux; nos. 25 and 72 for the viscounty of Falaise; and nos. 55 and 47 for the viscounty of Vire. In each the first number given is

for the October assembly and the second is for the one in November. It is not clear whether those present at the bailiwick assembly from the viscounty of Caen first chose their deputy, who then participated with the deputies of the other viscounties and those present for the first two estates in the election of the ecclesiastic and the noble, or whether all of the third estate of the viscounty of Caen who attended voted for each of the deputies of the other two orders and then chose their own representative. The latter seems more probable, for the result of the election of the deputy of the viscounty of Caen was always given in the procès-verbaux after that of the choice of the two individuals who were to stand for the other orders.

[5] For the bailiwick assemblies, see BN, MS. fr. 6,199, nos. 67, 42, 42 bis, and 46. For the viscounty of Avranches, see nos. 63 and 44; of Valognes, nos. 71 and 48; and of Carentan, nos. 69 and 43. The dependent bailiwick of Mortain did not participate in the bailiwick assembly, but for activities of this jurisdiction in late November see nos. 54, 4, 52, 56, 5, 6, 51, and 57.

[6] Only documents for the October meeting have been found. See BN, MS. fr. 6,199, no. 12 for the bailiwick; no. 9 for the viscounty of Orbec; no. 10 for Conches; and no. 11 for Beaumont-le-Roger.

[7] For the bailiwick assemblies, see BN, MS. fr. 6,199, nos. 68, 31, 32, and 33; for the viscounty of Pont-Audemer, nos. 7 and 8; of Auge, nos. 2, 3, and 27; and of Pont-de-l'Arche, nos. 24 and 39. The size of the delegation from the viscounty of Rouen was dictated by the presence of such a large city, but the documents are quite clear that the deputies elected were for the viscounty only, and not two for the town and one for the viscounty as later became the custom. Indeed, the powers given the deputies of the other viscounties seemingly authorized them to participate in the elections of the deputies of the viscounty of Rouen.

[8] For the viscounty of Caudebec, see BN, MS. fr. 6,199, nos. 21 and 34; for Montivilliers, nos. 22 and 49; for Neufchâtel, nos. 65 and 36; for Arques, nos. 70 and 53; and for Gournay, no. 20.

[9] For the bailiwick assembly, see BN, MS. fr. 6,199, no. 13; for the viscounty of

Domfront, nos. 14 and 29; for Argentan, nos. 15 and 40; for Perche, nos. 62 and 30; and for Verneuil, nos. 64 and 37.

[10] For the clergy of the bailiwick of Gisors, see BN, MS. fr. 6,199, nos. 61 and 28; for the nobility see nos. 18 and 50; for the viscounty of Andely, no. 17; for Gisors, nos. 60 and 26; for Lyons, nos. 59 and 38; for Vernon, no. 16; and for Pontoise, no. 19.

[11] BN, MS. fr. 6,199. Prentout, II, 46-57; III, 165-68.

[12] BN, MS. fr. 6,199.

[13] Ibid.

[14] Prentout, II, 50-80; III, 190-96. M. Baudot, "La Représentation de tiers état aux États provinciaux de Normandie," Revue historique de droit français et étranger, ser. 4, XXVI (1948), 164-65; and another article with the same title in Mém de l'ac. nationale des sciences, arts et belles-lettres de Caen, N.S. V (1929), 129-47.

[15] AC, Rouen, A 10, fols. 33-36v.

[16] IAD, Seine-inférieure, ed. Charles de Robillard de Beaurepaire (Paris, 1874), ser. G, II, 263.

[17] AC, Rouen, A 19, fols. 415v-30, 450. IAC, Seine-inférieure, ser. G, II, 271. B. Mun., Rouen, MS. 3,226 (5,741), Henry III to Matignon, October 8, 1576. The effort to prevent a royal official from being a deputy to the Estates General was in keeping with the rule against their serving in the provincial estates. Prentout, II, 87-89.

[18] AC, Rouen, A 20, fols. 382-93. IAD, Seine-inférieure, ser. G, II, 276. RPO, IV, pt. II, 8-9.

[19] AC, Rouen, A 20, fols. 429v-30 and 475v-78.

[20] C. de Robillard de Beaurepaire, "Pièces relatives aux États généraux de 1593," Bul. de la soc. de l'histoire de Normandie, IV, (1884-87), 390-403. Bernard, pp. 776-77.

[21] AC, Rouen, A 22, fols. 399v-411, 422v-33.

[22] Formes observées en 1649 et pendant les années suivantes pour l'élection et la députation de certains citoyens du bailliage de Rouen aux États généraux du Royaume (s.l.n.d.). Paul Logié, La Fronde en Normandie (Amiens, 1951-52), II, 94-95; III, 93-94.

[23] P. Blaizot, Jacques Germain, député du tiers état du bailliage de Cotentin aux États généraux de 1614 (Poitiers,

1906), pp. 12-16. Charles Fierville, "Le Cahier des doléances des trois ordres du duché et bailliage d'Alençon en 1560," Mém. lus à la Sorbonne dans les séances extraordinaire du comité impérial (histoire) (1876), 461-74. BN, MS. fr. 18,186, fols. 71v-73. Pierre-J. Odolant-Desnos, Mémoires historiques sur la ville d'Alençon (Alençon, 1787), II, 426-27.

[24] "Le Journal du sire de Gouberville," Mém. de la soc. des antiquaires de Normandie, ed. Eugène de Robillard de Beaurepaire, XXXI (1892), 669-78. P. Blaizot, "États généraux de Blois (1588). Procès-verbal de l'assemblée des députés de la vicomté de Valognes," Mém. de la soc. nationale académique de Cherbourg, XIX (1912), 145-50.

[25] RPO, II, 101; IV, pt. II, 45-46; VI, 36. BN, MS. fr. 16,236, fol. 235v.

[26] Pierre Carel, Histoire de la ville de Caen sous Charles IX, Henry III et Henry IV (Caen, 1886), pp. 187-202. RPO, IV, pt. II, 58-60; V, 33-34.

[27] RPO, IV, pt. I, 3; pt. II, 10-11, 58, 64-65, 75-76; V, 35-36. BN, MS. fr. 16,236, fol. 257. Bibl. de l'Institut, MS. 280, fol. 33v.

[28] The debate between Prentout and Baudot over when the plat pays began to be consulted is best solved by the argument that the change from individual summons to elections by viscounties and bailiwicks was a gradual one. The procès-verbaux found in BN, MS. fr. 6,199 seem to support this conclusion. See Baudot, Mém. de l'ac. ... de Caen, N.S. V (1929), 129-41.

[29] BN, MS. fr. 6,199, no. 9. Prentout, II, 76-77; III, 180-83, 190-96.

[30] Prentout, II, 87-89.

Chapter 6

[1] BN, MS. Dupuy 588, fols. 45, 59, 355; MS. C. C. Colbert 27, fol. 325.

[2] BN, MS, Périgord 24, fols. 336-40. P. de Bosredon, "Note sur les états du Périgord," Bul. de la soc. historique et archéologique du Périgord, II (1875), 297. L. de Cardenel, "Catalogue des assemblées des États de Périgord de 1378 à 1651," Bul. philologique et historique du comité des travaux historiques et scientifiques, (1938-39), 255-59.

[3] Eugène de Lépinois, Histoire de

Chartres (Chartres, 1858), II, 116-17, 601-2.

[4] BR, III, 727-29. Dumont, IV, pt. II, 35-37.

[5] BN, MS. fr. 26,324. Miss Elna-Jean Young made a study in my graduate seminar of about two fifths of the documents on the elections in Chartres in 1576. I am indebted to her for much of the material used in this paragraph.

[6] Lépinos, II, 293, 377-78. Kergestain-Lucien Merlet, Des Assemblées de communautés d'habitants dans l'ancien comté de Dunois (Châteaudun, 1887), 198-99.

[7] Lépinois, II, 419-26. Procez verbal contenant tout ce qui s'est faict et passé dans l'assemblée générale faict à Chartres (Paris, 1651), AN, O¹ 350.

[8] RPO, I, 26; II, 29; IV, pt. II, 28, 63-64, 70, 107-8; V, 36, 40-43; VI, 24, 139-40; VII, 32; VIII, 14. Mayer, XVI, 80-81, 87-88. Bibl. de l'Institut, MS. 280, fols. 34v-35. Archives Parlementaires de 1787 à 1860, eds. Jérôme Mavidal and Émile Laurent (Paris, 1867), I, 643-44. BR, III, 692-96.

[9] BN, MS. fr. 6,199, nos. 30 and 62. BR, III, 661-70. L. Duval, "L'Administration de la justice, la tenue des états provinciaux et les attributions du bailli dans le comté du Perche pendant les deux derniers siècles," Bul. de la soc. historique et archéologique de l'Orne, XI (1892), 95-118. RPO, IV, pt. II, 70-73. Merlet, p. 9, n. 2. Archives Parlementaires, I, 666-70. René Courtin, Histoire du Perche (Mortagne, 1893), pp. 385-87, pub. in Documents sur la province du Perche, Vol. II.

[10] Thomas Cauvin, États du Maine, députés et sénéchaux de cette province (Le Mans, 1839), pp. 8-12. BR, IV, 520-21.

[11] Cauvin, pp. 13-21.

[12] Bibl. de l'Institut, MS. 280. fols. 33v-34.

[13] Cauvin, pp. 21-45.

[14] Ibid., pp. 45-47. Capuchin convent at Paris, MS. 2,807, fols. 145-46v.

[15] RPO, III, 164-65; IV, pt. II, 21. BN, MS. fr. 16,631, p. 633; MS. 16,236, fol. 248v. Cauvin, pp. 19, 28.

[16] Documents relatifs à l'histoire du comté de Laval, ed. Honoré-J. Godbert (Laval, 1860), pp. 132-35.

[17] BR, III, 106-13. RPO, III, 175. AD, Seine et Oise, B 426.

[18] Charles Cuissard, "Ordonnance du bailli de Montargis pour la convocation des trois états de son bailliage et la nomination des députés aux états de Tours en 1484," Annales de la soc. historique et archéologique du Gâtinais, XII (1894), 104-7. Thomas Rymer, Foedera, Conventiones, Literae (The Hague, 1741), V, pt. IV, 94-95. Dumont, IV, pt. II, 25-26. BR, III, 856-65.

[19] Rymer, V, pt. IV, 95. BR, III, 761-67; 808-17. Dumont, IV, pt. II, 28-29.

[20] BN, MS. fr. 7,521, fols. 138v-40; MS. Dupuy 91, fols. 132-33v.

[21] B. Mun., Orléans, MS. 541 (427), fols. 42v-46.

[22] Ibid., fols. 65-69. J. Soyer, "Les députés du tiers représentant la ville et le bailliage d'Orléans aux États généraux de Blois en 1588," Bul. de la soc. archéologique et historique de l'Orléanais, XV (1908-10), 435-47.

[23] BN, MS. fr. 16,236, fol. 275v. RPO, III, 209-10, 214; IV, pt. II, 168; V, pt. I, 86-87; pt. II, 50.

[24] B. Mun., Orléans, MS. 541 (427), fols. 41-42.

[25] Ibid., fols. 13-24v, 37v-40.

[26] Ibid., fols. 24-30, 94v-98, 194-99.

[27] Ibid., fols. 101-2v.

[28] Rymer, V, pt. IV, 101-2. BR, III, 972-77.

[29] AC, Bourges, AA 37, procès-verbal of Berry, March 15, 1561. Thierry de Brimont, Le XVIᵉ siècle et les guerres de la Réforme en Berry (Paris, 1905), I, 229-31. Louis Raynal, Histoire du Berry (Bourges, 1847), IV, 21-26.

[30] Maurice de Bengy-Puyvallée, "Extraits des cahiers des assemblées du tiers état du duché de Berry en 1576 et 1588," Mém. de la soc. des antiquaires du centre, XLVI (1934-35), 129-58. Raynal, IV, 246-47. RPO, IX, 1-63. Bernard, pp. 599-600. FGC, II, 149-57. BN, MS. fr. 3,328, fols. 38-55, 58-67v; MS. Dupuy 91, fols. 122-29v.

[31] AD, Loiret, 8 G 142. AC, Bourges, AA 37, procès-verbal of Berry, March 1, 1649. Raynal, IV, 310.

[32] FGC, II, 131-36. See AC, Bourges, AA 37, and the municipal registers, BB 7-BB 18, for further evidence of the limited suffrage in Bourges.

[33] Journal de Jehan Glaumeau, Bourges, 1541-1562, ed. Alfred Hiver de Beauvoir (Bourges, 1867), pp. 114-15. Brimont, I, 228-31. AC, Bourges, AA 37,

procès-verbal of Berry, March 15, 1561. RPO, I, 174-75; III, 166; IV, pt. II, 22; V, pt. II, 47.

[34] AC, Bourges, AA 37. Raynal, IV, 246-47. BN, MS. fr. 3,328, fols. 58-67v; MS. Dupuy 91, fols. 122-29v.

[35] Jacques Soyer, Étude sur la communauté des habitants de Blois jusqu'au commencement du XVIe siècle (Paris, 1894), pp. 70-73. Alexandre Dupré, Étude sur les institutions municipales de Blois (Orléans, 1875), pp. 29-32, 69-70, extract from Mém. de la soc. archéologique et historique de l'Orléanais, XIV (1875). Louis-C. Bergevin and Alexandre Dupré, Histoire de Blois (Blois, 1847), II, 100-104.

[36] BR, III, 1100-1103. Dumont, IV, pt. II, 34-35.

[37] AC, Blois, register, Aug.-Nov., 1576. Bergevin and Dupré, II, 104-12.

[38] AC, Blois, register, July-Oct., 1614; Jan.-Feb., 1649; and Aug., 1651. Bergevin and Dupré, II, 112-14. FGC, I, 188-99.

[39] Charles Bouchet, "Cahier du tiers état Vendômois aux États généraux de 1614," Bul. de la soc. archéologique, scientifique et littéraire de Vendômois, XI (1872), 80-101, 145-64. BN, MS. fr. 7,525, fol. 34-34v.

[40] P. Viollet, "Élections des députés aux États généraux réunis à Tours en 1468 et en 1484," BEC, XXVII (1866), 24-28, 43-54. IAC, Amboise, ed. Casimir Chevalier (Tours, 1874), p. 52. Rymer, V, pt. IV, 93. For documents on the period 1421-24, see C. de Grandmaison, "Noveaux documents sur les États généraux du XVe siècle," Bul. de la soc. archéologique de Touraine, IV (1877-79), 139-55.

[41] BR, IV, 628-31; 675-86.

[42] Charles de Grandmaison, Plaintes et doléances de la province de Touraine aux États généraux du royaume (Tours, 1890), 1-108, extract from Bul. de la soc. archéologique de Touraine, VI, VII, VIII (1883-91). AC, Tours, AA 5. Mayer, XI, 165-69. RCG, I, 172-75. In 1506 the clergy and bourgeoisie of Tours elected their deputies together. Paul Viollet, Droit publique. Histoire des institutions politiques et administratives de la France (Paris, 1903), III, 194.

[43] Grandmaison, Plaintes et doléances ..., pp. 109-57. AC, Tours, AA 6. Abbé Desprez, Mémoire sur les États généraux (Lausanne, 1788), pp. 180-88.

FGC, II, 55-57, 81-83, 90-91, 99-102, 121-23. BN, MS. n. a. fr. 9,752, fols. 24-79v.

[44] FGC, II, 157-68. RPO, II, 134-35; VI, 34-35, 85-86, 104, 142-45, 293. Bibl. de l'Institut, MS. 280, fol. 33v.

[45] Grandmaison, "Cahier de remonstrances du tiers-état des villes et plat pays de Touraine pour les États généraux assignés à Tours en 1651," Bul. de la soc. archéologique de Touraine, IV (1877-79), 37-38. IAC, Chinon, ed. Henri Grimaud (Chinon, 1896), pp. 15-16.

[46] IAC, Amboise, pp. 52, 61-64, 77, 78, 194, 234, 456-89. BN, MS. n. a. fr. 3,377, fols. 220-30v. Grandmaison, Plaintes et doléances..., pp. 30, 35. RPO, IV, pt. II, 38-39, 66.

[47] BN, MS. n. a. fr. 9,752, fols. 81-173; MS. fr. 7,525, fol. 44-44v; MS. 18,186, fol. 21-21v. IAC, Amboise, pp. 64-65.

[48] AC, Angers, BB 13, fols. 130-34.

[49] BR, IV, 585-87. AC, Angers, BB 28, fols. 231-35, 244v-48. Barthélemy Roger, "Histoire d'Anjou," Revue de l'Anjou et de Maine et Loire, II (1853), pt. I, 407-23. Ernest Mourin, La Réforme et la Ligue en Anjou (Paris, 1856), pp. 7-22. "Journal de Jehan Louvet," Revue de l'Anjou et de Maine et Loire, III (1854), pt. I, 257-58. Histoire de l'estat de France tant de la républic que de la religion, sous le règne de François II, ed. Édouard Mennechet (Paris, 1836), pp. 295-307.

[50] Mourin, pp. 214-15. Albert Meynier, Cahier des gens du tiers estat du pays et duché d'Anjou en 1614 (Angers, 1905). Roger, II, pt. I, 447. Louvet, III, pt. II, 28-29, 134-36.

[51] Meynier. AC, Angers, BB 61, fols. 48-57; C. Port, "Cahier du tiers état de la sénéchaussée de Saumur aux États généraux de 1614," Revue historique, littéraire et archéologique de l'Anjou, I (1867), 203-10. Louvet, IV (1855), pt. I, 130-31, 137-39.

[52] A. Lemarchand, "Les doléances des Angevins en 1651, mémoire inédit," Revue de l'Anjou, X (1885), 173-85. Antonin Debidour, La Fronde angevine (Paris, 1877), pp. 170-81. Roger, II, pt. I, 515-16. IAC, Angers, ed. Célestin Port (Paris, 1861), pp. 455-56.

[53] RPO, VII, 18-19, 34-35, 39. BN, MS. fr. 18,186, fols. 135-36v, 240v-41. G. Esnault, "Convocation aux États généraux de 1651," Revue historique et

archéologique du Maine, X (1881), 375-78. Roger, II, pt. I, 515.

[54] AC, Loudun, AA 2. Mayer, XI, 170. RPO, II, 27; IV, pt. II, 22. M. Dumoustier de La Frond, Essais sur l'histoire de la ville de Loudun (Poitiers, 1778), pp. 101-2. BN, MS. fr. 18,186, fols. 35v-36; MS. fr. 20,154, fols. 1011-13v; MS. Dupuy 588, fol. 59.

[55] RPO, I, 168; II, 128-29; III, 174, 188-89, 207-8; IV, pt. II, 76-102, 182-84; V, pt. I, 41-42, 84, 112-13, pt. II, 142. Mayer, XV, 18.

[56] BR, IV, 772-73, 818-23, 851, 861-62. At least seven towns were represented in the assembly of Poitou to ratify the Treaty of Étaples in 1496. Rymer, V, pt. IV, 91.

[57] Bélisaire Ledain, "Les Maires de Poitiers," Mém. de la soc. des antiquaires de l'Ouest, ser. 2, XX (1897), 559. "Remonstrances du clergé et du tiers état de Poitou, 1560-1588," Archives historiques du Poitou, XX (1889), 325-52.

[58] AC, Poitiers, registre 42, pp. 532-39. AD, Vienne, C 608; G 399. Ledain, pp. 625-26 erred when he said that Rat represented the nobility at the Estates General, RPO. II, 27.

[59] RPO, II, 7.

[60] Ibid., III, 162-63, 176-77, 196-97, 207-8, 294. BN, Ms. fr. 16,631, p. 635. Archives historiques du Poitou, XXVII (1896), 35.

[61] AD, Vienne, C 608. AC, Poitiers, carton 7, nos. 178, 179; registre 48, pp. 56-62. Ledain, pp. 678-79. H. Ouvré, "Essai sur l'histoire de la Ligue à Poitiers," Mém. de la soc. des antiquaires de l'Ouest, XXI (1854), 148-51.

[62] RPO, IV, pt. II, 35, 83-102, 182-84; V, 84. Mayer, XIII, 225; XIV, 475-76; XV, 18. Bibl. de l'Institut, MS. 280, fol. 34v.

[63] Mayer, XVI, 127; XVII, 20. RPO, VI, 154-55; VII, 70. BN, MS. fr. 18,186, fols. 4v-5, 84-85.

[64] Lucien Lacroix, Ricelieu à Luçon, sa jeunesse; son épiscopat (Paris, 1890), pp. 205-7. Gabriel Hanotaux, Histoire du Cardinal de Richelieu (Paris, 1896), I, 148-51. AC, Poitiers, registre 69, pp. 17-19. L. Duval, "Extraits des registres de la commune de Niort, Mém. lus à la Sorbonne dans le séances extraordinaries du comité impérial des travaux historiques et des sociétés savantes

(histoire) (1867), pp. 549-51. AD, Vienne, C 608.

[65] AC, Poitiers, registre 100, pp. 211-21. G. Debien, "La Question des États généraux de 1649 et de 1651. La convocation et les élections en Haut-Poitou," Bul. de la soc. des antiquaires de l'Ouest, ser. 3, X (1935), 598-613. L. Merle, "Un Cahier de doléances d'une paroisse rurale pour les États généraux de 1649: Saint-Christophe-sur-Roc," Bul. de la soc. historique et scientifique des Deux-Sèvres, IX (1951), 86-91. I am indebted to Prof. Joseph M. Tyrrell, who is now preparing a history of the estates of Poitou, for calling my attention to these two articles.

[66] B. Mun., Poitiers, MS. 304 (26). Debien, pp. 619-30.

[67] "Diaire de Jacques Merlin," ed. Charles Dagibeaud, Archives historiques de la Saintonge et d'Aunis, V (1878), 238-40. E. Jourdan, Éphémérides historiques de La Rochelle (La Rochelle, 1861), I, 431. BN, MS. Clairambault 364, fol. 258; MS. Dupuy 588, fol. 59; and MS. fr. 18,187, fols. 135v-37. B. Mun., La Rochelle, MS. 150, fols. 51-52.

[68] IAC, Angoulême, ed. Émile Biais (Angoulême, 1889), p. 74. BN, MS. n. a. fr. 3,378, fols. 302-4v. Dujarric-Descombes, "Mémoire de ce qui s'est passé en la ville d'Angoulesme à l'assemblée des trois corps de la province d'Angoulmois, 1649," Bul. et mém. de la soc. archéologique et historique de la Charante, ser. 6, vol. V (1895). lxxxiii-lxxxvi.

Chapter 7

[1] Joseph Billioud, Les États de Bourgogne aux XIVe et XVe siècles (Dijon, 1922), pp. 25-57, 345-67. Henri Drouot, Mayenne et la Bourgogne, 1587-1596 (Paris, 1937), I, 94-99. Henri Beaune and Jules d'Arbaumont, La Noblesse aux États de Bourgogne, de 1350 à 1789 (Dijon, 1864) lists nobles convoked.

[2] P. Pélicier, "Voyage des députés de Bourgogne à Blois, 1483. Élection des députés de la Bourgogne aux États généraux de 1484," BEC, XLVII (1886), 357-69. Billioud, pp. 286-92, 393-94, 457-65. Masselin, pp. 719-20, 724, 739-41.

[3] Négociations, lettres et pièces diverses relatives au règne de François II.

CDI, ed. Louis Paris (Paris, 1841), pp. 632-33. Paul-M. Baudouin, Histoire du protestantisme et de la Ligue en Bourgogne (Auxerre, 1881), I, 121-38.

[4] AD, Côte-d'Or, C 3,063, fols. 70-94, 101-16. Baudouin, I, 156-71.

[5] AD, Côte-d'Or, C 3,067, fols. 32v-47; C 3,470, Henri III to Mayenne, Sept. 1, 1576. Baudouin, II, 193-94. Henri Drouot, La première Ligue en Bourgogne et les débuts de Mayenne, 1574-1579 (Dijon, 1937), pp. 93-99. Claude Perry, Histoire civile et ecclésiastique ancienne et moderne de la ville et cité de Chalon-sur-Saône (Chalon-sur-Saône, 1659), pp. 350-51.

[6] AD, Côte-d'Or, C 3,069, fols. 237-57.

[7] AD, Côte-d'Or, C 3,469, cahiers of the nobility and third estate of the bailiwick of Dijon.

[8] Baudouin, II, 181-83, 458-500. J. Garnier, "Documents relatifs à l'histoire des États généraux du royaume, conservés aux archives municipales de Dijon," Bul. du comité de la langue de l'histoire et des arts de la France, I (1852-53), 439-41. Correspondance de la mairie de Dijon, ed. Joseph Garnier (Dijon, 1870), II, 57-61.

[9] Garnier, Bul. du comité... de la France, I (1852-53), 441-43. Drouot, Mayenne et la Bourgogne..., I, 188-89.

[10] Bernard, pp. 765-68.

[11] Garnier, Bul. du comité... de la France, I (1852-53), 444-45. AD, Côte-d'Or, C 3,473.

[12] AC, Châtillon-sur-Seine, Affaires de la Ligue. États généraux de Blois. These documents have been published in part by C. Croix, "Documents sur la Ligue dans le bailliage de La Montagne: Les élections aux États généraux de 1588," Annales de Bourgogne, IX (1937), 307-12. Gustave Lapérouse, L'Histoire de Châtillon (Châtillon-sur-Seine, 1837), pp. 337-40. RPO, IV, pt. II, 6-7.

[13] Abbé Desprez, Mémoire sur les États généraux (Lausanne, 1788), pp. 171-75. Mayer, VII, 370-75.

[14] Baudouin, II, 187-90. AC, Avallon, AA 37. AD, Côte d'Or, C 3,473, procès-verbal of the clergy, 1651. Bernard, pp. 583-84. IAC, Avallon, ed. L. Prot (Avallon, 1883), p. 23.

[15] Hippolyte Abord, Histoire de la Réforme et la Ligue dans la ville d'Autun (Paris, 1855-87), I, 470-71; II, 5-7, 337-39; III, 331-32. IAD, Côte-d'Or, ed. Ferdinand Claudon (Dijon, (1926), ser. G, III, 437.

[16] H. Drouot, La première Ligue..., pp. 95-97. J.-P. Abel Jeandet, Pages inédites d'histoire de Bourgogne au XVIe siècle. Fragments des annales de la ville de Verdun-sur-Saône-et-Doubs (Dijon, 1893), pp. 32-33. Perry, pp. 350-51, 364, 424. Baudouin, II, 183-87.

[17] Jean Roussot, Un comté adjacent à la Bourgogne aux XVIIe et XVIIIe siècles. Le Mâconnais, pays d'états et d'élections (Mâcon, 1937), especially pp. 23-86.

[18] AD, Saône-et-Loire, C 505, nos. 2-6. AC, Mâcon, AA 10, nos. 14-23.

[19] AD, Saône-et-Loire, C 505, nos. 7-27. AC, Mâcon, AA 10, nos. 17, 32-38; BB 78, fols. 180-201v.

[20] Baudouin, II, 191-92. FGC, II, 51-53, 68-69, 72-73, 168-71. Bernard, pp. 785-91. BR, III, 610-22. AD, Yonne, G 1,725, nos. 1-5. The curés and parishes were not consulted when the custom was codified in 1507, BR, III, 584-91.

[21] AD, Saône-et-Loire, C 505, no. 31.

[22] L. Laroche, "Les États particuliers du Charolais," Mém. de la soc. pour l'histoire du droit et des institutions des anciens pays bourguignons, comtois et romands, VI (1939), 145-94.

[23] AC, Bourg, AA 12; BB 75, fols. 132v-33; BB 105, fol. 46-46v. AD, Saône-et-Loire, C 505, nos. 29, 30. Joseph Brossard, Mémoires historiques de la ville de Bourg. Extraits des registres municipaux de l'hôtel-de-ville (Bourg-en-Bresse, 1887), IV, 360. Bibl. de l'Institut, MS. 280, fols. 60-86. See Jules Baux, Nobiliaire du département de l'Ain (Bourg-en-Bresse, 1863), I, 357-492, for lists of nobles who attended the estates of Bresse from 1656 to 1789. A. Vayssière, "Les archives de l'Ain. Assemblées du clergé de Bresse et de Bugey," Ann. de la soc. d'émulation de l'Ain, IX (1876), 82-91. Armando Tallone, "Les États de Bresse," Annuaire de la soc. d'émulation de l'Ain, LV (1927), 272-344.

[24] Baux, II, 157-59. "Observations au sujet des listes de la noblesse du Bugey en 1651 et 1789," Rev. de la soc. littéraire, historique et archéologique du département de l'Ain, X (1881-82), 218-21. R. Pic. "Les États du Bugey, Les trois ordres, l'hôtel de province (1761-90)." Le Bugey. Bul. de la soc. scientifique,

historique et littéraire, I (1909), 113-18, 329-37; and "Les anciennes assemblées provinciales de la Savoie et du Bugey aux XIIIe et XIVe siècles," Le Bugey. Bul. de la soc. scientifique, historique et littéraire, II (1910), 627-35.

[25] Louis Ricard, Les Institutions judiciaires et administratives de l'ancienne France et spécialement du bailliage de Gex (Paris, 1886), pp. 165-68, 263-79. Octave Morel, Documents sur le pays de Gex conservés dans les archives cantonales de Genève et de Lausanne (Bourg, 1932), p. 32. Baux, II, 379-426. RPO, VI, 70.

Chapter 8

[1] A. Thomas, "Les États généraux sous Charles VII," Le Cabinet historique, ser. 2, II (1878), 212-21. Louis Caillet, Étude sur les relations de la commune de Lyon avec Charles VII et Louis XI (1417-1483) (Lyon, 1909), p. 436.

[2] Caillet, pp. 19, 28, 382, 403.

[3] Ibid., pp. 392-93, 436-37. The letter of convocation for March, 1428, has not been found.

[4] P. Viollet, "Élection des députés aux États généraux réunis à Tours en 1468 et en 1484," BEC, XXVII (1866), 28-30. Caillet, pp. 195-96. AC, Lyon, AA 147. B. Mun., Lyon, MS. 721, pp. 1-7.

[5] B. Mun., Lyon, MS. 721, pp. 183-88. Viollet, pp. 39-41.

[6] B. Mun., Lyon, MS. 721, pp. 191-201. AC, Lyon, BB 27, especially fols. 14v-15.

[7] AC, Lyon, AA 147, no. 3; BB 81, fols. 316v-34v. B. Mun., Lyon, MS. 721, pp. 9-27. Caillet, pp. 44-49. Maurice Pallasse, La Sénéchaussée et siège présidial de Lyon pendant les Guerres de Religion (Lyon, 1943), pp. 194-213.

[8] AC, Lyon, AA 147, nos. 9 and 10; BB 82, fols. 19v-28v.

[9] AC, Lyon, BB 94, fols. 137v-92. B. Mun., Lyon, MS. 721, pp. 29-41. Pallasse, p. 312.

[10] AC, Lyon, BB 121, fols. 148, 157-57v, 165-92. B. Mun., Lyon, MS. 721, pp. 101-5.

[11] AC, Lyon, BB 129, fols. 120-27v; BB 133, fols. 147-55. B. Mun., Lyon, MS. 721, pp. 157-62.

[12] AC, Lyon, BB 150, pp. 271-313;

AA 146, no. 1, cahier of the town of Lyon. B. Mun., Lyon, MS. 722, fols. 1-52.

[13] AC, Lyon, BB 200, pp. 197-205, 387-91. B. Mun., Lyon, MS. 722, fols. 55-58.

[14] BR, III, 1283-87. Dumont, IV, pt. II, 29-32. A. Vayssière, "Les États de Bourbonnais," Bul. de la soc. d'émulation du département de l'Allier, XVIII (1886), 361-414. Henry Faure, Histoire de Moulins (Moulins, 1900), I, 130-31. Mémoires du Marquis de Beauvais-Nangis, SHF, eds. Louis Monmerqué and Alphonse Taillandier (Paris, 1862), p. 139. BN, MS. fr. 18,186, fols. 51v-52v, 70-71.

[15] Registres consulaires de Villefranche, eds. Abel Besançon and Émile Longin, (Villefranche-sur-Saône, 1912-19), II, 236-37, 483-87; III, 44-45; and IV, 311-13.

[16] Jean B. Galley, Les États de Forez et les treize villes (Saint-Étienne, 1914), esp. pp. 39-47.

[17] J. Poulbrière, "Les Députés du Limousin et de La Marche aux divers États généraux de la France," Bul. de la soc. scientifique, historique et archéologique de la Corréze, XII (1890), 293-321. M. Clairefond, "Notice sur les députations de la province de Bourbonnais et du département de l'Allier aux grandes assemblées nationales depuis 1413 jusqu'en 1848," Bul. de la soc. d'émulation du département de l'Allier, I (1846-50), 242-65. BR, IV, 1135-37.

[18] For general accounts of the estates of Auvergne see Antoine Thomas, Les États provinciaux de la France centrale sous Charles VII (Paris, 1879), I, 29-58; Hippolyte Rivière, Histoire des institutions de l'Auvergne (Paris, 1874), I, 306-22; II, 25-33; and Antoine Bergier, Recherches historiques sur les États généraux et plus particulièrement sur l'origine, l'organisation et la durée des anciens États provinciaux d'Auvergne (Clermont-Ferrand, 1788).

[19] BR, IV, 1,214-19. BN, MS. fr. 3,086, fols. 98-109 is especially valuable for determining the composition of the estates, for the names of those who failed to obey the summons to attend the assembly of 1529 are given along with those who were present.

[20] AC, Clermont, Aa 3 i. Bergier, pt. I, 71-77; pt. II, 83-94. There is no rational explanation as to how thirteen localities became "good towns" and the rest remained in the unprivileged plat pays.

Some of the thirteen had no charter of privileges, and others had no fortifications until long after they had been accepted in the estates. Gilbert Rouchon, "Le Tiers état aux États provinciaux de Basse-Auvergne aux XVIe et XVIIe siècles," Bul. philologique et historique de comité des travaux historiques et scientifiques (1930-31), 171-72.

[21] Rouchon, pp. 165-79.

[22] Bergier, pt. I, 77-79; pt. II, 95-98.

[23] Ibid., pt. I, 80-87; pt. II, 112-20. AC, Clermont, Aa 3 bb. Rouchon, pp. 179-83. André Imberdis, Histoire de guerres religieuses en Auvergne pendant les XVIe et XVIIe siècles (Riom, 1846), pp. 167-70. RPO, III, 167-69. BN, MS. fr. 16,631, pp. 627-28.

[24] AC, Clermont, Aa 3 gg; Aa 3 11; Aa 3 rr. Bergier, pt. I, 87-110; pt. II, 124-66. Rouchon, pp. 179-83. Imberdis, 315-19, 575-78. BN, MS. fr. 16,236, fol. 296. RPO, IV, pt. II, 60-62, 228-29; V, pt. I, 35; pt. II, 48-49; VIII, 30-31.

[25] BR, IV, 1214-19. IAC, Aurillac, ed. Gabriel Esquer (Aurillac, 1907), I, 92-93. RPO, I, 24-25.

[26] AC, Saint-Flour, chap. v, article I, no. 9, 20. René de Ribier, "L'Assemblée des États particuliers de la Haute-Auvergne en 1649," Revue de la Haute-Auvergne, VI (1904), 134, 144-63.

[27] Bergier, pt. I, 23-24; pt. II, 108-9. RPO, II, 9; III, 170; IV, pt. II, 25-26. AC, Saint-Flour, chap. v, article I, no. 10.

[28] AC, Saint-Flour, chap. v, article I, nos. 14, 20, 28. AD, Cantal, C 433. Ribier, pp. 144-63.

[29] RPO, IV, pt. II, 26. AC, Saint-Flour, chap. v, article I, nos. 14-28. Ribier, 135-42.

[30] L. Despois, Histoire de l'autorité royale dans le comité de Nivernais (Paris, 1912), pp. 303-28. Mayer, VII, 302-5, 358-61. At the Estates General the deputies of Nevers usually, but not always, participated with the government of Orléans, but as the deputies of Saint-Pierre acted with Lyonnais, it is best to treat them together at this point. RPO, I, 168-69; III, 166, 181-82; IV, pt. II, 31; V, pt. II, 27, 32, 142; VI, 128-29.

[31] Masselin, p. 730. BR, III, 1164-89.

[32] Abbé Boutillier, "Documents inédits relatifs aux États généraux de 1560 à 1651 et conservés aux archives communales de Nevers," Bul. de la soc.

Nivernaise des sciences, lettres et arts, XI (1883), 230-31.

[33] B. Mun., Blois, MS. 89, fol. 1014. FGC, II, 12-15.

[34] Boutillier, 232-33. RPO, IV, pt. II, 102-4.

[35] Boutillier, 233-35. Mayer, XVI, pt. I, 47-51; XVII, 170-71. RPO, VI, 19, 84-85. BN, MS. fr. 18,186, fols. 48v-49.

[36] Boutillier, 235-37.

Chapter 9

[1] Paul Dognon, Les Institutions politiques et administratives du pays de Languedoc (Toulouse, 1895), pp. 195-325. Jean Albisson, Loix municipales et économiques de Languedoc (Montpellier, 1780), I, 316-437. Paul Gachon, Les États de Languedoc et l'édict de Béziers, 1632 (Paris, 1887), pp. 1-22. Baron Trouvé, Essai historique sur les États généraux de la province de Languedoc (Paris, 1818), I, 301-15.

[2] AD, Haute-Garonne, C 2,280, fols. 441-41v, 451-52.

[3] Ibid., 460-71.

[4] HL, XIII, 332.

[5] AC, Toulouse, AA 88, pp. 137-211; AA 16, no. 209; AA 20, no. 180; AA 22, no. 58. IAC, Toulouse, ed. E. Roschach (Toulouse, 1891), I, 520, 527, 303-4, 332-34. Germain de La Faille, Annales de la ville de Toulouse (Toulouse, 1701), II, 201-6, 345, 409, 466-67. Bernard, pp. 796-97.

[6] AD, Tarn, C 230. Representatives of the town of Toulouse and of eight dioceses submitted a cahier in 1560 in the name of the third estate of the seneschalsy. La Faille, II, preuves, 48-57.

[7] RPO, IV, pt. I, 19; pt. II, 18, 172-74.

[8] HL, XIII, 280-83; XIV, 209-39. The king annulled the elections and ordered a new meeting of the seneschalsy to name deputies on the grounds that the assembly had not been held at Toulouse, but not because it had been improperly convoked. HL, XIV, 301-3.

[9] AD, Haute-Garonne, C 957, fols. 388-90v. HL, XIV, 212-19. Thomas Puntous, "Les Assemblées de l'assiette dans le diocèse de Toulouse aux 17e et 18e siècles," Rec. de législation de Toulouse, V (1909), 185-225; and Un Diocèse civil de Languedoc: les États particuliers

du diocèse de Toulouse aux XVIIe et XVIIIe siècles (Paris, 1909), pp. 75-121. IAC, Haute-Garonne, ed. Adolphe Baudouin (Toulouse, 1878), ser. C, I, "notice."

[10] Élie-A. Rossignol, Assemblées du diocèse de Lavour (Paris, 1881).

[11] Jean Contrasty, Histoire de la cité de Rieux-Volvestre et de ses évêques (Toulouse, 1936), pp. 187-95. Trouvé, I, 349-53.

[12] HL, XIV, 210-13, 239-47.

[13] AD, Aude, V, C-1, no. 4. FGC, II, 199-216. IAC, Narbonne, ed. Germain Mouynès (Narbonne, 1872), ser. BB, I, 97, 274, 619.

[14] AD, Aude, XIII, C-2, and XXII, C-3. Élie-A. Rossignol, Assemblées du diocèse de Castres (Toulouse, 1878), pp. 1-35. Émile Appolis, Un Pays languedocien au milieu du XVIIIe siècle: le diocèse civil de Lodève (Albi, 1951), pp. 217-29. J. T. Lasserre, Recherches historiques sur la ville d'Alet et son ancien diocèse (Carcassonne, 1877), pp. 130-40. Trouvé, I, 344-47, 350-51, 355.

[15] FGC, II, 124-31, 206-8. Élie-A. Rossignol, Petits États d'Albigeois (Paris, 1875), pp. 1-50, 180. Trouvé, I, 353-55.

[16] Trouvé, I, 346. BN, MS. Languedoc, 131, fols. 64-66.

[17] AD, Ardeche, C 1,456, no. 11.

[18] BN, MS. Languedoc, 131, fols. 67-69.

[19] Léon Ménard, Histoire civile, ecclésiastique et littéraire de la ville de Nismes (Paris, 1755), VI, 79-83, and preuves, 19-29.

[20] See AD, Gard, C 629, for Nîmes in 1560 and 1561; C 641, pp. 726-28, for Nîmes in 1614; and C 1,209 for composition of estates of Uzès in 1576. Trouvé, I, 348-49. Ménard, VI, 281-90, 305, 311-13, and preuves, 267-88.

[21] Auguste Le Sourd, Essai sur les États de Vivarais depuis leurs origines (Paris, 1926), especially pp. 173-80.

[22] Ibid., pp. 63-86.

[23] F. André, "Procès-verbaux des délibérations des États de Gévaudan," Bul. de la soc. d'agriculture, sciences et arts du département de la Lozère, XXVII (1876), 10-12, 210-27. These procès-verbaux have been summarized by Gustave de Burdin, Documents historiques sur la province de Gévaudan (Toulouse, 1846-47), 2 vols. Jean

Roucaute, Le Pays de Gévaudan au temps de la Ligue (Paris, 1900), pp. 130-49; and Documents pour servir à l'histoire du pays de Gévaudan au temps de la Ligue (Paris, 1894), pp. 119-49. J. Deniau, "Les États particuliers du pays de Gévaudan," Soc. des lettres sciences et arts de la Lozère. Chroniques et mélanges, V (1930), 1-67.

[24] Étienne Delcambre, Contribution à l'histoire des États provinciaux. Les États du Velay des origines à 1642 (Saint-Étienne, 1938), especially pp. 88-96, 143-66, 328-30, 412-47. AD, Haute-Loire, 1 B 1,756, nos. 1 and 2.

[25] Oudot de Dainville, Archives de la ville de Montpellier (Montpellier, 1939), VII, 75-76. RCG, II, 182. RPO, II, 113-14. BN, MS. fr. 18,186, fols. 343-44v.

[26] G. Arnaud, Mémoire sur les États de Foix, 1608-1789 (Toulouse, 1904), pp. 1-40, 152-56.

[27] HL, XIII, 305-43; XIV, 364-65, 371-74, 380-82, 384-89.

Chapter 10

[1] Archives historiques du département de la Gironde, XXXV (1900), 72-75; XXVIII (1893), 44-108. P. de Bosredon, "Note sur les États du Périgord," Bul. de la soc. historique et archéologique de Périgord, II (1875), 297. BN, MS. Périgord 24, fols. 336-40. L. de Cardenal, "Catalogue des assemblées des États de Périgord de 1378 à 1651," Bul. philologique et historique du comité des travaux historiques et scientifiques, (1938-39), 255-59.

[2] BR, IV, 863-69. Some additional towns participated in 1496. Thomas Rymer, Foedera, conventiones, literae (The Hague, 1741), V, pt. IV, 103-4. For references to the estates of Saintonge during the Hundred Years War see: Denys d'Aussy, "La Saintonge pendant la guerre de cent ans," Bul. de la soc. des archives historiques de la Saintonge et de l'Aunis, XIV (1894), 217-21, 354-94.

[3] René Eschassériaux, Études, documents et extraits relatifs à la ville de Saintes (Saintes, 1876), pp. 416-20. Archives historiques de la Saintonge et de l'Aunis, VIII (1880), 241-55. Saintes probably also named the delegation in 1576, Eschassériaux, p. 275.

[4] B. Mun., La Rochelle, MS. 69, fols.

89-95. Archives historiques de la Saintonge et de l'Aunis, XLVI (1915), 34.

[5] BR, IV, 889-91.

[6] AD, Gironde, G 35. Alexandre Dupré, Élections du clergé de Guienne aux États généraux (Bordeaux, 1893), pp. 3-5, extract from La Revue catholique de Bordeaux, Aug. 10, 25, and Sept. 10, 1893. Archives historiques... de la Gironde, VIII (1866), 537-39.

[7] AD, Gironde, G 289, entry on Sept. 25, 1576. Jean de Gaufreteau, Chronique bordeloise (Bordeaux, 1877), I, 196-97. Archives municipales de Bordeaux, eds. Ariste Ducaunnès-Duval and Paul Courteault (Bordeaux, 1909), IX, 287.

[8] Raymond Guinodie, Histoire de Libourne et des autres villes et bourgs de son arrondissement (Bordeaux, 1845), I, 449-53. RPO, IV, pt. II, 11-12, 130, 163, 167; V, 83-84. BN, MS. fr. 16,236, fols. 325-26.

[9] AD, Gironde, G 599. Archives historiques... de la Gironde, X (1868), 1-11. Dupré, pp. 7-11.

[10] Archives Municipales de Bordeaux, II, 333-34; X, 287-89. Mayer, XVI, 118-19. BN, MS. fr. 18,186, fols. 21-22; MS. fr. 7,525, fols. 25v-26.

[11] AD, Gironde, H 281, nos. 6 and 7; H 642, fol. 23.

[12] Léon Cadier, La Sénéchaussée des Lannes sous Charles VII, administration royale et États provinciaux (Paris, 1885), pp. 49-52, extract from Revue de Béarn, Navarre et Lannes, III.

[13] Archives municipales de Bayonne. Délibérations du corps de ville. Registres Gascon (1484-1514), eds. Édouard Ducéré and others (Bayonne, 1890), I, 2-4, 282-88.

[14] Cadier, p. 54.

[15] BN, MS. Mélanges de Colbert 366, no. 318.

[16] BN, MS. C. C. Colbert 27, fols. 293-97v.

[17] RCG, I, 63. RPO, II, 12; IV, pt. I, 4; V, pt. II, 19; VI, 13-14. Bibl. de l'Institut, MS. 280, fol. 34v.

[18] RCG, I, 452. BN, MS. C. C. Colbert 27, fols. 293-97v. RPO, III, 156; IV, pt. II, 14; V, pt. II, 39-40, 65.

[19] Archives municipales de Bayonne. ... Registres Français (Bayonne, 1906), II, 400. M. Tartière, "Cahier du tiers état de la sénéchaussée des Lannes," Rev. des soc. savantes des départements, ser. 5, II (1870), 355. AD, Landres, H23.

Gabriel de Blaÿ de Gaïx, Histoire militaire de Bayonne (Bayonne, 1905), II, 189. IAC, Bayonne, ed. Édouard Dulaurens (Bayonne, 1894), I, 27. The three estates of the provostships of Saint-Sever assembled alone during the reign of Louis XI. Thus there may have been a tradition for individual action that made co-operation between the subordinate jurisdictions even more difficult. J.-C. Tauzin, "Louis XI et la Gascogne," Revue des questions historiques, LIX (1896), 436.

[20] Antoine Thomas, Les États provinciaux de la France centrale sous Charles VII (Paris, 1879), 2 vols. IAC, Haute-Vienne, ed. Alfred Leroux (Limoges, 1891), ser. C, xxxii-xxxvi. The composition of the estates of Haut- and Bas-Limousin was not given in the account of the assemblies to ratify the Treaties of Cambrai and Madrid. BN, MS. Mélanges de Colbert 369, nos. 364 and 365.

[21] Registres consularies de la ville de Limoges, ed. Émile Ruben (Limoges, 1869), II, 204, 220-22. Pierre Laforest, Limoges au XVIIe siècle (Limoges, 1862), p. 87. RPO, V, pt. II, 40-41. Chartes, chroniques et memoriaux pour servir à l'histoire de La Marche et du Limousin, eds. Alfred Leroux and Auguste Bosvieux (Tulle, 1886), pp. 189, 251, 252.

[22] G. Clément-Simon, "Rôle de la cotisation de la noblesse du Bas-Limousin pour les frais faits par ses députés aux États généraux d'Orléans en 1560," Archives historiques de la Corrèze, I (1903), 87-96. M. Combert, Histoire de la ville et du canton d'Uzerche (Tulle, 1853), p. 206.

[23] G. Clément-Simon, "Procès-verbal de l'assemblée des États provinciaux du Bas-Limousin, tenue à Tulle,... 1588," Archives historiques du Limousin, IX (1904), 320-64; also in Archives historiques de la Corrèze, II (1905), 320-64. BN, MS. fr. 16,236, fol. 248v. Gustave Clément-Simon, Tulle et le Bas-Limousin pendant les guerres de religion (Tulle, 1887), pp. 117-21.

[24] Combert, pp. 235-41. IAC, Corrèze, eds. A. Vayssière and A. Hugues (Tulle, 1889), III, 119. RPO, VIII, 29-30. Mayer, XVI, 124-26, 152-54. BN, MS. fr. 18,186, fols. 134v-35.

[25] Archives historiques du Limousin, IX (1904), 364-70; or Archives historiques de la Corrèze, II (1905), 364-70. BN, MS. fr. 18,186, fols. 111-12, 357v-59.

[26] IAC, Périgueux, ed. Michel Hardy (Périgueux, 1894), pp. 117, 251. P. de Bosredon, "Note sur les États du Périgord," Bul. de la soc. historique et archéologique du Périgord, II (1875), 289-98. Jean-Joseph Escande, Histoire du Périgord (Cahors, 1934), II, 319-24. Dumont, IV, pt. II, 32-34.

[27] AD, Dordogne, C 13, no. 10. IAC, Périgueux, p. 284.

[28] AC, Périgueux, AA 35. G. Picot, "Doléances du tiers état du Périgord, 1576," Rev. des soc. savantes des départements, ser. 7, VI (1882), 304-5.

[29] Louis de Cardenal, "Les États de Périgord sous Henri IV," L'Organisation corporative du moyen âge à la fin de l'ancien régime (Louvain, 1939), III, 163-81.

[30] AD, Dordogne, C 14, no. 1.

[31] Ibid., no. 2. AD, Périgueux, AA 38. R. Bernaret, "Tenue des États généraux à Périgueux en 1649," Bul. de la soc. historique et archéologique du Périgord, I (1874), 211-13. Les Jurades de la ville de Bergerac, ed. G. Charrier (Bergerac, 1899), VIII, 64-65, 268-69. Louis de Cardenal, "Les dernières réunions des trois ordres de Périgord avant la Révolution," L'Organisation corporative du moyen âge à la fin de l'ancien régime (Louvain, 1937), II, 111-27.

[32] AD, Lot, F 95 and F 96. Edmond Cabié, Guerres de religion dans le sud-ouest de la France et principalement dans le Quercy (Paris, 1906), 307-28, 864-65. M.-J. Baudel, Notes pour servir à l'histoire des États provinciaux du Quercy (Cahors, 1881).

[33] IAD, Lot-et-Garonne, ed. G. Tholin (Agen, 1885-98), ser. E. supplément, I, 28, 81, 138, 141, 262, 328, 334, 412, 417; II, 67, 87, 138. AC, Condom, BB 26, July 18-Aug. 30, 1614.

[34] Archives historiques... de la Gironde, XXXV (1900), 26-48.

[35] BN, MS. Mélanges de Colbert 369, no. 356.

[36] AC, Agen, AA 44, no. 3.

[37] AC, Agen, AA 45; CC 150. G. Tholin, "Les cahiers du pays d'Agenais au États généraux," Revue de l'Agenais, IX (1882), 505-14; X (1883), 5-16, 145-60, 244-59, 321-39, 408-16; also published separately under the title, Cahiers des doléances du tiers état du pays d'Agenais aux États généraux (Paris, 1885).

[38] AC, Agen, CC 150. Archives historiques... de la Gironde, XXXV (1900), 84-86. Tholin, Revue de l'Agenais, X (1883), 417-29, 507-22; XI, 112-25, 330-52.

[39] P. Parfouru and J. de Carsalade du Pont, "Comptes consulaires de la ville de Riscle de 1441 à 1507," Archives historiques de la Gascogne, XII (1892), I, xvii-xxvi, 281-82.

[40] M. A. Branet, "Les États d'Armagnac en 1631-1632," Bul. de la soc. archéologique du Gers, XIV (1913), 168-83, 214-29. Barbé, "Chronique," Bul. du comité d'histoire et d'archéologie de la province ecclésiastique d'Auch, II (1861), 610-11.

[41] J. Duffour, "Députés de l'Armagnac aux États généraux d'Orléans en 1649," Revue de Gascogne, LX (1924), 31-33. Paul Tierny, La Sénéchaussée d'Armagnac (Auch, 1893), p. 9.

[42] See AD, Haute-Garonne, C 3,795 for the cahier of Comminges in 1560; C 3,474 for the elections in 1561; C 3,570-72 for the elections in 1576; C 3,640-41 for the elections in 1588; C 3,652 for the elections in 1591; and C 3,659 for the elections in 1593. For 1614 see BN, MS. fr. 16,256, fols. 624-27. For the elections in the seneschalsy of Toulouse in 1576, see AD, Tarn, C 230. For general treatment of the estates of Comminges see Charles Higounet, Le Comté de Comminges des ses origines à son annexion à la couronne (Toulouse and Paris, 1949), II, 634-36; B. de Gorsse, "Cahier documental concernant le païs et les États de Comminges," Revue de Comminges, XLVI (1932), 6-28; and V. Fons, "Les États de Comminges," Mém. de la soc. archéologique du midi de la France, VIII (1861-65), 161-206.

[43] IAC, Verdun-sur-Garonne, ed. Jean-U. Devals (Montauban, 1875), ser. BB, p. 4. Abbé Galabert, "Note sur les États de Rivière-Verdun," Bul. de la soc. archéologique du midi de la France, X (1897), 105-10. Abbé Jean Contrasty, Histoire de Sainte-Foy-de-Peyrolières (Toulouse, 1917), pp. 198-210.

[44] Léon Cadier, Les États de Béarn depuis leurs origines jusqu'au commencement du XVIe siècle (Paris, 1888), pp. 186-87, 200-201, 312, 351.

[45] Louis de Froidour, Mémoire du pays et des États de Bigorre (Paris, 1892), pp. 143-89. Gustave Bascle de Lagrèze, Histoire du droit dans les Pyrénées (Paris, 1867), pp. 70-92. RPO, V, pt. II, 20.

[46] J. Artières, "Documents sur la ville de Millau," Archives historiques du Rouergue, VII (1930), 288, 381-82. AC, Rodez, BB 3, fols. 47-47v, 50v-69v. For general treatments of the estates see H. Affre, Dictionnaire des institutions, moeurs et coutumes de Rouergue (Rodez, 1903), pp. 161-66; and Marc-A. de Gaujal, Études historiques sur le Rouergue (Paris, 1858), I, 385-406.

[47] "Mémoire sur la tenue des États de Rouergue, écrit vers 1623, par Durieux, député du pays de Rouergue," Bul. philologique et historique du comité des travaux historiques et scientifiques (1885), 23-27.

[48] BN, MS. Clairambault, 364, fols. 277-79, 299.

[49] C. Valade, "Réunion des États de la province de Rouergue à Villefranche en 1649," Mém de la soc. des lettres, sciences et arts de l'Aveyron, XVII (1906-11), 438-44.

Chapter 11

[1] BN, MS. fr. 8,276, fols. 174-220v. An adequate summary of the procès-verbal of 1576 had been published by Charles de La Lande de Calan, "Documents inédits relatifs aux États de Bretagne de 1491 à 1589," Archives de Bretagne, XV (1909), pt. II, 73-96.

[2] BN, MS. fr. 8,277, pp. 551-53. See also, La Lande de Calan, XV (1909), pt. II, 279-300.

[3] AD, Ille-et-Vilaine, C 2,648, p. 588.

[4] Ibid., C 2,655, pp. 190-94.

[5] Ibid., C 2,648, pp. 595, 607, 610; C 2,655, pp. 64-65, 81, 122. In 1588 the deputies to the Estates General were empowered to receive municipal cahiers for consideration. BN, MS. fr. 8,277, pp. 551-53.

[6] Henri Sée, "Les États de Bretagne au XVIe siècle," Annales de Bretagne, X (1894-95), 10-15. Armand Rebillon, Les États de Bretagne de 1661 à 1789 (Rennes, 1932), pp. 80-128. La Lande de Calan, XV (1909), pt. II, 73-78, 279-83. AD, Ille-et-Vilaine, C 2,648, pp. 547-56.

[7] La Lande de Calan, XIV (1908), pt. I, 145. Mayer, X, 449. RPO, III, 158-59; IV, pt. II, 16. P. Thomas-Lacroix, "Les Bretons aux États généraux de 1614," Mém. de la soc. d'histoire et archéologie de Bretagne, XV (1934), 8-9. In 1576 a

letter of convocation was sent to the seneschal of Nantes, but that official does not seem to have convoked his jurisdiction. This error in the chancellery may have inspired the mayor and échevins to act. AC, Nantes, AA 78.

[8] AC, Grenoble, AA 39, no. 8.

[9] AC, Grenoble, BB 28, fols. 188v-92. IAC, Valence, ed. André Lacroix (Valence, 1914), p. 54. Nicolas Chorier, Histoire générale du Dauphiné (Lyon, 1672), II, 676. Pierre Cavard, La Réforme et les guerres de religion à Vienne (Vienne, 1950), pp. 198-202. BN, MS. fr. 16,631, pp. 625-27.

[10] IAC, Grenoble, ed. Marie-A. Prud-homme, (Grenoble, 1886), p. 150. AD, Isère, C 5, no. 27. B. Mun., Grenoble, MS. 2,313. BN, MS. fr. 18,723, fols. 246-47.

[11] Abbé A. Dussert, "Les États du Dauphiné aux XIVe et XVe siècles," Bul. de l'académie Delphinale, ser. 5, VIII (1914), 292-99; and "Les États du Dauphiné de la Guerre de Cent Ans aux Guerres de Religion," Bul. de l'académie Delphinale, ser. 5, XIII (1922), xiv-xv. André A. Fauché-Prunelle, Essai sur les anciennes institutions autonomes ou populaires des Alpes-Cottiennes-Briançonnaises (Grenoble, 1857), II, 489-612.

[12] Raoul Busquet, "Histoire des institutions," Les Bouches-du-Rhône, Encyclopédie départementale (Marseille, 1921), III, 448-544. Bernard Hildesheimer, Les Assemblées générales des communautés de Provence (Paris, 1935).

[13] BN, MS. Dupuy, 588, fols. 6-9v.

[14] RPO, II, 12; III, 211-12.

[15] AD, Bouches-du-Rhône, C 5, fols. 38-42; C 6, fol. 14-14v. Busquet, III, 284-95, 539-40. Honoré-G. de Coriolis, Dissertation sur les États de Provence (Aix, 1867), 241-45. RPO, IV, pt. 2, 109-10; V, 43, 49-50. Bibl. de l'Institut, MS. 280, fol. 36.

[16] AD, Bouches-du-Rhône, C 5, fol. 335.

[17] This assembly was attended by the syndics of the clergy and nobility and the deputies of 26 towns. AD, Bouches-du-Rhône, C 7, fols. 252v-53.

[18] AD, Bouches-du-Rhône, C 10, fols. 376-400v; C 107, fols. 549-55. RPO, V, pt. 2, 26.

[19] AD, Bouches-du-Rhône, C 2,068, cahier of the third estate, 1614; C 107, fols. 560-68; and C 5, fols. 42v-52. BN, MS. fr. 18,186, fols. 116-17v. RPO, I, 139, 141.

[20] AD, Bouches-du-Rhône, C 108, fols. 179v-85v. Busquet, III, 541, n. 4.

[21] Louis Méry and F. Guindon, Histoire analytique et chronologique des délibérations du corps et du conseil de la municipalité de Marseille (Marseille, 1841), I, 384-91. Bernard, pp. 566-67. See also Archives parlementaires de 1787 à 1860, eds. Jérôme Mavidal and Émile Laurent (Paris, 1867), I, 633-34, for Arles' defense of her right to name deputies of the two lay orders to the Estates General in 1789.

[22] Gaston Zeller, La Réunion de Metz à la France (1552-1648) (Paris, 1926), II, 259.

[23] M. J. Carsalade Du Pont, "Documents inédits sur la Fronde en Gascogne," Archives historiques de la Gascogne, I (1883), 12-28. IAD, Basses-Pyrénées, ed. Paul Raymond (Paris, 1865), III, 101. Beatrice F. Hyslop, A Guide to the General Cahiers of 1789 (New York, 1936), pp. 20-21. RPO, II, 32.

Chapter 12

[1] Les Oeuvres de maistre Guy Coquille, sieur de Romenay (Paris, 1666), I, 328. See also I, 322, 333-34. The chevaliers of the orders of the king also attended the ceremonial sessions of the Estates General.

[2] J. R. Major, The Estates General of 1560 (Princeton, 1951), pp. 86-91. Antoine Loisel, Institutes coutumières, eds. A. Dupin and E. Laboulaye (Paris, 1846), pp. 21-22. Mémoires et correspondance de Duplessis-Mornay (Paris, 1824), IV, 267-68. Raoul Patry, Philippe du Plessis-Mornay (Paris, 1933), p. 144. The Bishop of Langres went to Blois in 1576 to participate in the Estates General in his quality of duke and peer. He sat with the princes and peers at the opening ceremony, but did not serve with the other deputies. T. Pistollet de Saint-Ferjeux, "Langres pendant la Ligue," Mém. de la soc. historique et archéologique de Langres, II (1861-77), 106. RPO, II, 41.

[3] Masselin, pp. 392-95, 406-11, 488-89, 510-19, 704.

[4] Major, pp. 83-86. RPO, II, 113-14.

[5] RPO, V, pt. II, 2-3; VI, 4-5, 11-12, 14, 18-19, 77, 83.

[6] RPO, II, 134-35; VI, 34-35, 85-86, 104, 142-45, 293. Bibl. de l'Institut, MS. 280, fol. 33v.

[7] FGC, II, 250-51. RCG, I, 24-26, 308-13.

[8] RPO, II, 119, 266-67; III, 210-11, 295. RCG, II, 60-68, 174-75, 220-24, 355-64. Deputies from the University of Toulouse later joined the representatives from the other universities.

[9] FGC, II, 260. Bibl. de l'Institut, MS. 280. fols. 32v-33.

[10] Bernard, p. 3.

[11] RPO, VI, 176-77, 366-68; 489-91; VII, 204-5; VIII, 71-72, 151-52. Mayer, VII, 435-36; XVI, pt. I, 241-42; pt. II, 207-8; XVII, 227-9. BN, MS. fr. 18,186, fol. 245.

[12] RCG, II, 365-71; III, 168-77. RPO, IV, pt. I, 13.

[13] BN, MS. fr. 18,186, fol. 131. RPO, VI, 186-87.

[14] RPO, VI, 4, 553.

[15] AN, X^{1a} 1491, fols. 50v. 87-87v. Édouard Maugis, Histoire du Parlement de Paris (Paris, 1913), I, 655-73. Maugis overestimates the consistency of the attitude of Parlement toward the Estates General. G. Picot, "Le Parlement sous Charles VIII," Ac. des sciences morales et politiques. Séances et travaux, XXXVII (1877), 788-94.

[16] AN, X^{1a} 1598, fols. 168-69, 173-73v.

[17] Bernard, pp. 483-85, 800-801.

[18] Registres des délibérations du bureau de la ville de Paris, eds. Paul Guérin and Léon Le Grand (Paris, 1927), XVI, 33, n. 1.

[19] RPO, II, 100, 103; VI, 92, 95. Alexandre Dupré, Élections du clergé de Guienne aux États généraux (Bordeaux, 1893), pp. 7-11. J. R. Major, "The Third Estate in the Estates General of Pontoise," Speculum, XXIX (1954), 467.

[20] Amédée Combier, Étude sur le bailliage de Vermandois et siège présidial de Laon (Paris, 1874), pp. 88-92. Édouard Henry, La Réforme et la Ligue en Champagne et à Reims (Saint-Nicolas, 1867), p. 99.

Chapter 13

[1] I have published some of the conclusions reached in this chapter in "The Electoral Procedure for the Estates General of France and its Social Implications, 1484-1651," Medievalia et Humanistica, X

(1956), 131-50. I wish to express my appreciation to Medievalia et Humanistica for permission to reproduce this material here.

² Among the other towns that dominated the bailiwick assemblies were Rouen, Gien, Poitiers, Limoges, and Le Mans.

³ The principal municipal rivalries were Bellême and Mortagne in Perche; Clermont and Riom in Basse-Auvergne; Saint-Flour and Aurillac in Haute-Auvergne; Rodez and Villefranche in Rouergue; Dax, Saint-Sever, and Bayonne in Lannes; Tulle, Brive, and Uzerche in Bas-Limousin; and Maintes and Meulan.

⁴ Other jurisdictions exclusive of towns and plat pays whose right was challenged to have seats in the Estates General included Montdidier, Péronne, Roye, Niort, Fontenay, Luçon, Magny, Laval, Comminges, La Ferté Alais, Béziers, Vienne, Grasse, and Draguignan.

⁵ Included were deputies from the plat pays of the bailiwicks or seneschalsies of Orléans, Étampes, Basse-Auvergne, and Lyon.

⁶ Mayer, VII, 386-87. FGC, II, 53.

⁷ F. Dumont, "La noblesse et les États particuliers français," Studies Presented to the International Commission for the History of Representative and Parliamentary Institutions, XI (1952), 147-56 offers additional evidence for the increased participation of the nobility.

⁸ BR, III, 1100-1102; IV, 1135-37.

⁹ Ibid., II, 733-44, 777-81.

¹⁰ René Filhol, Le premier président Christofle de Thou et la réformation des coutumes (Paris, 1937) is a good biography, but it does not consider the question of the increase in suffrage.

¹¹ Registres des délibérations du bureau de la ville de Paris, ed. Paul Guérin (Paris, 1902) X, 329. G. Post has pointed to the importance of the maxim, quod omnes tangit, in the thirteenth century decision to convoke the deputies of the chapters, towns, and lesser nobles as well as the magnates. See his "A Roman Legal Theory of Consent, Quod Omnes Tangit, in Medieval Representation," Wisconsin Law Review (1950), pp. 66-78.

¹² They are Paris, Beauvais, Langres, Lyon, Villefranche-sur-Saône, Étampes,

Orléans, Vendôme, Amboise, La Rochelle, Caen, Rouen, Châtillon-sur-Seine, Toulouse, Saintes, Saint-Flour, Aurillac, Bordeaux, Limoges, Nantes, Morlaix, Marseille, and Arles. The other two towns are listed as Hybeix and Nortais in RPO, III, 158-59; IV, pt. II, 16, but I have been unable to identify them with the references available.

¹³ One exception to the nobles' policy of supporting the bourgeois of the privileged towns against the local royal officials may be found in Basse-Auvergne in 1576. There the nobility supported the effort of the plat pays to share with the thirteen "good towns" the privilege of speaking for the third estate. Local royal officials advocated a similar policy. G. Rouchon, "Le Tiers état aux états provinciaux de Basse-Auvergne aux XVIᵉ et XVIIᵉ siècles," Bul. philologique et historique du comité des travaux historiques et scientifiques, (1930-31), pp. 180-81.

¹⁴ The suffrage in Normandy also grew little during the sixteenth century, but here there was already a broad franchise in 1500.

¹⁵ For example, the fines established for the failure to attend the estates of Bas-Limousin in 1588 were as follows: bishop and viscounts, 50 écus; abbots and barons, 33 1/3 écus; priors, provosts, seigneurs, and consuls, 16 2/3 écus; curés and syndics of parishes, 8 1/3 écus. Archives historiques du Limousin, IX, 354.

¹⁶ François Olivier-Martin correctly argued that kings sought to reconcile, not exploit, differences that arose between the estates. See his Histoire du droit français des origines à la révolution (Paris, 1951), pp. 330-35, 358-59.

¹⁷ RPO, I, 139-41, 156.

Chapter 14

¹ G. Hérelle, "Documents inédits sur les États généraux tirés des archives de Vitry-le-François," Mém. de la soc. des sciences et arts de Vitry-le-François, IX (1878), 198-200. FGC, II, 24, 29, 33, 36-38, 43.

² In private law, women could be named proctors only in exceptional cases. Jean Masuer, La Practique (Paris, 1606), p. 76.

³ RPO, VIII, 29-30. Mayer, XVI, 124-

26, 152-54. In private law a <u>procureur</u> had to be at least 25 years of age. Masuer, p. 82.

[4] Hippolyte Abord, <u>Histoire de la Réforme et la Ligue dans la ville d'Autun</u> (Paris, 1855-87), II, 5-6.

[5] Louis Moréri, <u>Le Grand dictionnaire historique, ou le mélange curieux de l'histoire sacrée et profane</u> (Paris, 1759), X, 435.

[6] BN, MS. fr. 16,236, fols. 279, 325-26. AC, Bordeaux, AA 26, no. 1. <u>RPO</u>, IV, pt. II, 130, 163-64, 167; V, 83-<u>84</u>.

[7] BN, MS. fr. 18,186, fols. 343-44v; and MS. fr. 18,187, fols. 205v-6.

[8] They were: Pierre d'Amboise, Bishop of Poitiers, for Poitou and Loudun in 1484; Louis de Calembert, Archdeacon of Bellême, for Alençon and Perche; François de Neuville, Abbot of Grammont, for Bas-Limousin and Basse-Marche; Gabriel de Genevois, Abbot of Maures and Dean of Langres, for Bar-sur-Seine, Chaumont-en-Bassigny, and Langres; and Claude de Chanleu, Canon of Péronne, for Montdidier, Péronne, and Roye in 1576; François de Neuville, Abbot of Grammont, for Haut- and possibly Bas-Limousin and Haute- and Basse-Marche in 1588; Geoffroy de la Marthonie, Bishop of Amiens, for Amiens, Boulonnais, and Ponthieu in 1593; Jean de Bertier, Bishop of Rieux, for Toulouse and Valois; Raymond de la Marthonie, prior of Saint-Jean, provost and canon of the church of Notre Dame of Amiens, for Amiens and Montdidier; Antoine Thuet for Péronne and Roye; Gilles de Souvré, Bishop of Comminges, for Comminges and Rivière-Verdun; Armand Jean du Plessis, Bishop of Luçon, for Poitou and Loudun; and Philippe Hurault, Bishop of Chartres, for Blois, Chartres, Montfort-l'Amaury, and Mantes and Meulan in 1614. In addition, the clergy of Auxerre gave their proxy to a Paris canon in 1593, a month after the estates had commenced, in response to the canon's criticism for having chosen no one. Bernard, pp. 789-91.

[9] Moréri, II, 412.

[10] Bernard, p. 8. <u>Gallia Christiana</u> (Paris, 1770), XII, 95, <u>252</u>.

[11] Hérelle, pp. 257-60.

[12] AD, Haute-Garonne, C 3,572, pp. 15-16.

[13] Henri Prentout, <u>Les États provinci-</u> aux de Normandie (Caen, 1926), II, 87-90, extract from <u>Mém.</u> de la ac. nationale des sciences, <u>arts et belles-lettres de Caen</u>, N.S. II (1926). Thomas Cauvin, <u>États du Maine, députés et sénéchaux de cette province</u> (Le Mans, 1839), p. 19. C. Croix, "Documents sur la Ligue dans le bailliage de La Montagne. Les élections aux États généraux de 1588," <u>Annales de Bourgogne</u>, IX (1937), 307-12. Gustave Lapérouse, <u>L'Histoire de Châtillon</u> (Châtillon-sur-Seine, 1837), pp. 337-40. AD, Cote d'Or, C 3,069, fol. 247. BN, MS. fr. 18,186, fol. 199v.

[14] Moréri, VII, 493-98.

[15] Ibid., IV, 109-10.

[16] Bernard, pp. xxi-xxii, 48.

[17] RPO, III, 175, 296.

[18] For further details on the composition of the Estates General see Appendix B.

[19] Doucet, II, 462-63.

[20] Some other examples are the Foissy for La Montagne, the Anglure for Vitry, the Croix for Sézannes, the Joubert for Bazadois, the Pons de Cardaillac-Thémines for Quercy, the Boufflers for Beauvais, the Melun for Nemours, the Brichanteau for Melun, the Polignac for Velay, the La Valette for Toulouse, the Levis for Carcassonne, the Montraval for Basse-Auvergne, the Sindré for Bourbonnais, the Urfé for Forez, the Blanchefort for Nivernais, the Roncherolles for Gisors, the Bellay for Anjou, the La Châtre for Berry, the Angennes for Chartres, the Allonville for Étampes, the Mouchy for Boulonnais, and the Rambures for Ponthieu.

[21] Bernard, pp. 649-76.

[22] BN, MS. n. a. fr. 7,144, fols. 5v-7v. The baron was Louis de la Croix, Baron of Castries, one of the twenty-two nobles who held a hereditary seat in the estates of Languedoc.

[23] Some others were the Auvergne of Bazadois, the Estang and Bonnet of Bas-Limousin, the Couppé of Dreux, the Leroux of Carcassonne, the Muret of Basse-Auvergne, the Chabot and Sauret of Haute-Auvergne, the Scarron of Lyon, the Romier of Forez, the Barbier of Rouen, the Bonnyn and Lebègue of Berry, the Beauharnois of Orléans, and the Vias of Marseille.

[24] Sir William S. Holdsworth, <u>A History of English Law</u> (London, 1922-38), <u>IV</u>, 181.

[25] See Appendix C.

[26] J. E. Neale, The Elizabethan House of Commons (London, 1949), p. 309.

[27] Ibid., pp. 309-11.

[28] Some others were Jean de Bilhères-Lagraulas, Bishop of Lombez, diplomat, writer, and theologian; Jean de Rély, Rector of the University of Paris and co-translator of the first French Bible; Denis de Bar, Bishop of Tulle, astronomer; Claude d'Angennes, student of philosophy at Paris and of law at Bourges and Padua, member of the Parlement, and Bishop of Le Mans; André Frémyont, Archbishop of Bourges, student of law at Padua, president of the Parlement of Dijon, and the author of various pamphlets; Aimar Hennequin, Bishop of Rennes, translator of the confessions of Saint Augustine; Simon de Maillé, Archbishop of Tours and translator of Greek and Latin works; Arnaud de Pontac, Bishop of Bazas, student of Hebrew and Greek and the author of several books; and Charles de La Saussaye, Dean at Orléans and the author of the annals of his church.

[29] RCG, II, 182.

Chapter 15

[1] Thierry, II, 418. B. Mun., Blois, MS. 89, fol. 14v. See also the procès-verbaux of the various orders.

[2] Jean Roucaute, Documents pour servir à l'histoire du pays de Gévaudan au temps de la Ligue (Paris, 1894), pp. 138-49.

[3] Honoré-G. de Coriolis, Dissertation sur les États de Provence (Aix, 1867), p. 247. Jean-H. Mariéjol, Charles-Emmanuel de Savoie, duc de Nemours (Paris, 1938), p. 156. R. de Boysson, "La Ligue et l'Édict de Nantes en Périgord," Bul. de la soc. historique et archéologique du Périgord, XLVI (1919), 186.

[4] T. Pistollet de Saint-Ferjeux, "Langres pendant la Ligue," Mém. de la soc. historique et archéologique de Langres, II (1861-77), 137.

[5] Émile Jolibois, Histoire de la ville de Chaumont (Paris, 1856), p. 158. Henri Drouot, Mayenne et la Bourgogne, 1587-1596 (Paris 1937), II, 241. Bernard, pp. 802-3. Correspondance de la mairie de Dijon, ed. Joseph Garnier (Dijon, 1870), II, 435.

[6] AC, Lyon, BB 129, fols. 121-27v.

[7] J. Soyer, "Les députés du tiers représentant la ville et le bailliage d'Orléans aux États généraux de Blois en 1588," Bul. de la soc. archéologique et historique de l'Orléanais, XV (1908-10), 443. Roucaute, pp. 138-49. P. Thomas-Lacroix, "Les Bretons aux États généraux de 1614," Mém. de la soc. d'histoire et d'archéologie de Bretagne, XV (1934), 6-7.

[8] IAC, Périgueux, ed. Michel Hardy (Périgueux, 1894), p. 116.

[9] Canon Bosseboeuf, "Communication," Bul. trimestriel de la soc. archéologique de Touraine, XXVI (1935), 71-72. Henri Stein, Charles de France (Paris, 1919), p. 234.

[10] Louis Bergevin and Alexandre Dupré, Histoire de Blois (Blois, 1847), II, 8-14.

[11] Ordonnance of Aug. 2, 1561. A copy is at BN, F 46,821, no. 33.

[12] FGC, II, 27.

[13] Thierry, II, 409. C. de Grandmaison, "Nouveaux documents sur les États généraux du XVe siècle," Bul. de la soc. archéologique de Touraine, IV (1877-79), 143.

[14] BN, MS. fr. 8,277, p. 577.

[15] Roucaute, pp. 138-49. Soyer, pp. 443-44. Thomas-Lacroix, pp. 7-9.

[16] RCG, I, pp. 196-97, 400-401; II, 351; IV, 239. Isambert, XIV, 88, 211, 320-25.

[17] IAC, Amboise, ed. Casimir Chevalier (Tours, 1874), pp. 109, 390-91. Bernard, pp. 698-99.

[18] See chap. 16.

[19] RPO, pt. II, V, 22, 25, 43; VI, 87.

[20] BN, MS. fr. 8,277, pp. 577-78. AC, Grenoble, AA 39, no. 8. Coriolis, p. 251. Drouot, II, 242, n. 2.

[21] Thomas Cauvin, États du Maine, députés et sénéchaux de cette province (Le Mans, 1839), p. 39.

[22] Masselin, pp. 476-77. Thomas-Lacroix, p. 8.

[23] See Louis Moréri, Le Grande dictionnaire historique... (Paris, 1759), for genealogies.

[24] For examples of intermarriage between the members of the various estates, see Roland Mousnier, La venalité des offices sous Henri IV et Louis XIII (Rouen, 1945), pp. 60-63, 506-41.

[25] Thomas-Lacroix, pp. 3-6. Michel Jullien de Pommerol, Albret de Gondi, maréchal de Retz (Geneva, 1953), pp. 7-13,

266. For other examples of intermarriages between the nobility and third estate; of nobles of the sword becoming officeholders, and of officeholders becoming nobles of the sword, see Mousnier, pp. 60-63, 506-41; and Gaston Roupnel, La Ville et la campagne au XVIIe siècle, étude sur les populations du pays dijonnais (Paris, ed. of 1955), pp. 167-96.

²⁶ Thomas-Lacroix, pp. 11, 13.

Chapter 16

¹ A large part of the material for this chapter has been published in The Journal of Modern History, XXVII (1955), 217-29. I wish to express my appreciation for the permission to reprint sections of this article.

² C. de Grandmaison, "Nouveaux documents sur les États généraux du XVe siècle," Bul. de la soc. archéologique de Touraine, IV (1877-79), 142-43, 154-55.

³ Masselin, pp. 498-99.

⁴ Ibid., pp. 494-510.

⁵ HL, XII, 252-53. Joseph Billioud, Les États de Bourgogne aux XIVe et XVe siècles (Dijon, 1922), p. 464. AN, K 648, fol. 115.

⁶ AN, K 648, fol. 92.

⁷ IAC, Périgueux, ed. Michel Hardy (Périgueux, 1894), p. 251. Charles Samaran, La Maison d'Armagnac au XVe siècle (Paris, 1907), p. 241.

⁸ Thierry, II, 422-23. IAC, Laon, eds. A. Matton and Victor Dessein (Laon, 1883), p. 74. T. Boutiot and A. Babeau, "Documents inédits tirés des archives de Troyes et relatifs aux États généraux," Collection de documents inédits relatifs à la ville de Troyes (Troyes, 1878), I, 6-7.

⁹ RPO, IX, 288-90.

¹⁰ BN, MS. fr. 18,187, fols. 285v-87. For published documents on payment of deputies see especially RPO, IX, 288-345; and Mayer, VII, 390-99. There is a great deal of unpublished material in the provincial archives. AD, Gironde, C 3,894 is especially informative for the payment of the deputies of 1614.

¹¹ Amédée Combier, Étude sur le bailliage de Vermandois (Paris, 1874), pp. 85-88, 142-62.

¹² B. Mun., Rouen, MS. 967, no. 77.

B. Mun., Orléans, MS. 541 (427), fols. 32-35, 46. AD, Saône-et-Loire, C 550, no. 27. Archives historiques de la Corrèze, II (1905), 366-70.

¹³ G. Clément-Simon, "Rôle de la cotisation de la noblesse du Bas-Limousin pour les frais faits par ses députés aux États généraux d'Orléans en 1560," Archives historiques de la Corrèze, I, (1903), 87-96. Combier, pp. 150-55. A. de Calonne, "Réparation entre les gentilshommes tenant fiefs nobles en Ponthieu de l'idemnité allouée à messire André de Bourbon-Rubempré délégué aux États généraux de Blois en 1577," Mém. de la soc. des antiquités de Picardie, XIII (1873), 71-98. BN, MS. fr. 5,353, for Rouen. AD, Dordogne, C 14, no. 1, for Périgord. AD, Saône-et-Loire, C 550, no. 28, for Mâcon. AD, Côte-d'Or, C 3,470 and C 3,471 for La Montagne.

¹⁴ O. Morel, Documents sur le pays de Gex conservés dans les archives cantonales de Genève et de Lausanne (Bourg, 1932), p. 32. RPO, IX, 301-2. Thierry, II, 864-66.

¹⁵ Combier, pp. 155-62. AD, Côte-d'Or, C 3,471 and C 3,474.

¹⁶ Charles de La Lande de Calan, "Documents inédits relatifs aux États de Bretagne de 1491 à 1589," Archives de Bretagne, XV (1908-9), pt. I, 145-46; pt. II, 101. AD, Ille-et-Vilaine, C 2,649, p. 151. AD, Bouches-du-Rhône, C 3, fols. 12-13; C 107, fols. 146-47, 554v; C 5, fols. 40-40v, 335. Honoré-G. de Coriolis, Dissertation sur les États de Provence (Aix, 1867), pp. 247-49. AD, Haute-Garonne, C 2,280, fol. 471; C 2,281, fol. 52-52v; C 2,283, fol. 231; C 2,286, p. 103; C 2,294, fols. 331v-33, 337-40.

¹⁷ AD, Côte-d'Or, C 3,063, fols. 80v-86; C 3,469-C 3,472; C 3,474. RPO, IX, 298-302, 307-16. AD, Bourg, AA 12. AD, Saône-et-Loire, C 550, nos. 27 and 28.

¹⁸ Jean Déniau, La Commune de Lyon et la Guerre bourguignonne, 1417-1435 (Lyon, 1934), p. 265. B. Mun., Lyon, MS. 721, pp. 187-88, 191; MS. 722, fols. 51-52. IAC, Lyon, eds. Marie-C. Guigue, J. Vaësen and Georges Guigue (Lyon, 1887-1949), III, 259, 333; IV, 12, 122. AD, Lyon, BB 94, fols. 162, 169v; AA 147.

¹⁹ Thierry, II, 676-77, 973, 1039-41; III, 10. Boutiot and Babeau, I, 3-5, 24-25. Louis Méry and F. Guindon, Histoire analytique et chronologique, des actes et

délibérations du corps et du conseil de la municipalité de Marseille (Marseille, 1847), pp. 384-91.

[20] AD, Côte-d'Or, C 3,062, fol. 255.

[21] AD, Côte-d'Or, C 3,473. AD, Bouches-du-Rhône, C 2,069. Coriolis, pp. 251-52. AD, Saône-et-Loire, C 551, no. 24. The total cost of the assembly of 1626 was 199,660 livres, but the crown levied a supplementary tax of only 44,000 livres. Jeanne Petit, L'Assemblée des notables de 1626-1627 (Paris, 1936), pp. 67-68.

[22] AD, Bouches du Rhône, C 2,069, no. 4. Alexandre Dupré, Élections du clergé de Guienne aux États généraux (Bordeaux, 1893), pp. 7-11, extract from La Revue catholique de Bordeaux, Aug. 10, 25, and Sept. 10, 1893. AD, Côte-d'Or, C 3,069, fols. 245-56v. G. Arnaud, Mémoire sur les États de Foix, 1608-1789 (Toulouse, 1904), pp. 1-40, 152-56. AD, Haute-Garonne, C 3,572, pp. 15-16. Négociations, lettres et pièces diverses relatives au règne de François II. CDI, ed. Louis Paris (Paris, 1841), pp. 632-33.

[23] Masselin, pp. 510-11. AD, Ille-et-Vilaine, C 2,649, p. 151. Combier, pp. 150-55. Clément-Simon, "Rôle de la cotisation...," Archives historiques de la Corrèze, I, 87-96. Calonne, pp. 71-98. AD, Dordogne, C 14, no. 1. AD, Saône-et-Loire, C 550, no. 28.

[24] Grandmaison, pp. 142-43, 147-48, 154-55. Déniau, p. 265.

[25] Combier, pp. 144-62. AD, Amiens, BB 43, entry of Oct. 24, 1577. G. Hérelle, "Documents inédits sur les États généraux tirés des archives de Vitry-le-François," Bul. de la soc. des sciences et arts de Vitry-le-François, IX (1878), 212.

[26] Grandmaison, pp. 142-43, 147-48, 154-55. RPO, II, 225, 229; IX, 288-93, 298-309, 329-45. Mayer, VII, 391-99. BN, MS. fr. 18,187, fols. 285v87. Louis XI established the pay of the clergy and nobility who served in the Norman provincial estates at 3 livres per day and of the third estate at 2 livres per day. Henri Prentout, Les États provinciaux de Normandie (Caen, 1926), II, 137, extract from Mém. de l'ac. nationale des sciences, arts et belles-lettres de Caen, N.S., II (1926).

[27] B. Mun., Orléans, MS. 541 (427), fols. 32-35.

[28] J. Soyer, "Les députés du tiers représentant la ville et le bailliage d'Orléans aux États généraux de Blois en 1588," Bul. de la soc. archéologique et historique de l'Orléanais, XV (1908-10), 435-47.

[29] AD, Lyon, CC 1,354. IAC, Nevers, ed. François Boutillier (Nevers, 1876), pp. 88-89.

[30] "Diaire de Jacques Merlin," Archives historiques de la Saintonge et d'Aunis, V (1878), 237-40.

[31] RPO, IX, 288-90. La Lande de Calan, pt. I, 145. Abbé Millard and A. Roserot, "Procès-verbal de l'assemblée des trois ordres du bailliage de Chaumont (Haute-Marne) pour les États généraux convoqués à Orléans en 1649," Mém. de la soc. académique d'agriculture, des sciences, arts et belles lettres du département de l'Aube, XLVII (1883), 321-45.

[32] B. Mun., Lyon, MS. 721, pp. 187-88. AC, Lyon, BB 150, p. 306.

[33] Combier, pp. 85-92, 142-62. RPO, IX, 315-16. Bonnault d'Houët, Compiègne pendant les guerres de religion et la Ligue (Compiègne, 1910), pp. 199-200. BN, MS. fr. 5,353. Coriolis, p. 248.

[34] AD, Bouches-du-Rhône, C 5, fols. 40v, 355. IAC, Périgueux, p. 116. AC, Lyon, BB 94, fols. 162, 169v. AC, Amiens, CC 234, fol. 18; CC 236, fol. 16. J. Gosselin, "La Ligue à Péronne," La Picardie, XVI (1870), 271.

[35] Jules Flammermont, Histoire des institutions municipales de Senlis (Paris, 1881), pp. 99-100. Calonne, p. 77. RPO, VI, 55, IX, 318-28.

[36] Jacob Burckhardt, The Civilization of the Renaissance in Italy (London ed. of 1945), p. 57.

INDEX